Bisi Alimi

*The Nigerian Activist Changing LGBTQ Narratives –
Unauthorized*

Lina Toure

ISBN: 9781779696090
Imprint: Telephasic Workshop
Copyright © 2024 Lina Toure.
All Rights Reserved.

Contents

A Journey of Self-Discovery 27
Battling Personal and Professional Challenges 50

Bibliography 67
The Impact of International Activism 75

Taking Center Stage – Advocacy in Action 97
Taking Center Stage – Advocacy in Action 97
Fighting for LGBTQ Rights in Nigeria 102
Creating Safe Spaces for LGBTQ Individuals 127

Bibliography 149
Building Bridges with Religious Communities 151
Championing LGBTQ Rights on the African Continent 175

Bisi Alimi's Legacy and Continued Activism 199
Bisi Alimi's Legacy and Continued Activism 199
The Journey Towards a More Inclusive Nigeria 202
Global Impact and Advocacy Beyond Borders 226

Index 247

CONTENTS 1

Growing Up in Lagos

Growing up in Lagos, Nigeria, Bisi Alimi navigated a landscape rich in culture, vibrancy, and contradictions. Lagos, often referred to as the "City of Aquatic Splendor," is a bustling metropolis that serves as Nigeria's economic hub. However, beneath its lively exterior lies a complex social fabric woven with conservative values, particularly regarding gender and sexuality.

1.1.1 A Conservative Society

In Lagos, societal norms are heavily influenced by traditional beliefs and religious doctrines. The predominant religions—Christianity and Islam—impose strict moral codes that often marginalize those who do not conform to heteronormative standards. Bisi's early experiences in this conservative environment shaped his understanding of identity and acceptance.

$$\text{Social Norms} \rightarrow \text{Conformity} \rightarrow \text{Marginalization} \tag{1}$$

The pressure to conform was palpable, leading many, including Bisi, to grapple with their identities in silence. The stigma surrounding LGBTQ identities in Nigeria often manifests in both overt discrimination and subtle social exclusion.

1.1.2 Family Dynamics

Family plays a critical role in shaping one's identity, and for Bisi, this was no different. Growing up in a family that valued tradition, he faced the challenge of reconciling his emerging identity with familial expectations. His parents, while loving, held conventional views that left little room for deviation from the norm. This dynamic created an internal conflict for Bisi, who sought acceptance both from his family and himself.

1.1.3 The Influence of Religion

Religion in Nigeria is not just a belief system; it is a way of life that permeates every aspect of society. Bisi's exposure to religious teachings further complicated his understanding of his identity. The pervasive narrative that equates homosexuality with sin led to a profound sense of guilt and shame.

$$\text{Religious Teachings} + \text{Cultural Norms} \rightarrow \text{Internal Conflict} \tag{2}$$

This internal struggle was a catalyst for Bisi's later activism, as he sought to challenge these harmful narratives and promote a more inclusive understanding of love and identity.

1.1.4 Early Signs of Activism

Bisi's journey toward activism began in his teenage years. Despite the oppressive environment, he found solace in literature and art, which provided a means of expression and connection to the broader LGBTQ community. He began to question the societal norms that dictated his life and sought ways to advocate for change.

1.1.5 First Encounters with LGBTQ Community

Bisi's first encounters with the LGBTQ community were both exhilarating and terrifying. Online platforms became a refuge where he could connect with others who shared similar experiences. These interactions opened his eyes to the struggles faced by LGBTQ individuals in Nigeria and ignited a passion for advocacy.

1.1.6 Educational Pursuits

Education played a pivotal role in Bisi's life. He pursued his studies with a determination to understand the world around him. His academic journey exposed him to diverse perspectives and theories on gender and sexuality, equipping him with the knowledge necessary to challenge societal norms.

1.1.7 Discovering Personal Identity

As Bisi delved deeper into his studies and the LGBTQ community, he began to embrace his identity. This process of self-discovery was fraught with challenges, as he navigated the complexities of being a gay man in a society that vehemently opposed his existence.

$$\text{Self-Discovery} \rightarrow \text{Acceptance} \rightarrow \text{Activism} \qquad (3)$$

His journey toward acceptance became a powerful motivator for his future activism.

1.1.8 Coming Out and Acceptance

Coming out is a pivotal moment in the life of any LGBTQ individual, and for Bisi, it was no different. He faced the daunting task of revealing his identity to family and friends, a process that was met with mixed reactions. The fear of rejection loomed large, but Bisi's resolve to live authentically ultimately triumphed.

1.1.9 Promoting LGBTQ Rights in Nigeria

With a newfound sense of identity and purpose, Bisi began to actively promote LGBTQ rights in Nigeria. He engaged in grassroots organizing, raising awareness about the challenges faced by the LGBTQ community. His efforts were met with both support and hostility, reflecting the polarized views within Nigerian society.

1.1.10 Navigating Personal Relationships

Navigating personal relationships as an LGBTQ individual in Lagos presented unique challenges. Bisi faced the constant threat of societal backlash, which often infiltrated his relationships with friends and family. The pressure to conform to traditional expectations weighed heavily on him, yet he remained committed to forging connections based on authenticity and mutual respect.

In summary, Bisi Alimi's formative years in Lagos were marked by a struggle against societal norms, familial expectations, and religious influences. These experiences laid the groundwork for his future activism, as he emerged from a conservative society determined to advocate for LGBTQ rights and challenge the narratives that sought to silence him. His story is a testament to the resilience of the human spirit in the face of adversity and the power of self-acceptance.

Growing Up in Lagos

Growing up in Lagos, Nigeria, Bisi Alimi's early life was a vivid tapestry woven with the vibrant colors of a bustling city, yet shadowed by the oppressive realities of a conservative society. Lagos, known for its rich culture and diversity, is a city of contradictions. On one hand, it is a hub of creativity, music, and entrepreneurship; on the other, it is steeped in traditional values that often clash with modern ideals, particularly concerning sexual orientation and identity.

1.1.1 A Conservative Society

In a society where traditional norms dictate social behavior, the LGBTQ community faces significant challenges. The conservative nature of Nigerian society is deeply rooted in cultural practices and religious beliefs. The prevailing ideologies emphasize heteronormativity and often demonize any deviation from this norm. This societal backdrop created an environment where individuals like Bisi had to navigate their identities with caution.

1.1.2 Family Dynamics

Family plays a crucial role in shaping one's identity, particularly in a close-knit society like Nigeria. Bisi's family, while loving, held traditional views that often conflicted with his emerging identity. The pressure to conform to family expectations can be suffocating. In many cases, LGBTQ individuals experience rejection or disapproval from family members, leading to emotional turmoil. Bisi's journey illustrates the tension between familial love and the quest for personal authenticity.

1.1.3 The Influence of Religion

Religion is another powerful force in Nigerian society that shapes attitudes toward LGBTQ individuals. Predominantly influenced by Christianity and Islam, religious teachings often promote conservative values that marginalize those who identify as LGBTQ. This religious backdrop can lead to a culture of shame and secrecy, where individuals feel compelled to hide their true selves to avoid ostracization. Bisi's early experiences reflect the struggle of reconciling his identity with the religious expectations imposed upon him.

1.1.4 Early Signs of Activism

Despite the challenges, early signs of activism began to emerge in Bisi's life. Even as a child, he exhibited a strong sense of justice and an innate desire to challenge societal norms. This inclination was evident in his interactions with peers and his response to injustices he witnessed. The seeds of activism were sown early on, as he began to question the status quo and advocate for acceptance and equality.

1.1.5 First Encounters with LGBTQ Community

Bisi's first encounters with the LGBTQ community were pivotal moments in his life. These experiences provided him with a sense of belonging and affirmation. Meeting individuals who shared similar struggles helped him realize that he was not alone in his journey. These interactions were not without risk, as engaging with the LGBTQ community in Nigeria often comes with the threat of violence and discrimination.

1.1.6 Educational Pursuits

Education played a significant role in shaping Bisi's worldview. Attending school in Lagos exposed him to diverse perspectives and ideas. However, the educational system often mirrored societal biases, with limited discussions on sexual orientation and gender identity. Bisi's pursuit of knowledge became a double-edged sword; while it broadened his horizons, it also highlighted the gaps in understanding and acceptance within his community.

1.1.7 Discovering Personal Identity

The journey of self-discovery is a complex and often painful process for many LGBTQ individuals. For Bisi, recognizing and embracing his identity as a gay man was fraught with challenges. Societal stigma and internalized homophobia created barriers to self-acceptance. However, through introspection and support from friends, he began to embrace his true self, paving the way for his future activism.

1.1.8 Coming Out and Acceptance

Coming out is a significant milestone in the life of any LGBTQ individual. For Bisi, this moment was both liberating and terrifying. The fear of rejection loomed large, yet the desire for authenticity propelled him forward. His decision to come out to friends and family marked a turning point, leading to a mix of acceptance and backlash. This experience underscored the varying degrees of acceptance within families and communities, highlighting the ongoing struggle for LGBTQ rights in Nigeria.

1.1.9 Promoting LGBTQ Rights in Nigeria

As Bisi navigated his identity, he became increasingly aware of the systemic injustices faced by the LGBTQ community in Nigeria. This awareness ignited a passion for advocacy, as he sought to promote LGBTQ rights and challenge discriminatory laws. His early efforts laid the groundwork for a lifelong commitment to activism, as he endeavored to change the narrative surrounding LGBTQ identities in Nigeria.

1.1.10 Navigating Personal Relationships

Navigating personal relationships as an LGBTQ individual in a conservative society can be particularly challenging. Bisi's experiences reflect the complexities of forming meaningful connections while grappling with societal expectations. The fear of rejection and societal backlash often hindered his ability to fully engage in romantic relationships. However, these challenges also fostered resilience and a deeper understanding of the importance of supportive networks.

In conclusion, growing up in Lagos shaped Bisi Alimi's identity and activism in profound ways. The interplay of cultural, familial, and religious influences created a landscape fraught with challenges, yet it also served as a catalyst for his journey toward self-acceptance and advocacy. Through his experiences, Bisi emerged as a powerful voice for change, challenging the narratives that seek to marginalize LGBTQ individuals in Nigeria and beyond.

ERROR. thisXsection() returned an empty string with textbook depth = 3.
ERROR. thisXsection() returned an empty string with textbook depth = 3.
ERROR. thisXsection() returned an empty string with textbook depth = 3.

Family Dynamics

When we talk about family dynamics, we're diving into a pool of emotions, expectations, and sometimes, a whole lot of drama. You know, the kind of drama that makes you want to binge-watch a reality show, but instead, you're living it. For Bisi Alimi, growing up in Lagos, Nigeria, family dynamics were like a game of chess—strategic, tense, and full of unexpected moves.

In a conservative society where traditional values reign supreme, Bisi's family was no exception. Picture this: a Nigerian household where religion and cultural expectations are the cornerstones of family life. You've got parents who are trying to uphold the family name, while you're over here just trying to figure out if you can wear that fabulous outfit without getting side-eyed. It's like trying to cook jollof rice while the fire is way too hot—things can get messy real quick!

The Role of Tradition and Expectations

In many African families, there's this unspoken rulebook that everyone is expected to follow. And let me tell you, Bisi's family had that book on lock. The expectations were clear: get an education, find a good job, marry someone of the opposite sex, and produce grandchildren. But what happens when you don't fit into that mold? You become the subject of family meetings, whispered conversations, and the occasional "What will people say?" That's right, the dreaded phrase that haunts many LGBTQ individuals—because let's be real, in a conservative society, the opinions of others can feel heavier than a bag of rice.

Bisi's journey through family dynamics was a rollercoaster of emotions. On one hand, there was love and support; on the other, there were the weighty expectations and the fear of disappointing those who raised you. It's like being in a relationship where your partner wants you to be yourself, but also wants you to change everything about yourself. Confusing, right?

Navigating Acceptance and Rejection

As Bisi began to explore his identity, the dynamics within the family started to shift. The early signs of activism were budding, and with them came the realization that coming out could lead to acceptance or rejection. Imagine sitting at the dinner table, trying to muster the courage to drop the "I'm gay" bombshell while your mom is serving up some spicy efo riro. The moment feels monumental, like the climax of a blockbuster movie.

However, the reality was that not everyone was ready for that conversation. Bisi faced rejection from some family members, and it hit harder than a punchline that falls flat. The disappointment was palpable, and it was clear that acceptance was not a given. This led to a series of emotional battles—feeling isolated yet fiercely determined to stand up for who he was.

The Influence of Religion

Now, let's talk about religion because, in many Nigerian families, that's the big elephant in the room. For Bisi, religion was both a comfort and a source of conflict. The teachings he grew up with were often at odds with his identity. It's like trying to fit a square peg into a round hole while everyone around you is chanting, "Just pray harder!"

Bisi's family, like many others, held strong religious beliefs that often condemned homosexuality. This created an internal struggle for him—how do you honor your family's beliefs while also being true to yourself? It's a classic case of "damned if you do, damned if you don't."

Finding Common Ground

Despite the challenges, Bisi's journey was not without moments of connection. Through open dialogues and heartfelt conversations, he began to bridge the gap between his identity and his family's expectations. It wasn't easy, but Bisi's ability to articulate his experiences helped some family members understand his perspective.

He often used humor to diffuse tense situations—because if there's one thing that can ease the tension, it's laughter. Imagine Bisi cracking jokes about the absurdity of societal expectations while simultaneously sharing his truth. It's like a comedy special where the punchline is acceptance, and the audience is slowly warming up.

The Impact of Family Dynamics on Activism

Ultimately, the family dynamics that Bisi navigated played a significant role in shaping his activism. The challenges he faced at home fueled his desire to fight for LGBTQ rights, not just for himself but for others who felt the same rejection. It was as if every moment of pain transformed into a stepping stone toward greater advocacy.

Bisi's experiences highlight a crucial theory in family dynamics: the concept of *family resilience*. This theory suggests that families can adapt to challenges and emerge stronger. In Bisi's case, while there were moments of rejection, there were also moments of love and support that helped him persevere.

In conclusion, family dynamics are complex, especially in a conservative society like Nigeria. Bisi Alimi's journey illustrates that while the road to acceptance can be fraught with obstacles, it also holds the potential for growth, understanding, and ultimately, change. So, as we delve deeper into Bisi's life, let's remember that family isn't just about blood; it's about the bonds we create and the love we share, even amidst the chaos.

The Influence of Religion

Religion plays a pivotal role in shaping societal norms and values, particularly in conservative societies like Nigeria. In this context, it is essential to understand how religious beliefs intersect with issues of sexual orientation and gender identity. Nigeria is predominantly religious, with Islam and Christianity being the two major faiths. These religions often espouse traditional views on sexuality, which can lead to significant challenges for LGBTQ individuals seeking acceptance and rights.

Religious Doctrines and LGBTQ Issues

Many religious doctrines explicitly condemn homosexuality. For instance, certain interpretations of the Bible and the Quran emphasize heterosexual relationships as the only acceptable form of love and partnership. This condemnation is often rooted in specific verses that are cited to justify exclusion and discrimination. For example, Leviticus 18:22 states, "You shall not lie with a male as with a woman; it is an abomination." Similarly, in Islamic texts, homosexuality is frequently viewed as a sin, leading to societal stigmatization of LGBTQ individuals.

The adherence to these doctrines creates a framework where LGBTQ identities are not only marginalized but also demonized. This is particularly evident in Nigeria, where the Same-Sex Marriage Prohibition Act of 2014 was largely supported by religious groups. The Act not only criminalizes same-sex marriage but also imposes penalties for individuals who advocate for LGBTQ rights, reflecting the profound influence of religious beliefs on legal and social structures.

The Role of Religious Institutions

Religious institutions in Nigeria often serve as gatekeepers of moral values, exerting significant influence over public opinion and policy-making. Pastors, imams, and other religious leaders are powerful figures whose sermons can shape the attitudes of their congregations. Many leaders use their platforms to preach against homosexuality, reinforcing negative stereotypes and fostering an environment of fear and hostility toward LGBTQ individuals.

For example, some churches and mosques have organized campaigns against LGBTQ rights, framing their opposition as a defense of family values and societal norms. This mobilization can lead to a culture of intolerance, where LGBTQ individuals face harassment, violence, and discrimination not just from society at large but also from their own religious communities.

Personal Experiences and Activism

Bisi Alimi's journey as an LGBTQ activist is emblematic of the struggle against the influence of religion on personal identity and societal acceptance. Growing up in a conservative religious environment, Bisi faced immense pressure to conform to heteronormative standards. His early experiences of rejection from family and community due to his sexual orientation were deeply intertwined with their religious beliefs.

Despite these challenges, Bisi's activism has highlighted the need for dialogue within religious communities. He has advocated for a reinterpretation of religious texts that emphasizes love, acceptance, and compassion rather than condemnation. By engaging with religious leaders and communities, Bisi aims to challenge misconceptions and promote a more inclusive understanding of faith that embraces diversity in sexual orientation.

Interfaith Dialogue and Inclusion

Recognizing the power of religion in shaping societal attitudes, Bisi Alimi and other activists have initiated interfaith dialogues aimed at bridging the gap between LGBTQ individuals and religious communities. These dialogues focus on fostering understanding and empathy, encouraging religious leaders to consider the lived experiences of LGBTQ individuals within their congregations.

Through storytelling and personal testimonies, activists have sought to humanize the LGBTQ experience, countering the dehumanizing narratives often perpetuated by religious teachings. By sharing their journeys, LGBTQ individuals can challenge the stereotypes that fuel discrimination and advocate for a more inclusive interpretation of religious doctrine.

The Path Forward

The influence of religion on LGBTQ rights in Nigeria presents a complex challenge. However, it also offers an opportunity for transformative change. As more LGBTQ individuals and allies engage with religious communities, there is potential for a shift in attitudes and beliefs. By promoting an inclusive dialogue that respects both faith and sexual identity, activists can work towards a more equitable society.

In conclusion, while the influence of religion in Nigeria has historically contributed to the marginalization of LGBTQ individuals, it also holds the potential for positive change. Through advocacy, education, and interfaith dialogue, there is hope for a future where religious beliefs coexist with acceptance and respect for diversity in sexual orientation and gender identity. The journey is fraught with challenges, but the resilience of activists like Bisi Alimi continues to inspire a movement towards inclusivity and understanding.

Early Signs of Activism

Bisi Alimi's journey toward activism didn't start with grand speeches or protests. No, it began in the heart of Lagos, where the vibrant streets were alive with the hustle of life, but also filled with the quiet whispers of oppression. Growing up in a conservative society, Bisi was often caught between the expectations of his family and the burgeoning realization of his identity. It was in these early years that the seeds of activism were sown, nurtured by experiences that would later blossom into a full-fledged campaign for LGBTQ rights.

The first signs of Bisi's activism emerged in subtle ways. As a young boy, he was acutely aware of the societal norms that dictated behavior, especially regarding sexuality. The Nigerian cultural landscape was heavily influenced by traditional values and religious beliefs that painted homosexuality as a taboo. Bisi's early experiences were marked by a profound sense of injustice; he observed how peers who were different faced ridicule and ostracism.

One pivotal moment in Bisi's early life was his exposure to the concept of human rights during his education. The introduction of subjects that discussed equality and justice sparked a fire within him. He began to question why certain groups were marginalized and why love was conditional. This intellectual awakening was not just a personal journey but a collective one. Bisi realized he was not alone; there were others who felt the weight of societal expectations pressing down on them.

In the classroom, Bisi often engaged in discussions about fairness and equality, challenging his peers and teachers alike. His boldness to speak out against discrimination, even in small ways, was an early indication of his activist spirit. For instance, when a classmate was bullied for being perceived as different, Bisi took a stand, defending his friend and confronting the bullies. This act of solidarity was not without its consequences; he faced backlash from both peers and authority figures, but it only fueled his resolve.

Bisi's involvement in school clubs and community initiatives also laid the groundwork for his activism. He participated in debates and forums that addressed social issues, often advocating for inclusivity and respect for all individuals, regardless of their sexual orientation. This engagement provided him with a platform to voice his concerns and connect with like-minded individuals. The camaraderie formed in these spaces was essential, as it fostered a sense of belonging and purpose.

As the influence of religion loomed large in his upbringing, Bisi grappled with the conflicting messages he received. The church, a cornerstone of Nigerian society, often preached against homosexuality, labeling it a sin. However, Bisi's interpretation of faith began to evolve. He sought out progressive religious groups that embraced LGBTQ individuals, learning that spirituality could coexist with his identity. This exploration was crucial; it highlighted the importance of finding allies within the very institutions that often perpetuated discrimination.

In addition to his educational pursuits, Bisi's early encounters with the LGBTQ community were transformative. He discovered underground networks and safe spaces where individuals could express themselves without fear of persecution. These gatherings were filled with laughter, tears, and shared stories of resilience. It was here that Bisi witnessed the power of community and the strength that comes from standing together. The courage displayed by those around him inspired him to embrace his identity fully and to advocate for change.

Bisi's early activism was not just about personal liberation; it was about envisioning a more equitable society. He began to understand the broader implications of his experiences. The problems faced by the LGBTQ community were systemic and deeply rooted in societal norms. He recognized that to effect change, one must challenge the status quo, and this realization became a driving force in his life.

Theoretical frameworks of activism, such as the Social Movement Theory, elucidate Bisi's early experiences. According to this theory, social movements arise when individuals recognize a discrepancy between their current situation and their desired state of affairs. Bisi's awareness of injustice and his subsequent actions exemplified this principle. He understood that activism was not merely a reaction to oppression but a proactive stance to create a better future.

In conclusion, the early signs of Bisi Alimi's activism were marked by a series of personal and communal experiences that shaped his worldview. From challenging societal norms in school to finding solace within the LGBTQ community, Bisi's journey was a testament to the power of resilience and the importance of allyship. These formative years laid the foundation for a lifetime of advocacy, setting the stage for his future endeavors in the fight for LGBTQ rights in Nigeria and beyond.

First Encounters with LGBTQ Community

Growing up in Lagos, Bisi Alimi's first encounters with the LGBTQ community were nothing short of transformative. In a society steeped in conservative values, where discussions about sexual orientation were often met with disdain, Bisi's initial exposure to the community was a revelation. It was like stepping into a vibrant world filled with colors, freedom, and acceptance—an experience that contrasted sharply with the grayness of societal norms he had known.

Bisi's first encounter occurred during his university years. He was a young man eager to explore his identity, and it was during this period that he stumbled upon a small gathering organized by a local LGBTQ group. The event was held discreetly in a community center, a safe haven for those who sought solace and connection. As he entered the room, he felt a mix of excitement and apprehension. The atmosphere was electric, filled with laughter, discussions, and a palpable sense of belonging.

Here, Bisi witnessed the power of community. People shared their stories—stories of struggle, love, and resilience. He listened as individuals spoke candidly about their experiences of coming out, facing discrimination, and finding acceptance. This was a stark contrast to the whispers and judgment he had faced in his daily life. It was in this space that he realized he was not alone; there were others who understood his journey, who had walked similar paths, and who were ready to fight for their rights.

One poignant moment stood out to Bisi. A young woman shared her story of being disowned by her family after coming out. Her voice trembled as she recounted the pain of rejection, but it was also filled with strength as she spoke about finding a new family within the LGBTQ community. Bisi felt a surge of empathy and solidarity. This was not just a group of individuals; it was a movement—a movement that sought to challenge the status quo and redefine what it meant to be LGBTQ in Nigeria.

However, this newfound sense of belonging came with its own set of challenges. The fear of being outed loomed large. Bisi understood the risks that came with being associated with the LGBTQ community in a country where homosexuality was criminalized. The societal stigma was pervasive; it was a constant reminder that acceptance was not guaranteed. He grappled with the duality of wanting to be part of this vibrant community while also fearing the repercussions it could bring.

In the following months, Bisi became more involved with the LGBTQ group. He attended meetings, participated in discussions, and even helped organize events. His activism began to take shape as he learned about the legal battles facing the community. He discovered the Same-Sex Marriage Prohibition Act, a law that not only criminalized same-sex relationships but also provided a legal framework for discrimination. This knowledge ignited a fire within him—he was determined to advocate for change.

Bisi's early encounters with the LGBTQ community also exposed him to the intersectionality of identities. He met individuals from diverse backgrounds—different ethnicities, religions, and socio-economic statuses. This diversity enriched his understanding of the struggles faced by LGBTQ individuals in Nigeria. It was not just about sexual orientation; it was about race, class, and gender identity. He learned that the fight for LGBTQ rights was intricately linked to broader human rights issues.

As he navigated through this journey, Bisi also encountered skepticism from some members of the LGBTQ community. There were debates about the effectiveness of activism and the best strategies to employ in a hostile environment. Some believed in a more radical approach, while others advocated for gradual change through dialogue and education. These discussions were crucial in shaping Bisi's perspective on activism. He realized that there was no one-size-fits-all solution; the path to equality would require a multifaceted approach.

The significance of these early encounters cannot be overstated. They were foundational in Bisi's evolution as an activist. He learned the importance of solidarity, the need for safe spaces, and the value of shared experiences. These encounters laid the groundwork for his future endeavors, fueling his passion for advocacy and his commitment to promoting LGBTQ rights in Nigeria.

In retrospect, Bisi's first encounters with the LGBTQ community were not merely moments of personal discovery; they were pivotal in shaping the narrative of activism in Nigeria. They highlighted the need for visibility, the importance of community support, and the relentless pursuit of justice. Bisi Alimi emerged from these experiences not just as a participant but as a leader—ready to challenge the norms, confront the injustices, and pave the way for future generations.

In conclusion, Bisi's initial interactions with the LGBTQ community in Lagos were transformative. They provided him with a sense of belonging, ignited his passion for activism, and equipped him with the knowledge and support needed to confront the challenges ahead. These encounters marked the beginning of a journey that would not only change his life but also impact the lives of countless others in the fight for LGBTQ rights in Nigeria.

Educational Pursuits

Bisi Alimi's educational journey is a testament to resilience and determination in the face of adversity. Growing up in Lagos, Nigeria, Bisi was acutely aware of the societal constraints imposed on him due to his sexual orientation. However, he recognized early on that education would be a vital tool for empowerment.

The Importance of Education

Education serves as a foundation for personal and societal growth. In Bisi's case, it became a means to challenge the status quo and advocate for change. As he pursued his studies, he began to understand the complexities of societal norms and the legal frameworks surrounding LGBTQ rights.

$$\text{Empowerment} = \text{Education} + \text{Awareness} \qquad (4)$$

This equation reflects Bisi's belief that knowledge and awareness are essential components of empowerment, particularly for marginalized communities.

Challenges in the Educational System

Despite his aspirations, Bisi faced significant challenges within the Nigerian educational system. The conservative societal values often permeated educational institutions, creating an environment where discussions about sexual orientation were taboo. This lack of representation and understanding made it difficult for Bisi and others like him to fully engage in their educational pursuits.

For instance, during his time at the University of Lagos, Bisi encountered hostility from both peers and faculty when he attempted to initiate conversations about LGBTQ issues. The fear of retribution and stigma often silenced voices that sought to challenge prevailing norms. This environment led to feelings of isolation and frustration, but it also ignited a fire within Bisi to become an advocate for change.

Finding Support and Inspiration

In the midst of these challenges, Bisi found solace and inspiration in literature and the arts. He discovered the works of authors and activists who had paved the way for LGBTQ rights globally. This exposure not only broadened his perspective but also provided him with role models who demonstrated the power of education as a catalyst for change.

Bisi became involved in student organizations that focused on human rights and social justice, which allowed him to connect with like-minded individuals. These experiences reinforced the idea that education could be a powerful tool for advocacy.

The Role of Higher Education

Pursuing higher education became a critical step for Bisi in his journey toward activism. After completing his undergraduate studies, he sought opportunities abroad, where he could engage with more progressive educational environments.

During his time studying in the United Kingdom, Bisi was exposed to diverse perspectives on LGBTQ rights, which further fueled his passion for activism. He learned about the legal frameworks that protected LGBTQ individuals in more liberal societies and the ongoing struggles faced by activists around the world. This knowledge equipped him with the tools necessary to advocate for change back home in Nigeria.

Advocacy Through Education

Bisi's educational pursuits did not end with his formal studies. He recognized the importance of continuing education as a means to empower others within the LGBTQ community. He began organizing workshops and seminars aimed at educating individuals about their rights and the importance of advocacy.

One notable initiative was the establishment of support networks that provided educational resources for LGBTQ youth. These networks aimed to foster a sense of belonging and community, allowing individuals to express themselves freely and learn about their rights in a safe environment.

Conclusion

Bisi Alimi's educational journey highlights the transformative power of education in the fight for LGBTQ rights. Through his experiences, he learned that education is not merely about acquiring knowledge; it is about challenging oppressive systems and advocating for change.

As Bisi often states, "Knowledge is power, and with power comes the responsibility to uplift others." His commitment to education continues to inspire a new generation of activists who are determined to create a more inclusive society.

In summary, Bisi's educational pursuits were marked by challenges, resilience, and a relentless drive to advocate for LGBTQ rights. His journey underscores the importance of education as a tool for empowerment and social change, demonstrating that even in the face of adversity, the pursuit of knowledge can lead to transformative activism.

Discovering Personal Identity

In the vibrant and bustling city of Lagos, where the cacophony of life intertwines with the whispers of tradition, Bisi Alimi embarked on a profound journey of self-discovery. This journey was not merely about understanding his sexual orientation; it was about unraveling the layers of his identity in a society that often viewed such explorations with skepticism and disdain.

Understanding Identity Formation

The process of discovering one's personal identity is complex and multifaceted. According to Erik Erikson's theory of psychosocial development, individuals navigate various stages throughout their lives, each characterized by a specific conflict that must be resolved to develop a healthy personality. In the context of LGBTQ individuals, the stage of identity versus role confusion is particularly salient. Bisi's experiences in Lagos exemplify this struggle, as he grappled with societal expectations while seeking to understand who he truly was.

$$I = f(P, S) \tag{5}$$

Where I represents identity, P symbolizes personal experiences, and S denotes societal influences. This equation illustrates the interplay between individual experiences and societal pressures in shaping identity.

Cultural and Societal Influences

Growing up in a conservative society, Bisi faced immense pressure to conform to heteronormative expectations. The influence of family dynamics played a crucial role in shaping his understanding of self. His family, like many others in Nigeria, adhered to traditional values that often marginalized LGBTQ identities. This led to a profound internal conflict for Bisi, as he navigated the expectations of his family while yearning for authenticity.

Moreover, the pervasive influence of religion in Nigerian society cannot be understated. Many religious teachings promote a narrative that stigmatizes non-heterosexual identities, creating an environment where individuals like Bisi often feel compelled to suppress their true selves. This internalized homophobia can lead to significant psychological distress, as individuals wrestle with feelings of shame and isolation.

Early Signs of Activism

Despite these challenges, Bisi began to recognize the early signs of activism within himself. His journey of self-discovery was marked by moments of courage and defiance against societal norms. For instance, during his time in school, he found solace in literature and art that celebrated diversity and challenged the status quo. This exposure ignited a passion for advocacy, as he realized that his experiences were not isolated but shared by many others in his community.

First Encounters with the LGBTQ Community

Bisi's first encounters with the LGBTQ community were pivotal in his journey. Attending clandestine gatherings and connecting with like-minded individuals provided him with a sense of belonging that he had long sought. These interactions were not without risk, as the societal backlash against LGBTQ individuals in Nigeria is severe. Yet, the empowerment he felt in these spaces was transformative. It was here that he began to embrace his identity fully, understanding that he was not alone in his struggles.

The Role of Education in Identity Formation

Education played a significant role in Bisi's journey of self-discovery. As he pursued higher education, he was exposed to diverse perspectives and ideologies that challenged the traditional narratives he had grown up with. This exposure fostered critical thinking and self-reflection, allowing him to question the societal norms that had previously constrained him.

Through academic exploration, Bisi encountered theories of gender and sexuality that resonated with his experiences. The works of scholars such as Judith Butler and Michel Foucault provided frameworks for understanding the fluidity of identity and the social constructs surrounding it. This intellectual engagement was crucial in solidifying his understanding of himself as a queer individual navigating a complex world.

Coming Out and Acceptance

The culmination of Bisi's journey towards discovering his personal identity was his decision to come out. This moment was not merely an act of self-affirmation; it was a declaration of resistance against the oppressive societal norms that sought to silence him. Coming out is often framed as a linear process, but for Bisi, it was a series of ongoing dialogues with himself and those around him.

The acceptance he sought was not just from his family but from a broader society that had long marginalized LGBTQ individuals. This quest for acceptance was fraught with challenges, as he faced rejection and hostility from some quarters. Yet, each act of defiance, each moment of vulnerability, brought him closer to a community that celebrated him for who he was.

The Power of Visibility

Bisi's journey of self-discovery underscored the power of visibility in the LGBTQ community. By embracing his identity and advocating for LGBTQ rights, he became a beacon of hope for others navigating similar paths. His story resonated with many, illustrating that the journey of self-discovery is not a solitary endeavor but a collective struggle for acceptance and equality.

In conclusion, Bisi Alimi's exploration of his personal identity was a transformative journey shaped by cultural, societal, and educational influences. His experiences reflect the broader narrative of LGBTQ individuals in conservative societies, highlighting the importance of self-acceptance, community, and activism in the quest for identity. As he continues to advocate for change, Bisi's story serves as a testament to the resilience of the human spirit in the face of adversity.

Coming Out and Acceptance

Coming out is a pivotal moment in the lives of many LGBTQ individuals, often serving as a crucial step toward personal authenticity and societal acceptance. For

Bisi Alimi, this journey was not just a personal revelation but a political statement that challenged the conservative norms of Nigerian society. In a country where being gay can lead to severe repercussions, the act of coming out is layered with complexity and danger.

The Process of Coming Out

The process of coming out can be understood through several psychological frameworks. One of the most recognized theories is Cass's Model of Sexual Identity Formation, which outlines six stages: identity confusion, identity comparison, identity tolerance, identity acceptance, identity pride, and identity synthesis. Each stage represents a progression from confusion and fear to acceptance and pride in one's identity.

For Bisi, the initial stage of identity confusion was marked by feelings of isolation. Growing up in Lagos, he faced societal pressures that dictated strict norms around masculinity and heterosexuality. The conflict between his identity and societal expectations created a tumultuous internal struggle. He recalls, "I felt like I was living a lie. I was trying to fit into a mold that was never meant for me."

Cultural and Religious Influences

The conservative nature of Nigerian society, deeply intertwined with religious beliefs, often exacerbates the challenges faced by LGBTQ individuals. In many cases, coming out is met with rejection from family and community, which can lead to mental health issues such as depression and anxiety. Bisi faced these challenges head-on, understanding that acceptance from others was often tied to deeply rooted cultural and religious beliefs.

In a society where homosexuality is often condemned, Bisi's decision to come out was not just an act of self-affirmation; it was a challenge to the status quo. He noted, "Coming out in Nigeria is like walking into a lion's den. You know you might not make it out alive, but you do it anyway because you have to." This metaphor illustrates the extreme risks associated with coming out in a conservative environment.

Family Dynamics and Acceptance

Family acceptance plays a crucial role in the coming out process. Research indicates that supportive family dynamics can significantly reduce the negative impacts of discrimination and stigma. In Bisi's case, his family initially struggled with his identity. His mother, a devout Christian, grappled with the teachings of her faith against the love for her son. However, through open dialogue and education, Bisi was able to foster a sense of understanding within his family.

This aligns with the concept of *family resilience*, which emphasizes the ability of families to adapt and thrive despite adversity. Bisi's journey reflects the potential for transformation within familial relationships, demonstrating that acceptance can evolve over time. "It took time, but my family learned to see me as their son first and foremost, not just my sexuality," he shared.

Community and Support Networks

The significance of community support cannot be understated. For many LGBTQ individuals, finding a safe space is crucial in navigating the complexities of coming out. Bisi found solace in connecting with other LGBTQ individuals who shared similar experiences. This sense of belonging was instrumental in his journey, as it provided a counter-narrative to the rejection he faced from broader society.

$$\text{Support Network} = \{\text{Friends, Allies, LGBTQ Organizations}\}$$

This equation highlights the components of a robust support network that can facilitate acceptance and foster resilience. Bisi's involvement with local LGBTQ organizations not only empowered him but also laid the groundwork for advocacy efforts aimed at changing societal perceptions.

The Role of Visibility and Advocacy

Bisi's coming out was not merely a personal act; it became a catalyst for activism. His visibility as an openly gay man in Nigeria challenged stereotypes and provided a platform for dialogue. By sharing his story, he inspired others to embrace their identities and advocate for change.

Visibility theory posits that representation matters. Bisi's public persona as an LGBTQ activist has contributed to a gradual shift in societal attitudes toward homosexuality in Nigeria. He remarked, "When you see someone like you standing tall, it gives you the strength to do the same." This statement underscores the importance of role models in the coming out process.

Challenges of Acceptance

Despite the progress made, challenges remain. The societal backlash against LGBTQ individuals in Nigeria is still prevalent, with many facing violence, discrimination, and ostracism. Bisi has faced threats and intimidation as a result of his activism, highlighting the ongoing risks associated with being openly gay in a conservative society.

The struggle for acceptance is ongoing, and Bisi's narrative illustrates the resilience required to navigate this journey. He emphasizes the importance of creating safe spaces for LGBTQ individuals, where they can share their experiences without fear of judgment. "We need to build communities where love and acceptance are the norms, not the exceptions," he asserts.

Conclusion

In conclusion, Bisi Alimi's journey of coming out and seeking acceptance is a powerful testament to the resilience of the human spirit. His story reflects the complexities faced by LGBTQ individuals in conservative societies, emphasizing the importance of family support, community networks, and visibility in the advocacy for acceptance. As he continues to champion LGBTQ rights, Bisi remains a beacon of hope for many navigating their own paths toward authenticity and acceptance in a world that often resists change.

Promoting LGBTQ Rights in Nigeria

Promoting LGBTQ rights in Nigeria is akin to navigating a minefield while blindfolded—difficult, dangerous, and often disheartening. The societal landscape in Nigeria is heavily influenced by conservative values, deeply rooted traditions, and a legal framework that criminalizes same-sex relationships. This section delves into the multifaceted challenges faced by activists, the theoretical frameworks that underpin their work, and the examples of resilience and courage that illuminate the path forward.

Theoretical Frameworks

At the core of LGBTQ rights advocacy in Nigeria lies the intersectionality theory, which posits that various social identities (such as race, gender, and sexuality) intersect to create unique modes of discrimination and privilege. This framework is crucial for understanding the specific struggles faced by LGBTQ individuals in Nigeria, where cultural, religious, and societal factors converge to create a hostile environment.

Moreover, the social constructivism theory emphasizes that sexual orientation and gender identity are not merely biological but are shaped by societal norms and values. This understanding is vital for activists as they challenge the misconceptions surrounding LGBTQ identities, advocating for a broader acceptance that transcends traditional views.

Challenges Faced

Promoting LGBTQ rights in Nigeria is fraught with challenges, including:

- **Legal Barriers:** The Same-Sex Marriage Prohibition Act of 2014 serves as a significant legal obstacle, imposing severe penalties for same-sex relationships. This law not only criminalizes LGBTQ identities but also creates an environment where discrimination is legally sanctioned.

- **Cultural Stigma:** Nigerian society is predominantly conservative, with strong religious beliefs that often view homosexuality as an abomination. This cultural stigma fosters an atmosphere of fear and silence among LGBTQ individuals, discouraging them from seeking support or advocating for their rights.

- **Violence and Intimidation:** Activists face threats of violence and intimidation from both state and non-state actors. Reports of harassment, physical assaults, and even killings of LGBTQ individuals underline the dangerous reality of advocating for rights in such a hostile environment.

- **Limited Resources:** Many LGBTQ organizations in Nigeria operate with limited funding and resources, making it challenging to sustain advocacy efforts, provide support services, and raise awareness about LGBTQ issues.

Strategies for Advocacy

Despite these challenges, activists in Nigeria have employed various strategies to promote LGBTQ rights:

- **Community Building:** Creating safe spaces for LGBTQ individuals is paramount. Activists have established support groups and networks that provide emotional support, legal assistance, and resources for mental health. These safe havens foster a sense of belonging and community among individuals who often feel isolated.

- **Education and Awareness:** Raising awareness about LGBTQ rights is critical in challenging societal misconceptions. Activists conduct workshops, seminars, and outreach programs to educate the public about sexual orientation and gender identity, emphasizing that love and acceptance should transcend societal norms.

- **Engagement with Allies:** Building coalitions with human rights organizations, feminist groups, and other marginalized communities amplifies the LGBTQ voice. By collaborating with allies, activists can leverage resources and create a united front against discrimination.

- **Utilizing Social Media:** In an era where social media serves as a powerful tool for advocacy, Nigerian activists have harnessed platforms like Twitter, Instagram, and Facebook to raise awareness, share personal stories, and mobilize support. Online campaigns have gained traction, allowing activists to reach a broader audience and challenge the narrative surrounding LGBTQ identities.

Examples of Impact

Despite the oppressive environment, there are notable examples of LGBTQ advocacy making a difference in Nigeria:

- **The Nigerian Queer Community:** Organizations like *The Initiative for Equal Rights (TIERs)* and *Queer Alliance Nigeria* have been at the forefront of promoting LGBTQ rights, providing essential services, and advocating for policy changes. Their work has not only raised awareness but has also fostered solidarity within the LGBTQ community.

- **Media Representation:** The portrayal of LGBTQ individuals in Nigerian media has been a contentious issue. However, some filmmakers and writers have courageously tackled LGBTQ themes, challenging stereotypes and sparking conversations about acceptance and understanding. These creative expressions serve as a form of activism, pushing the boundaries of societal norms.

- **International Support:** The global LGBTQ community has rallied behind Nigerian activists, providing resources, funding, and visibility. International organizations have pressured the Nigerian government to uphold human rights and have highlighted the plight of LGBTQ individuals in Nigeria on global platforms.

Conclusion

Promoting LGBTQ rights in Nigeria is a daunting task, characterized by immense challenges and societal resistance. However, the resilience of activists, the power of community, and the ongoing dialogue around sexual orientation and gender identity signal a gradual shift toward acceptance. By embracing intersectionality and leveraging the support of allies, LGBTQ advocates continue to fight for a future where love knows no boundaries, and every individual can live authentically without fear of persecution.

$$\text{Advocacy Impact} = \text{Community Engagement} + \text{Education} + \text{Alliances} + \text{Visibility} \tag{6}$$

As the struggle for LGBTQ rights in Nigeria persists, it is imperative to recognize the courage of those at the forefront, ensuring that their voices are heard and their rights are respected.

Navigating Personal Relationships

Navigating personal relationships can be a complex endeavor, especially for LGBTQ activists like Bisi Alimi, who operate within a conservative society that often stigmatizes their identities. This section delves into the intricacies of personal relationships in the context of activism, exploring the challenges faced, the strategies employed, and the transformative power of supportive connections.

The Challenge of Acceptance

For many LGBTQ individuals, including Alimi, the journey to self-acceptance is often fraught with emotional turmoil. Growing up in Lagos, where traditional values dominate, Alimi faced the dual challenge of reconciling his identity with societal expectations. Research indicates that the process of coming out can significantly impact personal relationships, often leading to a mix of support and rejection from family and friends [?].

$$\text{Acceptance} = \text{Understanding} + \text{Empathy} - \text{Prejudice} \tag{7}$$

This equation illustrates that acceptance in personal relationships hinges on the presence of understanding and empathy, while being diminished by prejudice. Alimi's experience exemplifies this; his journey involved not only self-acceptance but also seeking acceptance from those around him.

Building Support Networks

As Alimi embarked on his activism, he recognized the importance of building a robust support network. Studies show that social support plays a crucial role in the mental health and well-being of LGBTQ individuals [?]. Alimi sought out like-minded individuals and organizations that shared his vision for equality, creating a community that provided emotional and practical support.

$$\text{Support Network} = \text{Allies} + \text{Community} + \text{Shared Goals} \qquad (8)$$

In this equation, the strength of a support network is determined by the presence of allies, a sense of community, and shared goals. Alimi's ability to connect with other activists not only empowered him but also fostered a sense of belonging, which is vital for anyone navigating the often tumultuous waters of personal relationships in the LGBTQ community.

Navigating Family Dynamics

Family relationships can be particularly challenging for LGBTQ activists. Alimi's initial struggle with his family's acceptance is a common narrative among many LGBTQ individuals. The impact of family rejection can lead to feelings of isolation and distress, as noted in various psychological studies [?].

$$\text{Family Acceptance} = \text{Communication} + \text{Education} - \text{Fear} \qquad (9)$$

This equation suggests that family acceptance can be enhanced through open communication and education while being hindered by fear—fear of the unknown and fear of societal judgment. Alimi's journey involved not only coming out to his family but also engaging them in conversations about LGBTQ issues, gradually transforming their perceptions.

Romantic Relationships and Activism

Romantic relationships present their own set of challenges for LGBTQ activists. Alimi's experiences highlight the delicate balance between personal love life and public activism. The pressure of activism can strain relationships, as partners may struggle with the public scrutiny that comes with being associated with a prominent activist.

$$\text{Relationship Stability} = \text{Communication} + \text{Shared Values} - \text{External Pressure} \qquad (10)$$

In this context, relationship stability is influenced by effective communication and shared values, while external pressures—such as media attention and societal expectations—can create significant stress. Alimi's ability to communicate openly with his partners about the challenges of activism has been essential in maintaining healthy relationships.

Friendship and Solidarity

Friendships play a pivotal role in the lives of LGBTQ activists, providing a sanctuary of understanding and solidarity. Alimi has often emphasized the importance of friendships forged in the fires of activism. These relationships not only offer emotional support but also serve as a platform for collective action.

$$\text{Friendship} = \text{Trust} + \text{Shared Experiences} + \text{Mutual Support} \quad (11)$$

This equation underscores that friendship thrives on trust, shared experiences, and mutual support. Alimi's friendships with fellow activists have been a source of strength, enabling them to face adversity together while amplifying their collective voice in the fight for LGBTQ rights.

The Role of Intersectionality

Navigating personal relationships as an LGBTQ activist also requires an understanding of intersectionality—the interconnected nature of social categorizations such as race, class, and gender. Alimi's activism is deeply informed by his experiences as a Black gay man in Nigeria, which shapes his relationships both personally and professionally.

$$\text{Intersectionality} = \text{Identity} + \text{Context} + \text{Power Dynamics} \quad (12)$$

Here, intersectionality is viewed as a function of identity, context, and power dynamics. Alimi's ability to navigate these complexities allows him to build relationships that are not only supportive but also inclusive of diverse perspectives within the LGBTQ community.

Conclusion

In conclusion, navigating personal relationships as an LGBTQ activist is a multifaceted endeavor that involves acceptance, support, and the complexities of family dynamics. Bisi Alimi's journey illustrates the importance of building strong networks, fostering communication, and understanding the role of intersectionality in relationships. By embracing these challenges, activists can cultivate meaningful connections that empower both their personal lives and their advocacy efforts.

A Journey of Self-Discovery

Facing Discrimination

Facing discrimination is a harsh reality for many individuals within the LGBTQ community, particularly in conservative societies like Nigeria. Bisi Alimi's journey is a testament to the struggles that come with being openly gay in a country where societal norms are steeped in traditional values and where legal frameworks often fail to protect marginalized groups. This section delves into the various forms of discrimination Bisi encountered, the societal and psychological implications, and the theoretical frameworks that help us understand these experiences.

Types of Discrimination

Discrimination can manifest in numerous ways, including:

- **Social Discrimination:** This includes ostracism, exclusion from social groups, and verbal abuse. Bisi often faced ridicule and hostility from peers, which is a common experience for many LGBTQ individuals in Nigeria. The fear of being rejected by friends and family can lead to internalized homophobia, where individuals struggle to accept their own identities.

- **Economic Discrimination:** This occurs when LGBTQ individuals are denied job opportunities or promotions based on their sexual orientation. Bisi experienced this firsthand, as many employers in Nigeria are reluctant to hire openly gay individuals due to the prevailing stigma.

- **Legal Discrimination:** The Same-Sex Marriage Prohibition Act of 2014 is a prime example of legal discrimination in Nigeria. This law not only criminalizes same-sex relationships but also provides a legal basis for harassment and violence against LGBTQ individuals. Bisi's advocacy work aimed to challenge such laws and promote legal reforms.

- **Physical Violence:** Reports of violence against LGBTQ individuals are alarmingly high in Nigeria. Bisi has shared stories of friends who faced brutal attacks simply for being who they are. This physical threat is a constant reminder of the risks associated with visibility in a hostile environment.

Psychological Impacts

The psychological effects of facing discrimination can be profound. Many individuals report experiencing anxiety, depression, and feelings of worthlessness. The constant threat of violence and social rejection can lead to a state of hyper-vigilance, where individuals feel they must constantly monitor their behavior to avoid drawing attention to their sexual orientation.

Bisi has openly discussed his mental health struggles as a result of discrimination. He emphasizes the importance of seeking support from mental health professionals who understand the unique challenges faced by LGBTQ individuals. The stigma surrounding mental health in many African societies can compound these issues, making it difficult for individuals to seek help.

Theoretical Frameworks

To better understand the discrimination faced by Bisi and others in the LGBTQ community, we can draw on several theoretical frameworks:

- **Intersectionality:** Coined by Kimberlé Crenshaw, intersectionality explores how various social identities (such as race, gender, and sexual orientation) intersect to create unique experiences of oppression. Bisi's identity as a gay man in Nigeria positions him at the crossroads of multiple forms of discrimination, including homophobia and racism.

- **Minority Stress Theory:** This theory posits that individuals from marginalized groups experience chronic stress due to their social position. This stress can lead to mental health issues and decreased well-being. Bisi's activism can be seen as a response to this stress, as he seeks to create a more supportive environment for LGBTQ individuals in Nigeria.

- **Social Identity Theory:** This theory suggests that a person's sense of who they are is based on their group membership. For Bisi, embracing his identity as a gay man has been a powerful act of defiance against the discrimination he faces. By publicly advocating for LGBTQ rights, he challenges the negative stereotypes associated with his identity.

Examples of Discrimination

Bisi's own experiences provide a vivid illustration of the discrimination faced by LGBTQ individuals in Nigeria. During his early years, he faced bullying in school, where classmates would taunt him for his perceived differences. This social ostracism not only affected his self-esteem but also fueled his desire to connect with others in the LGBTQ community.

In his advocacy work, Bisi has encountered government officials who dismiss his concerns about human rights violations. He recalls a particularly disheartening meeting where a government representative laughed off the idea of LGBTQ rights, stating that homosexuality is "un-African." Such dismissive attitudes highlight the systemic nature of discrimination and the challenge of changing deeply ingrained societal beliefs.

Moreover, Bisi has faced threats from individuals who oppose his activism. He recounts an incident where he received a message threatening violence if he continued to speak out for LGBTQ rights. This experience underscores the physical dangers that accompany advocacy in a repressive environment.

Conclusion

Facing discrimination is an ever-present reality for Bisi Alimi and many others in the LGBTQ community. Understanding the various forms of discrimination, their psychological impacts, and the theoretical frameworks that explain these experiences is crucial for fostering empathy and support. Bisi's resilience in the face of such adversity serves as an inspiration for many, reminding us that the fight for equality is ongoing and that every voice matters in the struggle for justice.

Embracing Activism

In the vibrant yet tumultuous landscape of Nigeria, where societal norms often clash with individual identities, Bisi Alimi found himself at a crossroads. The moment he embraced activism was not merely a decision; it was a declaration of war against oppression, ignorance, and the pervasive stigma surrounding the LGBTQ community. This section delves into the transformative journey of Bisi as he transitioned from a reluctant participant in his own life to a fierce advocate for change.

The roots of activism can often be traced back to personal experiences of discrimination and marginalization. For Bisi, the awakening began with the realization that he could no longer remain silent in the face of injustice. The theory of *social identity* plays a crucial role here; it posits that an individual's self-concept is derived from perceived membership in social groups. Bisi's identity as a gay man in a conservative society fueled his desire to fight for not only his rights but for those of countless others who felt voiceless.

Bisi's early experiences with discrimination were not isolated incidents but rather reflections of a larger systemic issue. In Nigeria, the Same-Sex Marriage Prohibition Act of 2014 served as a stark reminder of the legal and social barriers that LGBTQ individuals faced. The law not only criminalized same-sex relationships but also perpetuated a culture of fear and violence. Bisi's first encounter with activism came when he decided to speak out against this draconian legislation. He understood that silence would only embolden the oppressors, and thus, he chose to use his voice as a weapon.

However, embracing activism was not without its challenges. Bisi faced significant backlash from his community, family, and even friends. The fear of ostracism and violence loomed large, yet it was this very fear that galvanized him. The psychological theory of *cognitive dissonance* explains the internal conflict that arises when one's beliefs are challenged by their actions. Bisi experienced this dissonance as he navigated his dual identity: a gay man and an activist in a society that vehemently opposed both.

To combat these challenges, Bisi sought out allies within the LGBTQ community. He found strength in numbers, discovering that collective action could amplify their voices. The concept of *collective efficacy*—the belief in the group's ability to achieve goals—became a cornerstone of his activism. Organizing rallies and protests, Bisi mobilized the community to stand together against the oppressive laws and societal norms that sought to silence them.

One of the pivotal moments in Bisi's activism was his participation in the first-ever LGBTQ conference in Nigeria. Here, he met other activists who shared similar struggles and aspirations. The conference served as a catalyst for Bisi, igniting a fire within him to not only advocate for change in Nigeria but to also connect with international organizations. He realized that the fight for LGBTQ rights was not confined to Nigeria; it was a global struggle that required solidarity across borders.

Bisi's activism was also marked by the use of social media as a powerful tool for visibility. In a world where traditional media often shunned LGBTQ narratives, platforms like Twitter and Facebook provided a space for marginalized voices to be heard. Bisi understood the significance of *digital activism*, where hashtags and online campaigns could mobilize support and raise awareness on a scale previously unimaginable. His viral posts and videos challenged stereotypes and educated the public on LGBTQ issues, proving that visibility was a form of resistance.

As Bisi embraced his role as an activist, he also confronted the harsh realities of mental health struggles. The toll of activism can be heavy, often leading to burnout and feelings of isolation. Bisi's journey included seeking therapy and building a support network of fellow activists who understood the emotional weight of their work. This aspect of his activism highlighted the importance of self-care and resilience in the face of adversity.

In conclusion, Bisi Alimi's embrace of activism was a multifaceted journey marked by personal revelations, collective action, and the relentless pursuit of justice. His story serves as a testament to the power of resilience and the impact of standing up against oppression. As he navigated the complexities of identity, community, and activism, Bisi became not just a voice for the LGBTQ community in Nigeria, but a beacon of hope for marginalized individuals around the world. The challenges he faced only strengthened his resolve, proving that embracing activism is not just a choice; it is a calling to create a world where love knows no boundaries.

Finding Allies

In the journey of activism, the importance of finding allies cannot be overstated. Allies serve as a crucial support system, amplifying voices, sharing resources, and fostering a culture of solidarity. For Bisi Alimi, navigating the often treacherous waters of LGBTQ activism in Nigeria required not just courage, but also the strategic cultivation of alliances with individuals and organizations that shared a commitment to equality and human rights.

The Need for Allies

Activism can often feel like an uphill battle, especially in a conservative society where LGBTQ rights are frequently dismissed or outright attacked. Research in social movements, such as Tilly's (2004) theory of collective action, suggests that successful movements often rely on a network of allies. This network can provide legitimacy, resources, and protection against backlash. In the context of LGBTQ activism in Nigeria, where societal stigma and legal repercussions are prevalent, finding allies becomes a matter of survival and effectiveness.

Types of Allies

Bisi Alimi identified several types of allies throughout his activism:

- **Local Allies:** These are individuals within Nigeria who understand the cultural context and can navigate the local landscape. They include fellow activists, supportive family members, and friends who stand in solidarity against discrimination.

- **International Allies:** Organizations and activists outside Nigeria, such as Human Rights Watch or Amnesty International, have been instrumental in providing support, resources, and a global platform for local issues. Their involvement can help draw international attention to human rights violations in Nigeria.

- **Institutional Allies:** These are organizations, such as NGOs and advocacy groups, that have established networks and resources dedicated to LGBTQ rights. Collaborating with such institutions can offer legal support, funding, and strategic advice.

- **Academic Allies:** Scholars and researchers who study LGBTQ issues can provide valuable insights and data to support advocacy efforts. Their research can lend credibility to claims made by activists and help in framing the narrative around LGBTQ rights in Nigeria.

Building Relationships

Finding allies is not merely about identifying potential supporters; it requires building genuine relationships based on trust and mutual respect. Bisi Alimi's approach involved engaging with various communities, attending events, and participating in dialogues that fostered understanding and collaboration. For example, he often emphasized the need for intersectionality, recognizing that allies from different backgrounds—be it race, gender, or class—could enrich the movement and broaden its appeal.

Challenges in Finding Allies

While the pursuit of allies is essential, it is not without challenges. One of the primary obstacles is the pervasive stigma surrounding LGBTQ identities in Nigeria. Many potential allies may fear social ostracism or professional repercussions for associating with LGBTQ individuals. This fear can lead to a reluctance to engage openly, which can hinder the formation of effective alliances.

Additionally, there is often a lack of awareness about LGBTQ issues among potential allies. Many individuals may hold misconceptions or biases that prevent them from fully understanding the struggles faced by the LGBTQ community. Bisi Alimi tackled this issue through education and advocacy, hosting workshops and discussions aimed at dispelling myths and fostering a culture of empathy.

Examples of Successful Alliances

One notable success in Bisi Alimi's journey was the collaboration with local human rights organizations. By partnering with groups like the Nigerian Human Rights Commission, Bisi was able to leverage their resources and networks to amplify the LGBTQ message. Together, they organized campaigns that highlighted the need for anti-discrimination laws and safe spaces for LGBTQ individuals.

Another significant alliance was formed with international organizations, which provided platforms for Bisi to speak at global conferences. These opportunities not only raised awareness about the dire situation for LGBTQ individuals in Nigeria but also attracted the attention of potential allies within the international community. For instance, speaking at the United Nations allowed Bisi to connect with diplomats and activists from various countries, creating a ripple effect that brought international scrutiny to Nigeria's human rights record.

The Power of Solidarity

Ultimately, the strength of an activist's message is magnified by the solidarity of allies. Bisi Alimi's story illustrates how finding allies can transform the landscape of activism. When individuals come together, united by a common cause, they create a powerful force for change. This solidarity not only provides emotional and psychological support but also strengthens the movement's capacity to challenge oppressive systems.

In conclusion, finding allies is an essential component of activism, particularly in challenging environments like Nigeria. Bisi Alimi's journey demonstrates that through strategic relationships, education, and a commitment to solidarity, activists can amplify their voices and create meaningful change. As the LGBTQ rights movement continues to evolve, the importance of finding and nurturing allies will remain a cornerstone of effective advocacy.

Dealing with Social Stigma

Social stigma presents one of the most formidable challenges for individuals within the LGBTQ community, particularly in conservative societies like Nigeria. This section delves into the nature of social stigma, its implications on personal and communal levels, and the strategies employed by Bisi Alimi and other activists to combat it.

Understanding Social Stigma

Social stigma refers to the negative attitudes and beliefs that society holds against certain groups, often leading to discrimination and exclusion. Erving Goffman, a prominent sociologist, defined stigma as an attribute that is deeply discrediting, reducing an individual from a whole and usual person to a tainted, discounted one [?]. In the context of LGBTQ individuals in Nigeria, stigma manifests through derogatory language, social ostracism, and systemic discrimination.

Theoretical Framework

Theories surrounding stigma can be categorized into several frameworks, including Labeling Theory and Social Identity Theory.

- **Labeling Theory** posits that the labels society assigns to individuals can significantly affect their self-identity and behavior. When LGBTQ individuals are labeled negatively, they may internalize these labels, leading to feelings of shame and isolation.

- **Social Identity Theory** emphasizes that individuals derive part of their identity from the groups they belong to. For LGBTQ individuals in a stigmatizing society, this can result in a fractured identity, where their sexual orientation conflicts with societal expectations.

Problems Arising from Social Stigma

The repercussions of social stigma are profound and multifaceted:

1. **Mental Health Issues:** Stigmatized individuals often experience higher rates of anxiety, depression, and suicidal ideation. A study by Meyer (2003) highlights that perceived stigma can lead to a phenomenon known as "minority stress," which exacerbates mental health challenges among LGBTQ individuals.

2. **Social Isolation:** Stigma can result in individuals feeling alienated from their communities. This isolation can hinder access to support networks, making it more challenging to engage in activism or seek help.

3. **Economic Disadvantages:** Discrimination in employment and housing can stem from societal stigma, leading to economic instability for LGBTQ individuals. Many may face job loss or difficulty in securing housing due to their sexual orientation.

Bisi Alimi's Approach to Combatting Stigma

Bisi Alimi's activism has been instrumental in addressing and challenging the stigma surrounding LGBTQ individuals in Nigeria. His approach encompasses various strategies:

- **Visibility and Representation:** Alimi emphasizes the importance of visibility in combating stigma. By sharing his own story and experiences, he humanizes LGBTQ individuals, challenging the negative stereotypes perpetuated by society. He famously stated, "The more we talk about our stories, the more we take away the power of stigma."

- **Education and Awareness Campaigns:** Alimi has been involved in numerous educational initiatives aimed at dispelling myths about LGBTQ individuals. By providing factual information and fostering dialogue, these campaigns work to reduce ignorance and fear, which are often at the root of stigma.

- **Building Support Networks:** Alimi understands the critical role of community in overcoming stigma. He has worked to establish safe spaces for LGBTQ individuals to connect, share experiences, and support one another. These networks not only provide emotional support but also empower individuals to advocate for their rights collectively.

Examples of Activism Against Stigma

Several initiatives and movements led by Alimi and his allies illustrate the fight against social stigma:

1. **Pride Events:** Organizing pride events in Nigeria, despite the legal and social risks, serves to celebrate LGBTQ identities and foster community solidarity. These events challenge societal norms and assert the right to exist openly and proudly.

2. **Media Engagement:** Alimi has utilized various media platforms to amplify LGBTQ voices. By engaging with journalists and participating in interviews, he has been able to shift narratives around LGBTQ issues, showcasing the diversity and richness of LGBTQ lives in Nigeria.

3. **Collaboration with Allies:** Alimi collaborates with non-LGBTQ allies, including human rights organizations and sympathetic political figures, to

advocate for broader societal change. This coalition-building is crucial in challenging the stigma that exists not only against LGBTQ individuals but also against those who support them.

Conclusion

Dealing with social stigma is a complex and ongoing struggle for LGBTQ individuals in Nigeria. However, through the relentless efforts of activists like Bisi Alimi, there is hope for a more inclusive future. By fostering understanding, building community, and challenging negative narratives, the tide of stigma can be turned, paving the way for acceptance and equality.

Exploring Activism Abroad

Activism is a global language, and when Bisi Alimi decided to explore activism abroad, he was not just stepping outside Nigeria; he was stepping into a world of possibilities, challenges, and transformative encounters. This journey was not merely a physical relocation but an intellectual and emotional expedition that allowed him to broaden his understanding of LGBTQ rights and the multifaceted nature of activism.

The Global Landscape of LGBTQ Activism

The first step in exploring activism abroad involved understanding the global landscape of LGBTQ rights. Different countries exhibit varying degrees of acceptance and legal protection for LGBTQ individuals. For instance, countries like Canada and the Netherlands have made significant strides in LGBTQ rights, including the legalization of same-sex marriage and the implementation of anti-discrimination laws. In contrast, many African nations still grapple with stringent laws against homosexuality, often rooted in colonial-era statutes.

Bisi's exploration took him to international conferences, where activists from around the world gathered to share their experiences, strategies, and aspirations. These gatherings often serve as melting pots of ideas, where the exchange of knowledge can lead to innovative approaches in advocacy. Bisi learned that while the challenges faced by LGBTQ communities in different regions may vary, the underlying themes of discrimination, violence, and the quest for acceptance are universally shared.

Building Alliances with Global Activists

One of the most significant aspects of Bisi's journey was the opportunity to build alliances with global activists. These connections were not just about networking; they were about forming a coalition of voices united by a common goal. For example, during a conference in Amsterdam, Bisi met activists from Eastern Europe who were facing severe backlash from their governments. Their stories resonated with him, highlighting the importance of solidarity in the fight for human rights.

The collaboration with international activists also opened doors for knowledge exchange. Bisi was introduced to various advocacy techniques, such as community organizing and digital activism, which he could adapt to the Nigerian context. The concept of *intersectionality*, introduced by legal scholar Kimberlé Crenshaw, became particularly relevant here. Intersectionality emphasizes that individuals experience discrimination in varying degrees based on overlapping identities, such as race, gender, and sexual orientation. Understanding this concept helped Bisi to appreciate the complexities within the LGBTQ movement and the necessity of inclusive advocacy.

Challenges of International Activism

However, exploring activism abroad was not without its challenges. Bisi encountered the problem of *cultural appropriation*, where activists from the Global North sometimes imposed their narratives and solutions onto communities in the Global South without fully understanding the local context. This highlighted the need for a nuanced approach to activism that respects local cultures while advocating for universal human rights.

Moreover, the issue of funding in international activism became apparent. Many grassroots organizations in Nigeria struggled to secure funding, while larger organizations in the West often had more resources but sometimes lacked the local insights necessary for effective advocacy. Bisi recognized that for activism to be truly effective, it must be locally driven. He began advocating for a model of *funding equity*, where resources were allocated to support local activists rather than imposing external agendas.

Utilizing Technology for Global Advocacy

In the digital age, technology emerged as a powerful tool for activism. Bisi leveraged social media platforms to amplify the voices of Nigerian LGBTQ individuals, showcasing their stories to a global audience. This not only raised awareness but also fostered a sense of community among those who felt isolated.

The power of visibility cannot be overstated; as Bisi often said, "When you see someone like you, fighting for your rights, it gives you hope."

He also participated in online campaigns that highlighted the plight of LGBTQ individuals in Nigeria, bringing international attention to local issues. For instance, the #FreeNigeria campaign garnered global support, leading to increased pressure on the Nigerian government to address human rights violations against LGBTQ individuals.

The Role of International Institutions

International institutions also played a crucial role in Bisi's exploration of activism abroad. Organizations such as the United Nations and Amnesty International provided platforms for activists to voice their concerns on a global stage. Bisi took part in lobbying efforts at the UN, advocating for the inclusion of LGBTQ rights in discussions on human rights. This engagement was pivotal, as it not only raised awareness but also held governments accountable for their treatment of LGBTQ individuals.

Conclusion: A Broader Vision for Activism

Ultimately, Bisi Alimi's exploration of activism abroad enriched his understanding of the LGBTQ movement and its complexities. He returned to Nigeria with a broader vision, one that encompassed not only local struggles but also global interconnectedness. His journey underscored the importance of collaboration, cultural sensitivity, and the utilization of technology in advocacy. As he often reminded his peers, "We are not alone in this fight; our struggles are interconnected, and together, we can create a world where everyone can love freely and live authentically."

In summary, exploring activism abroad was a transformative experience for Bisi Alimi, one that equipped him with the tools, knowledge, and networks necessary to continue his fight for LGBTQ rights in Nigeria and beyond. The journey was not just about crossing borders; it was about breaking barriers and building bridges in the pursuit of equality for all.

Establishing Connections with LGBTQ Organizations

In the journey of LGBTQ activism, establishing connections with organizations dedicated to the cause is not just beneficial; it is essential. For Bisi Alimi, this meant creating a network that would amplify his voice and the voices of countless others in Nigeria. These connections provided a platform for collaboration, resource sharing, and collective action, which are vital in a landscape often marked by hostility and discrimination.

The Importance of Networking

Networking within the LGBTQ community serves multiple purposes. It allows activists to share experiences, strategies, and resources. According to the Social Network Theory, relationships and connections can significantly influence the flow of information and support among individuals within a community. This theory posits that the more interconnected individuals are, the stronger their collective power becomes. For Bisi, establishing these connections meant not just finding allies but also creating a robust support system that could withstand the pressures of activism in a conservative society.

Challenges in Establishing Connections

However, the process of establishing these connections is fraught with challenges. In a country like Nigeria, where LGBTQ identities are often criminalized and stigmatized, many organizations operate underground or face severe backlash. This leads to a lack of visibility and resources, making it difficult for activists to find each other. Bisi faced numerous obstacles, including:

- **Fear of Repercussions:** Many individuals are hesitant to engage with LGBTQ organizations due to fear of persecution, both from the government and society.

- **Limited Resources:** Many local organizations operate on shoestring budgets, limiting their ability to reach out and connect with others.

- **Cultural Barriers:** In a conservative society, cultural norms often dictate that LGBTQ individuals remain silent about their identities, further isolating them from potential allies.

Despite these challenges, Bisi recognized the importance of building a coalition. He began by reaching out to existing LGBTQ organizations, both locally and internationally, to share knowledge and resources.

Strategies for Connection

Bisi employed several strategies to establish these vital connections:

1. **Utilizing Social Media:** In an age where digital platforms can transcend geographical barriers, Bisi leveraged social media to connect with LGBTQ activists worldwide. Platforms like Twitter and Facebook became critical tools for outreach and collaboration.

2. **Participating in Conferences:** Attending international LGBTQ conferences allowed Bisi to meet activists from different backgrounds. These events provided a space for sharing experiences and strategies, fostering a sense of global solidarity.

3. **Creating Safe Spaces:** Bisi emphasized the need for safe spaces where LGBTQ individuals could gather without fear of judgment or persecution. This included organizing community meetings and support groups that encouraged open dialogue.

4. **Building Alliances with Human Rights Organizations:** By collaborating with broader human rights organizations, Bisi was able to amplify LGBTQ issues within the larger context of human rights advocacy. This approach not only increased visibility but also garnered support from allies who may not have identified as LGBTQ.

Impact of Connections on Activism

The connections Bisi established had a profound impact on his activism. They provided him with the necessary support to tackle issues such as discrimination, legal barriers, and social stigma. For instance, through collaboration with international organizations, Bisi was able to secure funding for local initiatives aimed at educating the public about LGBTQ rights.

Moreover, these connections facilitated the sharing of best practices. Bisi learned from the experiences of activists in other countries who faced similar challenges. For example, he drew inspiration from the strategies employed by LGBTQ activists in South Africa, who successfully mobilized public support for equality through grassroots campaigns.

Case Study: Collaboration with Global LGBTQ Leaders

One notable example of Bisi's successful connections was his collaboration with global LGBTQ leaders during the United Nations Human Rights Council sessions. By joining forces with international activists, he was able to bring attention to the plight of LGBTQ individuals in Nigeria. This collaboration not only increased visibility for the issues at hand but also pressured the Nigerian government to reconsider its stance on LGBTQ rights.

Conclusion

Establishing connections with LGBTQ organizations is crucial for effective activism. For Bisi Alimi, these connections transformed his journey from a solitary fight for acceptance to a collaborative movement for change. By leveraging the power of networking, he not only amplified his voice but also the voices of countless others, creating a ripple effect that continues to inspire future generations of activists. The journey is ongoing, but through these connections, the dream of a more inclusive society becomes increasingly attainable.

The Power of Visibility

In the realm of activism, visibility holds immense power. For LGBTQ individuals, being seen and heard can transform not only personal experiences but also societal narratives. Visibility serves as a beacon of hope, illuminating paths for those who may feel isolated or oppressed. It is an essential tool in the fight for equality, as it challenges stereotypes, breaks down barriers, and fosters understanding.

Theoretical Framework

The concept of visibility in LGBTQ activism is grounded in several theoretical frameworks. One such framework is **Queer Theory**, which posits that identity is not fixed but fluid, and that societal norms around gender and sexuality are socially constructed. This theory emphasizes the importance of representation and visibility in challenging normative narratives. Judith Butler, a prominent figure in queer theory, argues that visibility can disrupt the binary understanding of gender and sexuality, allowing for a more nuanced understanding of identity.

Another relevant theory is the **Social Identity Theory**, which suggests that individuals derive a sense of self from their group memberships. For LGBTQ individuals, visibility can reinforce a sense of belonging within the community, while also fostering solidarity and collective action. The more LGBTQ individuals are visible, the more they can challenge the stigma associated with their identities.

Problems of Invisibility

Despite the power of visibility, many LGBTQ individuals face significant barriers that contribute to their invisibility. In conservative societies, where traditional norms dominate, being openly LGBTQ can lead to discrimination, violence, and ostracism. This societal pressure often forces individuals to hide their identities, leading to internalized stigma and mental health struggles.

The consequences of invisibility are profound. Research has shown that LGBTQ individuals who are not visible or who feel they cannot express their identities are at a higher risk for mental health issues, including depression and anxiety. A study by the *American Psychological Association* found that LGBTQ youth who experience high levels of stigma are more likely to engage in self-harm and suicidal ideation.

Examples of Visibility in Action

Bisi Alimi's journey exemplifies the transformative power of visibility. As one of Nigeria's first openly gay men, Alimi has used his platform to advocate for LGBTQ rights and challenge societal norms. His appearance on a Nigerian television show in 2004 was groundbreaking; it not only marked a significant moment in Nigerian media but also sparked conversations about LGBTQ identities in a country where such discussions were largely taboo.

Moreover, Alimi's work extends beyond personal visibility. He has actively promoted the visibility of LGBTQ issues on international platforms, addressing homophobia and advocating for anti-discrimination laws. By sharing his story and experiences, he has inspired countless others to embrace their identities and fight for their rights.

Another powerful example of visibility is the impact of social media. Platforms like Twitter, Instagram, and TikTok have provided LGBTQ individuals with spaces to express themselves, share their stories, and connect with others. The viral hashtag campaigns, such as #LoveIsLove and #Pride, have mobilized communities and raised awareness about LGBTQ issues globally. These digital spaces allow for a diverse range of voices to be heard, challenging the dominant narratives perpetuated by mainstream media.

The Role of Allies

Visibility is not solely the responsibility of LGBTQ individuals; allies play a crucial role as well. Allies can amplify LGBTQ voices, advocate for inclusive policies, and challenge discriminatory practices within their spheres of influence. The visibility of allies can help normalize LGBTQ identities and create a more accepting environment.

For instance, public figures who openly support LGBTQ rights can significantly impact societal perceptions. When celebrities come out or advocate for LGBTQ issues, they leverage their visibility to challenge stereotypes and promote acceptance. This phenomenon was evident when celebrities like Ellen DeGeneres and Laverne Cox became vocal advocates for LGBTQ rights, contributing to a broader cultural shift towards acceptance.

Conclusion

The power of visibility in LGBTQ activism cannot be overstated. It is a catalyst for change, fostering understanding, challenging stigma, and inspiring future generations. While barriers to visibility remain, the ongoing efforts of activists like Bisi Alimi and the support of allies are paving the way for a more inclusive society. As visibility continues to expand, it holds the potential to reshape narratives, empower individuals, and ultimately transform the world into a more accepting place for all.

Advocacy for Anti-Discrimination Laws

In the fight for LGBTQ rights, advocacy for anti-discrimination laws serves as a fundamental pillar in the quest for equality and justice. These laws are designed to protect individuals from discrimination based on sexual orientation, gender identity, and other characteristics. For Bisi Alimi, advocating for these laws was not just a professional endeavor but a deeply personal mission rooted in his own experiences and struggles.

Theoretical Framework

At the core of anti-discrimination advocacy lies the principle of equality, which asserts that all individuals should be treated equally under the law. The legal framework surrounding anti-discrimination can be understood through various theories, including:

1. **Social Justice Theory**: This theory emphasizes the importance of fairness and equality in society. It posits that systemic inequalities must be addressed through legal reforms, ensuring that marginalized communities receive the same protections as others.

2. **Human Rights Framework**: International human rights laws, such as the Universal Declaration of Human Rights (UDHR), advocate for the protection of all individuals regardless of their sexual orientation or gender identity. Article 1 of the UDHR states, "All human beings are born free and equal in dignity and rights."

3. **Intersectionality**: Coined by Kimberlé Crenshaw, this framework explores how various forms of discrimination (e.g., race, gender, sexual orientation) intersect and compound one another. Recognizing intersectionality is crucial in crafting anti-discrimination laws that address the unique challenges faced by individuals at the intersections of these identities.

Problems Faced in Advocacy

Despite the theoretical underpinnings supporting anti-discrimination laws, advocates like Bisi Alimi face significant challenges:

1. **Political Resistance**: In Nigeria, where Alimi's advocacy began, the political landscape is often hostile to LGBTQ rights. The Same-Sex Marriage Prohibition Act of 2014 exemplifies this resistance, criminalizing same-sex relationships and further entrenching discrimination.

2. **Cultural Stigma**: Societal attitudes towards LGBTQ individuals are often rooted in cultural and religious beliefs. This stigma can hinder the acceptance of anti-discrimination laws, as communities may view such legislation as a threat to traditional values.

3. **Legal Barriers**: Existing laws may not provide adequate protections for LGBTQ individuals, creating a legal environment where discrimination can flourish. This lack of legal recourse exacerbates the vulnerability of LGBTQ individuals in various aspects of life, including employment, healthcare, and housing.

Examples of Advocacy Efforts

Bisi Alimi's advocacy for anti-discrimination laws has taken many forms, with notable examples including:

1. **Public Campaigns**: Alimi has utilized social media platforms to raise awareness about the importance of anti-discrimination laws. His campaigns often highlight personal stories of individuals who have faced discrimination, humanizing the issue and fostering empathy among the broader public.

2. **Collaboration with NGOs**: Partnering with local and international non-governmental organizations (NGOs) has been a strategic move for Alimi. These collaborations amplify voices and provide resources for advocacy efforts. For instance, working with organizations like OutRight Action International has helped bring global attention to the plight of LGBTQ individuals in Nigeria.

3. **Engagement with Policymakers**: Alimi has actively engaged with policymakers to advocate for the inclusion of anti-discrimination provisions in

legislation. By presenting data and personal testimonies, he has aimed to persuade lawmakers of the necessity for legal protections.

The Role of Education and Awareness

Education plays a crucial role in the advocacy for anti-discrimination laws. Alimi has emphasized the need for educational programs that inform both the public and lawmakers about LGBTQ issues. By fostering understanding and empathy, these programs can help dismantle the stereotypes and misconceptions that fuel discrimination.

$$\text{Awareness} = \text{Education} + \text{Empathy} + \text{Action} \qquad (13)$$

This equation encapsulates the idea that increasing awareness about LGBTQ rights requires a combination of education, empathy towards the struggles faced by LGBTQ individuals, and actionable steps to create change.

Looking Ahead

The road to enacting anti-discrimination laws is fraught with obstacles, but the efforts of activists like Bisi Alimi have laid a strong foundation for future progress. As awareness grows and more individuals join the fight, the push for legal protections will continue to gain momentum. Alimi's vision for a Nigeria where LGBTQ individuals can live freely and without fear is not just a dream—it is a goal that can be achieved through persistent advocacy, education, and the unwavering belief in the principles of equality and justice.

In conclusion, advocacy for anti-discrimination laws is essential for creating a more inclusive society. Bisi Alimi's work exemplifies the power of activism in challenging oppressive systems and fostering a culture of acceptance. The journey may be long, but with each step taken towards equality, the dream of a just society becomes more attainable.

Building Alliances within Nigerian Society

In the quest for LGBTQ rights in Nigeria, Bisi Alimi recognized that building alliances within Nigerian society was not merely beneficial; it was essential for fostering a more inclusive environment. Alimi's approach was rooted in the understanding that change could not occur in isolation. Instead, it required a coalition of diverse voices that transcended the LGBTQ community, engaging with various societal sectors including religion, politics, education, and culture.

Theoretical Framework

The theory of intersectionality provides a critical lens through which to analyze the dynamics of building alliances. Coined by Kimberlé Crenshaw, intersectionality posits that individuals experience overlapping identities that can lead to unique forms of discrimination or privilege. For instance, LGBTQ individuals in Nigeria often face compounded challenges due to their gender, ethnicity, and socio-economic status. Understanding these intersections allows activists like Alimi to tailor their advocacy strategies to resonate with broader societal issues, thereby fostering alliances with non-LGBTQ groups who may also face discrimination.

Challenges in Building Alliances

Despite the potential for collaboration, several challenges hindered the formation of these alliances. The conservative nature of Nigerian society, heavily influenced by religious beliefs and cultural norms, often stigmatized LGBTQ identities. Many potential allies were hesitant to engage with LGBTQ issues due to fear of backlash or ostracism from their communities. For example, a prominent religious leader who might sympathize with LGBTQ rights could face significant repercussions from their congregation, making it risky to publicly support Alimi's initiatives.

Moreover, the Nigerian government's stance on LGBTQ rights, exemplified by the Same-Sex Marriage Prohibition Act of 2014, created a hostile environment for open discussions. This legislation not only criminalized same-sex relationships but also imposed severe penalties on individuals and organizations advocating for LGBTQ rights. As a result, many potential allies were deterred from forming alliances, fearing legal repercussions or social ostracism.

Strategies for Building Alliances

Alimi employed several strategies to overcome these challenges and build meaningful alliances:

- **Engaging with Religious Leaders:** Alimi sought to engage in dialogues with progressive religious leaders who were open to discussing LGBTQ issues. By framing the conversation around love, acceptance, and human rights, he was able to find common ground. For instance, Alimi collaborated with a group of interfaith leaders who advocated for compassion and understanding, thereby creating a platform for dialogue that included LGBTQ perspectives.

- **Collaboration with Human Rights Organizations:** Alimi recognized the importance of aligning with established human rights organizations that had a broader mandate. By collaborating with groups like Amnesty International and Human Rights Watch, Alimi was able to leverage their resources and networks to amplify the message of LGBTQ rights. This partnership not only provided legal support but also helped to legitimize the movement within a wider human rights framework.

- **Utilizing Media for Advocacy:** Alimi understood the power of media in shaping public perception. He utilized various media platforms to tell personal stories of LGBTQ individuals, humanizing the struggle for rights. By showcasing these narratives, he was able to challenge stereotypes and foster empathy among the general public. For example, Alimi's participation in interviews and documentaries highlighted the everyday realities of LGBTQ Nigerians, making the issues more relatable to a broader audience.

- **Education and Awareness Campaigns:** Alimi initiated educational programs aimed at dispelling myths about LGBTQ individuals. These campaigns targeted schools, universities, and community centers, focusing on fostering understanding and acceptance. By collaborating with educators and youth organizations, Alimi was able to reach younger generations, instilling values of inclusivity and respect from an early age.

- **Cultural Engagement:** Recognizing the importance of culture in Nigerian society, Alimi engaged with artists, musicians, and writers to promote LGBTQ narratives through various forms of art. Events such as art exhibitions and music festivals provided platforms for LGBTQ expression and fostered discussions about identity and acceptance. This cultural engagement helped to normalize LGBTQ presence in public discourse.

Examples of Successful Alliances

One notable example of successful alliance-building was the collaboration between LGBTQ activists and women's rights organizations. Both groups faced similar challenges in a patriarchal society, and by joining forces, they were able to amplify their voices. This coalition organized protests against gender-based violence, highlighting the intersection of gender and sexual orientation. Such collaborations not only strengthened the advocacy for LGBTQ rights but also fostered a sense of solidarity among marginalized groups.

Another example was Alimi's partnership with local businesses to create safe spaces for LGBTQ individuals. By encouraging businesses to adopt inclusive policies and practices, Alimi helped to establish environments where LGBTQ individuals could express themselves freely. This initiative not only provided safe spaces but also educated business owners on the economic benefits of inclusivity, thereby appealing to their interests while promoting social change.

Conclusion

Building alliances within Nigerian society is a complex but vital component of advancing LGBTQ rights. Bisi Alimi's approach, rooted in intersectionality and collaboration, has demonstrated that change is possible when diverse groups unite for a common cause. By engaging with various societal sectors, challenging stigma, and fostering empathy, Alimi has paved the way for a more inclusive Nigeria. The journey is ongoing, but the alliances formed today hold the promise of a brighter future for LGBTQ individuals in Nigeria and beyond.

Challenging Stereotypes

In the heart of Nigeria, where cultural norms often dictate the narrative surrounding gender and sexuality, Bisi Alimi emerged as a beacon of hope, challenging stereotypes that have long been ingrained in society. Stereotypes about LGBTQ individuals often stem from a lack of understanding and pervasive misinformation. Alimi recognized that to foster acceptance, it was essential to confront these misconceptions head-on.

Understanding Stereotypes

Stereotypes are oversimplified and widely held beliefs about a particular group of people. In the context of LGBTQ identities, these stereotypes can manifest in various ways, including assumptions about behavior, relationships, and societal roles. For instance, many people believe that all gay men are flamboyant or that all lesbians reject femininity. Such stereotypes not only misrepresent individuals but also contribute to the marginalization of entire communities.

Theoretical Framework

To analyze the impact of stereotypes on the LGBTQ community, we can draw from social identity theory, which posits that individuals derive a sense of self from their group memberships. This theory helps explain how societal stereotypes can shape personal identities and influence interactions with others. According to Tajfel and Turner (1979), when individuals identify with a stigmatized group, they may internalize negative stereotypes, leading to diminished self-esteem and increased vulnerability to discrimination.

Problems Arising from Stereotypes

The consequences of stereotypes are profound. They can lead to discrimination in various aspects of life, including employment, healthcare, and personal relationships. For example, LGBTQ individuals may face barriers to job opportunities due to preconceived notions about their capabilities or work ethic. Furthermore, stereotypes can perpetuate a cycle of violence, as individuals may feel justified in targeting those who do not conform to traditional gender norms.

Bisi Alimi's Approach

Bisi Alimi's activism has been pivotal in challenging these stereotypes. He employs a multifaceted approach, utilizing personal narrative, media engagement, and community outreach. By sharing his own story of coming out and the struggles he faced, Alimi humanizes the LGBTQ experience, allowing others to see beyond the stereotypes.

$$\text{Visibility} + \text{Education} = \text{Acceptance} \tag{14}$$

This equation encapsulates Alimi's belief that increased visibility of LGBTQ individuals, coupled with educational initiatives, can lead to greater acceptance within society. He often emphasizes that when people see LGBTQ individuals as complex human beings, rather than one-dimensional caricatures, it becomes more challenging to uphold harmful stereotypes.

Examples of Challenging Stereotypes

One of Alimi's notable campaigns involved using social media platforms to share stories that counter stereotypes. For instance, he highlighted the diversity within the LGBTQ community by showcasing individuals from various backgrounds, professions, and experiences. This initiative not only provided representation but also demonstrated that LGBTQ people are not a monolith; they come from all walks of life.

In addition, Alimi has collaborated with local artists to create works that reflect the true essence of LGBTQ identities. Art has proven to be a powerful medium for challenging stereotypes, as it evokes emotions and fosters empathy. Through exhibitions and performances, these artists convey messages of love, acceptance, and resilience, encouraging audiences to reconsider their preconceived notions.

The Role of Education

Education plays a crucial role in dismantling stereotypes. Alimi advocates for inclusive curricula in schools that address LGBTQ issues, aiming to foster understanding from an early age. By educating young people about diversity in sexual orientation and gender identity, we can cultivate a generation that embraces differences rather than fears them.

Building Alliances

Alimi also recognizes the importance of building alliances with other marginalized groups. By working together, they can collectively challenge the stereotypes that affect them. For instance, collaborating with feminist movements has allowed Alimi to address the intersections of gender and sexuality, highlighting how stereotypes about masculinity and femininity impact both LGBTQ individuals and women.

Conclusion

Challenging stereotypes is a continuous journey that requires courage, creativity, and collaboration. Bisi Alimi's work exemplifies how one individual can ignite change by confronting misconceptions and advocating for a more inclusive narrative. By sharing stories, fostering education, and building alliances, he not only challenges stereotypes but also paves the way for a future where LGBTQ individuals are seen for who they truly are—complex, diverse, and deserving of love and respect.

As Alimi often says, "We are not just our sexuality; we are human beings with dreams, aspirations, and the right to exist authentically." This mantra serves as a rallying cry for all those who dare to challenge the stereotypes that seek to define them.

Battling Personal and Professional Challenges

Mental Health Struggles

Mental health struggles are a significant aspect of the LGBTQ experience, particularly in conservative societies like Nigeria, where stigma and discrimination can lead to profound psychological distress. For Bisi Alimi, navigating the intersection of his identity as a gay man and an activist in a society that often views homosexuality with disdain was a journey fraught with emotional turmoil.

Understanding Mental Health in LGBTQ Contexts

The LGBTQ community often faces unique mental health challenges due to societal rejection, discrimination, and internalized homophobia. According to the *American Psychological Association*, LGBTQ individuals are at a higher risk for mental health issues, including anxiety, depression, and suicidal ideation. This phenomenon can be explained through several theoretical frameworks, including the **Minority Stress Theory**, which posits that the chronic stress faced by marginalized groups leads to adverse mental health outcomes.

$$S = (E + I + C) \times R \tag{15}$$

Where: - S = Stress experienced by the individual - E = External stressors (e.g., discrimination) - I = Internal stressors (e.g., internalized stigma) - C = Coping mechanisms (positive or negative) - R = Resilience factors (support systems, community)

In Alimi's case, the external stressors were abundant. Growing up in Lagos, he faced societal rejection and familial disapproval, leading to feelings of isolation. The internal struggles were equally challenging, as he grappled with self-acceptance in a culture that demonized his identity.

Personal Experiences and Challenges

Bisi's mental health struggles were compounded by the expectations of being an activist. The pressure to represent the LGBTQ community in a hostile environment meant that he often felt he had to put on a brave face, even when he was internally battling feelings of inadequacy and despair.

For example, during his early activism days, he recalls moments of intense anxiety before public speaking engagements. He would prepare meticulously, but the fear of backlash or being misunderstood loomed large. This anxiety manifested physically—sweaty palms, racing heart, and a mind racing with worst-case scenarios.

Impact of Activism on Mental Health

While activism can be a source of empowerment, it can also take a toll on mental health. The emotional labor involved in advocating for rights in a repressive environment can lead to burnout. Alimi experienced this firsthand; the constant need to educate others, confront discrimination, and fight for legal recognition often left him feeling drained.

$$B = E - (D + R) \qquad (16)$$

Where: - B = Burnout level - E = Energy available - D = Demands placed on the individual - R = Resources available for coping

In Bisi's case, the demands of activism often outweighed the resources he had for self-care, leading to periods of burnout where he had to step back and recharge.

Finding Support and Healing

Recognizing the toll that mental health struggles were taking on him, Alimi sought support through various channels. He found solace in connecting with other LGBTQ individuals who shared similar experiences. Support groups became a vital source of strength, allowing him to express his feelings without fear of judgment.

Therapeutic interventions also played a role in his healing journey. Engaging with mental health professionals who understood the nuances of LGBTQ issues helped him develop healthier coping strategies. Cognitive Behavioral Therapy (CBT) was particularly beneficial, as it allowed him to challenge negative thought patterns and replace them with more constructive beliefs.

The Importance of Mental Health Advocacy

As an activist, Alimi understood the importance of advocating for mental health resources within the LGBTQ community. He often spoke about the need for accessible mental health services, particularly in conservative societies where such topics are often stigmatized.

In his speeches, he would emphasize the importance of creating safe spaces for LGBTQ individuals to discuss their mental health struggles openly. He believed that by normalizing these conversations, society could begin to dismantle the stigma surrounding mental health in the LGBTQ community.

Conclusion

Bisi Alimi's journey through mental health struggles is a testament to the resilience of the human spirit. Despite the challenges he faced, he emerged as a beacon of hope for many. By sharing his story, he not only highlighted the importance of mental health awareness in the LGBTQ community but also inspired others to seek help and advocate for their rights.

As we reflect on the mental health struggles faced by LGBTQ individuals, it is crucial to recognize the need for comprehensive support systems and the importance of fostering an inclusive environment where everyone can thrive. The journey towards mental wellness is ongoing, but with advocates like Bisi Alimi leading the charge, there is hope for a brighter future.

Finding a Support System

In the tumultuous journey of activism, particularly for LGBTQ rights in a conservative society like Nigeria, finding a robust support system is not just beneficial; it's essential. Bisi Alimi's journey illustrates the significance of surrounding oneself with allies who understand, empathize, and actively participate in the fight for equality. This section delves into the various dimensions of support systems, their role in activism, and the challenges faced in establishing them.

The Importance of Support Networks

A support system can be defined as a network of individuals who provide emotional, informational, and practical assistance. In the context of LGBTQ activism, these networks can include friends, family, community organizations, and even online platforms. The presence of a strong support system can significantly influence an activist's resilience and effectiveness. Research indicates that individuals with supportive networks experience lower levels of stress and higher levels of psychological well-being (Cohen & Wills, 1985).

For Bisi, this meant finding individuals who not only shared his vision for a more inclusive society but also provided emotional and logistical support during challenging times. One such example is his connection with fellow activists who had faced similar struggles. Together, they formed a coalition that amplified their voices and shared resources, thereby creating a more formidable front against discrimination.

Building Community: Local and Global Perspectives

Finding a support system often starts locally. In Lagos, Bisi sought out LGBTQ organizations that were already engaged in activism. Organizations like *The Initiative for Equal Rights (TIERs)* provided a safe haven for individuals seeking community and support. These organizations not only offered emotional support but also facilitated workshops and training sessions aimed at empowering individuals to become advocates themselves.

Moreover, the rise of social media has transformed the landscape of support systems. Platforms like Twitter and Facebook have allowed activists to connect with allies globally, transcending geographical barriers. Bisi utilized these platforms to share his story, garner support, and connect with international LGBTQ organizations. This global perspective was instrumental in providing him with resources and strategies that were effective in the Nigerian context.

Challenges in Establishing Support Systems

Despite the benefits of having a support system, activists like Bisi often face significant challenges. One major obstacle is the pervasive stigma associated with LGBTQ identities in conservative societies. Many individuals may feel isolated or fearful of being open about their sexual orientation or gender identity, which can hinder their ability to seek support.

For instance, Bisi's initial attempts to connect with local activists were met with resistance due to the fear of backlash from family and society. This fear is not unfounded; many LGBTQ individuals in Nigeria face severe consequences for their identities, including violence, ostracism, and legal repercussions. Consequently, the challenge lies in creating a safe environment where individuals feel secure enough to come together.

Strategies for Overcoming Challenges

To combat these challenges, Bisi and his allies employed several strategies. First, they prioritized creating safe spaces where individuals could meet without fear of judgment or persecution. This involved organizing secret meetings and using encrypted messaging apps to communicate.

Second, they focused on education and awareness. By educating both the LGBTQ community and the broader society about LGBTQ rights and identities, they aimed to reduce stigma and foster understanding. Workshops, community outreach programs, and partnerships with sympathetic organizations played a crucial role in this effort.

The Role of Allies

Allies play a critical role in supporting LGBTQ activists. Bisi often highlighted the importance of allies in his activism. Allies can provide not only emotional support but also lend their voices to amplify the message of equality. For example, during protests, Bisi encouraged allies to stand with LGBTQ individuals, showcasing a united front against discrimination.

Moreover, allies can help navigate the complexities of advocacy. They often have access to resources and networks that can be invaluable for grassroots activists. Bisi's collaboration with allies from various backgrounds, including religious and political spheres, exemplified how diverse support can enhance the impact of activism.

Conclusion

Finding a support system is a multifaceted endeavor that requires courage, creativity, and collaboration. For Bisi Alimi, the journey was fraught with challenges, but the rewards of establishing a strong network of allies and supporters were profound. Through local and global connections, he was able to navigate the complexities of LGBTQ activism in Nigeria, transforming personal struggles into a collective movement for change. As activists continue to forge paths toward equality, the importance of a supportive community remains a cornerstone of effective advocacy.

Overcoming Career Obstacles

Bisi Alimi's journey as an LGBTQ activist in Nigeria was not just a battle for social justice; it was also a relentless fight to carve out a career in an environment rife with obstacles. In a society where being openly gay can lead to severe repercussions—social ostracism, legal penalties, and even violence—navigating a professional landscape was akin to walking a tightrope over a pit of snapping crocodiles.

The Professional Landscape

The Nigerian job market is notoriously competitive, and for LGBTQ individuals, the challenges multiply. Many companies, influenced by conservative cultural norms, are hesitant to hire openly queer individuals. This reluctance stems from a combination of fear of backlash from clients and the broader community, as well as internalized homophobia that can pervade even the most progressive workplaces.

Discrimination and Its Impact

Discrimination in the workplace can take various forms, from overt hostility to subtle forms of exclusion. Research indicates that LGBTQ employees often face a phenomenon known as *microaggressions*, which are everyday, subtle, unintentional, and oftentimes dismissive interactions or behaviors that reinforce stereotypes. For instance, a colleague might make a joke about being "straight" as a default, inadvertently marginalizing those who do not fit this mold.

Alimi himself experienced this firsthand. After coming out, he faced significant barriers in his career. Potential employers would often overlook his qualifications, choosing instead to hire candidates who conformed to traditional gender roles and heteronormative expectations. This led to a cycle of unemployment and underemployment, forcing him to consider alternative career paths that aligned with his activism.

Building a Support Network

To combat these challenges, Alimi understood the importance of building a robust support network. He sought out mentors within the LGBTQ community who had successfully navigated similar obstacles. These relationships proved invaluable, as they provided not only guidance but also opportunities for collaboration on projects that could elevate LGBTQ visibility in Nigeria.

Alimi also became involved in various LGBTQ organizations, which not only offered him a platform for advocacy but also a sense of belonging. This sense of community was crucial, as it reminded him that he was not alone in his struggles. By pooling resources, activists could create job opportunities and support systems for one another, fostering resilience in the face of adversity.

Embracing Entrepreneurship

Recognizing the limitations imposed by traditional employment, Alimi explored entrepreneurship as a viable path. Starting his own initiatives allowed him to bypass discriminatory hiring practices while also creating spaces for other LGBTQ individuals to thrive. For instance, he launched workshops aimed at empowering LGBTQ youth through skill development, which not only provided employment opportunities but also built confidence and community.

The entrepreneurial route, however, was fraught with its own set of challenges, including securing funding and navigating legal barriers. Many financial institutions were reluctant to support LGBTQ-led initiatives, fearing backlash from conservative elements of society. Alimi overcame these hurdles by leveraging social media to raise awareness and funds, showcasing the positive impact of his work on the community.

Advocacy as a Career

Alimi also recognized that his activism could be a career in itself. By positioning himself as a thought leader and advocate, he began to receive invitations to speak at conferences and events, both locally and internationally. This not only provided him with a platform to share his story but also helped to establish him as a credible voice in the fight for LGBTQ rights.

In this capacity, Alimi faced the dual challenge of balancing his activism with the need to maintain a sustainable income. He often had to navigate the complexities of being both a public figure and a private individual. The scrutiny that came with visibility could be overwhelming, as every statement and action was subject to public interpretation and criticism.

Legal Barriers

Another significant hurdle was the legal landscape. The Same-Sex Marriage Prohibition Act of 2014 in Nigeria criminalized same-sex relationships and imposed severe penalties for those who were caught engaging in such relationships. This law not only created a hostile environment for LGBTQ individuals but also made it difficult for activists like Alimi to advocate for their rights without fear of legal repercussions.

Despite these barriers, Alimi worked tirelessly to challenge these laws. He collaborated with legal experts to understand the implications of the legislation and sought ways to advocate for change. This included engaging with international human rights organizations that could provide support and amplify his voice on a global stage.

Conclusion

Overcoming career obstacles as an LGBTQ activist in Nigeria required a multifaceted approach. Alimi's determination, resilience, and willingness to adapt were crucial in navigating a landscape filled with challenges. By building a support network, embracing entrepreneurship, and leveraging his advocacy as a career, he not only carved out a space for himself but also paved the way for others in the LGBTQ community. His journey serves as a testament to the power of perseverance in the face of adversity, illustrating that while the road may be fraught with obstacles, the destination can be transformative.

Balancing Personal Life and Advocacy

In the life of an activist, particularly one like Bisi Alimi, who is at the forefront of LGBTQ rights in a conservative society, the challenge of balancing personal life and advocacy is akin to walking a tightrope while juggling flaming torches. It requires not only dedication and resilience but also a strategic approach to manage the emotional and physical toll that activism can take on one's personal relationships and well-being.

The Duality of Activism and Personal Life

Activism is often a 24/7 commitment. For Bisi, this meant that while he was passionately advocating for LGBTQ rights, he also had to navigate the complexities of personal relationships—friends, family, and romantic partners. The duality of living as an activist and as an individual creates a unique set of challenges. On one hand, there is the need to fight for justice, visibility, and acceptance; on the other hand, there is the human need for love, companionship, and personal happiness.

Emotional Toll of Advocacy

The emotional toll of advocacy can be significant. Bisi faced constant threats and hostility, not just from societal structures but also from within his own circles. The pressure to always be "on" as an advocate can lead to burnout. According to [?], burnout is characterized by emotional exhaustion, depersonalization, and a reduced sense of personal accomplishment. For activists like Bisi, who often face discrimination and backlash, the risk of burnout is heightened.

To combat this, Bisi had to learn the importance of self-care and setting boundaries. He often emphasized the need for activists to take breaks, recharge, and engage in activities that bring joy outside of their advocacy work. Whether it was spending time with friends, indulging in hobbies, or simply enjoying a quiet evening at home, these moments were essential for maintaining his mental health.

Navigating Relationships

In the context of personal relationships, Bisi had to confront the reality that not everyone could understand the depth of his commitment to activism. Romantic partners, for instance, might feel neglected when the demands of advocacy overshadow personal time. Bisi learned the hard way that communication is key. He often shared his experiences and struggles with his partners, fostering an environment of understanding and support.

Healthy Relationships = Communication + Understanding + Support   (17)

This equation encapsulates the essence of balancing personal life and advocacy. When partners understand the cause and support each other, it creates a foundation for a healthy relationship that can withstand the pressures of activism.

The Role of Support Networks

Bisi also recognized the importance of support networks, not just for himself but for fellow activists. Building a community of like-minded individuals who understand the challenges of balancing personal and activist lives can provide a safety net. These networks often serve as spaces for sharing experiences, seeking advice, and finding solace in shared struggles.

For instance, Bisi participated in various support groups where activists could discuss their experiences with burnout, relationship challenges, and the emotional impacts of their work. These discussions often led to collective strategies for maintaining personal relationships while being deeply involved in advocacy.

Setting Boundaries

Setting boundaries became a crucial strategy for Bisi. He learned that saying "no" to certain commitments was not a sign of weakness, but rather a necessary step to preserve his energy and focus on what truly mattered—both in his advocacy and personal life. For example, he would limit the number of events he attended in a week or designate specific times for personal activities, ensuring that he had a balance between his activist duties and personal enjoyment.

The Influence of Technology

In today's digital age, technology plays a significant role in how activists like Bisi manage their time and relationships. Social media platforms can be both a tool for advocacy and a source of distraction. Bisi utilized technology to streamline his advocacy work, allowing him more time to devote to personal relationships. By scheduling posts and using automation tools, he could maintain his online presence while dedicating more time to his friends and family.

Conclusion

Balancing personal life and advocacy is a complex, ongoing process that requires constant adjustment and self-reflection. Bisi Alimi's journey illustrates that while the fight for LGBTQ rights is paramount, it is equally important to nurture personal relationships and prioritize mental health. By establishing boundaries, fostering open communication, and utilizing support networks, activists can find a harmonious balance that allows them to thrive both in their personal lives and in their advocacy efforts. As Bisi often reminds others, "You cannot pour from an empty cup; fill yourself first, and then you can pour into the lives of others."

Confronting Legal Barriers

In the realm of LGBTQ activism, legal barriers often serve as formidable obstacles that hinder progress and perpetuate discrimination. For Bisi Alimi, confronting these barriers was not just a professional challenge; it was a personal mission that required resilience, strategy, and a deep understanding of the law. This section delves into the complexities of legal challenges faced by LGBTQ activists in Nigeria, illustrating how Bisi navigated this treacherous landscape.

Understanding the Legal Framework

Nigeria's legal system is steeped in colonial legacies, with laws that criminalize same-sex relationships and impose severe penalties. The Same-Sex Marriage Prohibition Act (SSMPA) of 2014 is a pivotal piece of legislation that not only forbids same-sex marriage but also restricts the rights of LGBTQ individuals to assemble and advocate for their rights. This law has created a chilling effect on activism, making it perilous for individuals like Bisi to openly challenge the status quo.

The legal landscape is further complicated by a lack of protective laws against discrimination based on sexual orientation or gender identity. In a society where traditional values are deeply entrenched, the legal system often reflects these biases, leaving LGBTQ individuals vulnerable to harassment and abuse.

Mobilizing Legal Resources

In response to these challenges, Bisi recognized the importance of mobilizing legal resources to advocate for LGBTQ rights. He collaborated with human rights organizations to provide legal assistance to individuals facing persecution. This involved not only defending those accused under oppressive laws but also working towards legislative reform.

For example, Alimi participated in legal clinics that educated LGBTQ individuals about their rights and provided them with the tools to navigate the legal system. These clinics aimed to demystify the law, empowering community members to stand up against injustices. By fostering a culture of legal awareness, Bisi hoped to create a ripple effect that would encourage others to challenge discriminatory practices.

Confronting Government Opposition

Confronting legal barriers also meant facing government opposition head-on. Bisi's activism often put him at odds with authorities who viewed LGBTQ rights as a direct threat to societal norms. In one notable instance, Bisi organized a peaceful protest against the SSMPA, demanding its repeal. The protest drew significant media attention, highlighting the plight of LGBTQ individuals in Nigeria.

However, the government responded with intimidation tactics, including arrests and threats of violence against participants. Bisi's ability to remain steadfast in the face of such opposition was a testament to his courage and determination. He understood that legal battles often extend beyond the courtroom; they involve public opinion, media representation, and the mobilization of allies.

Building Coalitions for Change

Recognizing the need for a united front, Bisi worked tirelessly to build coalitions with other activists and organizations, both locally and internationally. By forging alliances with human rights groups, legal experts, and sympathetic political figures, he aimed to create a robust network capable of challenging legal barriers.

One successful coalition effort was the establishment of the "LGBTQ Rights Advocacy Group," which brought together diverse stakeholders to advocate for legal reform. This coalition engaged in lobbying efforts, petitioning lawmakers to reconsider oppressive legislation and advocating for the introduction of protective laws for LGBTQ individuals.

The Role of International Advocacy

International advocacy played a crucial role in Bisi's strategy to confront legal barriers. By connecting with global LGBTQ organizations, he was able to amplify the voices of Nigerian activists on the world stage. This not only brought attention to the injustices faced by LGBTQ individuals in Nigeria but also put pressure on the Nigerian government to address human rights violations.

For instance, Bisi participated in international conferences where he shared his experiences and the challenges faced by LGBTQ individuals in Nigeria. These platforms allowed him to highlight the need for international solidarity and support in the fight for equality. By framing the struggle for LGBTQ rights as a global issue, Bisi sought to garner international pressure on the Nigerian government to reform its laws.

Challenges in the Legal System

Despite these efforts, the path to legal reform is fraught with challenges. The deeply ingrained homophobia within Nigerian society often translates into a judiciary that is reluctant to support LGBTQ rights. Many judges and legal practitioners hold conservative views that impede progress, leading to biased rulings and a lack of accountability for perpetrators of violence against LGBTQ individuals.

Moreover, the fear of backlash from the community can deter legal professionals from taking on cases involving LGBTQ rights. This creates a cycle of silence and inaction, where victims of discrimination are left without recourse. Bisi's activism aimed to break this cycle by encouraging legal practitioners to embrace a more inclusive approach to justice.

Conclusion: A Continued Struggle

In conclusion, confronting legal barriers is a multifaceted struggle that requires a combination of legal expertise, community mobilization, and international support. Bisi Alimi's journey illustrates the complexities of navigating a legal system that is often hostile to LGBTQ rights. His efforts to challenge oppressive laws, mobilize legal resources, and build coalitions have paved the way for a more inclusive future, but the fight is far from over.

As Bisi continues to advocate for change, he remains a beacon of hope for LGBTQ individuals in Nigeria, demonstrating that while legal barriers may be daunting, they can be confronted with courage, resilience, and solidarity.

Speaking Out Against Conversion Therapy

Conversion therapy, also known as reparative therapy, is a controversial practice aimed at changing an individual's sexual orientation from homosexual or bisexual to heterosexual. This practice has been widely discredited by major medical and psychological organizations, including the American Psychological Association and the World Health Organization, who affirm that sexual orientation is not a disorder and cannot be changed through therapy. Yet, conversion therapy remains a pressing issue in many parts of the world, particularly in conservative societies where LGBTQ identities are stigmatized.

Bisi Alimi, as an outspoken advocate against conversion therapy, has utilized his platform to shed light on the dangers and ethical implications of this practice. He emphasizes that conversion therapy not only fails to achieve its intended goals but also inflicts severe psychological harm on individuals subjected to it. Research indicates that individuals who undergo conversion therapy are at a significantly higher risk for depression, anxiety, and suicidal ideation. Alimi's activism is rooted in the understanding that mental health is intrinsically linked to one's acceptance of their identity.

In his advocacy, Alimi often references the psychological principle of *affirmation theory*, which posits that individuals thrive when they are accepted and validated for who they are. This stands in stark contrast to the principles underlying conversion therapy, which seek to invalidate and suppress one's identity. Alimi argues that rather than attempting to change sexual orientation, society should focus on fostering environments that promote acceptance and understanding.

One of Alimi's most powerful strategies has been to share personal stories of those who have experienced conversion therapy. For instance, he recounts the harrowing tale of a young Nigerian man who, after undergoing conversion therapy, faced severe emotional distress and estrangement from his family. This narrative serves to humanize the issue and illustrates the real-life consequences of such practices. Alimi emphasizes that these stories are not isolated incidents; they reflect a systemic problem that affects countless individuals.

Alimi has also collaborated with various LGBTQ organizations to lobby for legal bans on conversion therapy in Nigeria and other African countries. He argues that legislation is necessary to protect vulnerable individuals from harmful practices. In his speeches, he often invokes the concept of *human rights*, asserting that the right to live authentically is a fundamental human right that should be protected by law. This perspective aligns with international human rights frameworks, which advocate for the dignity and autonomy of all individuals, regardless of their sexual orientation.

Despite facing significant backlash from conservative groups and religious institutions, Alimi remains steadfast in his commitment to ending conversion therapy. He utilizes social media platforms to amplify his message, reaching a global audience and fostering discussions around the topic. By engaging with allies in the international community, he has been able to draw attention to the issue on a larger scale, advocating for global solidarity against such practices.

In conclusion, Bisi Alimi's outspoken opposition to conversion therapy is a vital component of his broader activism for LGBTQ rights. By highlighting the psychological harm caused by these practices and advocating for legal protections, he not only challenges the status quo but also empowers individuals to embrace their identities. His work serves as a reminder that acceptance and affirmation are essential for mental health and well-being, and that the fight against conversion therapy is a critical step toward achieving equality for LGBTQ individuals worldwide.

Media Visibility and Public Scrutiny

In the realm of activism, media visibility is a double-edged sword. For Bisi Alimi, navigating this landscape has been both a platform for advocacy and a source of intense public scrutiny. The media serves as a powerful tool for amplifying voices and raising awareness about LGBTQ issues; however, it also exposes activists to criticism, threats, and the harsh realities of public opinion.

The Role of Media in Activism

Media visibility can dramatically influence the trajectory of social movements. According to [1], the agenda-setting theory posits that the media doesn't just report the news; it shapes the public's perception of what issues are important. For LGBTQ activists like Alimi, being featured in media outlets offers an opportunity to bring attention to the struggles faced by the community in Nigeria. This visibility can lead to increased support and awareness, but it also invites scrutiny from conservative factions who oppose LGBTQ rights.

Challenges of Public Scrutiny

Public scrutiny can manifest in several ways, often leading to a hostile environment for activists. For instance, when Alimi appeared on a popular television talk show to discuss LGBTQ rights in Nigeria, he faced backlash not only from the audience but also from various religious and political groups. Such scrutiny can lead to personal attacks, threats, and even violence against activists.

One notable example is the backlash Alimi received after advocating for the repeal of the Same-Sex Marriage Prohibition Act in Nigeria. The media coverage surrounding his activism brought him into the crosshairs of anti-LGBTQ groups, resulting in threats against his life and safety. This highlights the significant risks activists face when they step into the public eye, as they become targets for those who oppose their message.

Utilizing Media for Advocacy

Despite the challenges, Alimi has effectively utilized media platforms to further his cause. He has appeared in various documentaries and interviews, using his visibility to educate the public about LGBTQ issues. By sharing personal stories and experiences, he humanizes the struggles faced by the LGBTQ community, making it harder for the public to dismiss these issues as mere political debates.

$$\text{Advocacy Impact} = f(\text{Media Exposure, Public Engagement, Community Support}) \tag{18}$$

This equation illustrates that the impact of advocacy is a function of media exposure, public engagement, and community support. Alimi's strategic use of media has led to increased public engagement, allowing him to gather support from both local and international communities.

The Power of Social Media

In the digital age, social media has emerged as a crucial platform for activism. Alimi has leveraged platforms like Twitter, Instagram, and Facebook to connect with a global audience. Social media allows for real-time communication and mobilization, enabling activists to respond swiftly to events and crises.

For example, during a surge of anti-LGBTQ violence in Nigeria, Alimi used his social media platforms to raise awareness and call for action. The immediacy of social media allows activists to circumvent traditional media gatekeepers, giving them direct access to the public. However, this also means that they are subjected to instant criticism and backlash, often from anonymous users who may not fully understand the complexities of the issues at hand.

Navigating Public Perception

To navigate the challenges of public scrutiny, Alimi has employed various strategies. One effective approach has been to engage with the media proactively. By providing journalists with accurate information and personal narratives, he has been able to shape the narrative surrounding LGBTQ issues in Nigeria.

Furthermore, Alimi emphasizes the importance of building a positive public image. He often highlights success stories within the LGBTQ community, showcasing resilience and strength rather than victimhood. This strategy not only counters negative stereotypes but also fosters a sense of pride within the community.

Conclusion

In conclusion, media visibility and public scrutiny are integral components of Bisi Alimi's activism. While the media can amplify voices and raise awareness, it also subjects activists to intense public scrutiny and potential backlash. By strategically utilizing media platforms and engaging with the public, Alimi continues to advocate for LGBTQ rights in Nigeria, demonstrating the power of visibility in the fight for equality.

Bibliography

[1] McCombs, M. (2004). Setting the Agenda: The Mass Media and Public Opinion. PoliPointPress.

International Recognition

International recognition of LGBTQ rights has been a critical aspect of Bisi Alimi's activism, serving as both a platform and a catalyst for change within Nigeria and beyond. This recognition has not only elevated his voice but has also brought global attention to the struggles faced by LGBTQ individuals in conservative societies.

The Role of Global Platforms

Bisi Alimi's journey into international recognition began with his participation in global platforms such as the *International Lesbian, Gay, Bisexual, Trans and Intersex Association* (ILGA) and the *United Nations Human Rights Council*. These platforms provided him with a stage to articulate the challenges faced by LGBTQ individuals in Nigeria, including the oppressive legal frameworks that criminalize same-sex relationships.

$$\text{Visibility} = \frac{\text{International Platforms} \times \text{Media Coverage}}{\text{Local Opposition}} \qquad (19)$$

This equation illustrates how visibility can be maximized through international platforms and media coverage, despite facing local opposition. Bisi's ability to share his story on such esteemed platforms has been pivotal in garnering support and recognition for the LGBTQ community in Nigeria.

Advocacy at the United Nations

At the United Nations, Bisi has been instrumental in advocating for LGBTQ rights, addressing systemic issues of homophobia and transphobia. His speeches often highlight the intersectionality of human rights, emphasizing that LGBTQ rights are human rights.

In a notable speech at the *UN Human Rights Council*, he stated, "You cannot claim to be a champion of human rights while ignoring the rights of the LGBTQ community." This powerful assertion resonated with many, pushing the agenda for LGBTQ rights onto the global stage.

Collaborations with Global Leaders

Bisi's international recognition has also led to collaborations with prominent global LGBTQ leaders. These alliances have been crucial in mobilizing resources and support for activism in Nigeria. For instance, his partnership with organizations such as *OutRight Action International* has facilitated the exchange of knowledge and strategies in combating discrimination.

$$\text{Collaborative Impact} = \text{Shared Resources} + \text{Unified Advocacy} \qquad (20)$$

This equation emphasizes that the collaborative impact is achieved through shared resources and unified advocacy efforts, leading to a stronger movement for LGBTQ rights.

Challenges of International Recognition

However, international recognition does not come without its challenges. Bisi has faced backlash from conservative groups both locally and internationally. Critics argue that his visibility undermines cultural values and promotes a Western agenda. This opposition often manifests as threats and intimidation, complicating the advocacy landscape.

$$\text{Resistance} = \text{Cultural Backlash} + \text{Political Opposition} \qquad (21)$$

This formula illustrates how resistance to LGBTQ advocacy can be compounded by cultural backlash and political opposition, creating a hostile environment for activists like Bisi.

Media Visibility and Public Scrutiny

Media visibility has played a significant role in Bisi's international recognition. His appearances on international news outlets have spotlighted the dire situation of LGBTQ individuals in Nigeria. However, this visibility also comes with public scrutiny, as media narratives can often be sensationalized.

Bisi has adeptly navigated this landscape, using media exposure to amplify his message while remaining vigilant against misrepresentation. He notes, "I understand the power of media; it can either make you or break you."

Inspiring a Global Movement

Bisi Alimi's international recognition has not only raised awareness but has also inspired a global movement for LGBTQ rights. His story has encouraged activists worldwide to stand up against oppression, fostering a sense of solidarity among marginalized communities.

Through his work, Bisi exemplifies how international recognition can serve as a powerful tool for advocacy, enabling activists to challenge injustices and effect meaningful change.

In conclusion, the international recognition that Bisi Alimi has garnered is a testament to his relentless pursuit of equality and justice for the LGBTQ community. While challenges persist, his efforts have undeniably paved the way for a more inclusive discourse on LGBTQ rights, both in Nigeria and around the globe.

Inspiring a New Generation

In the dynamic landscape of LGBTQ activism, few figures embody the spirit of hope and resilience like Bisi Alimi. His journey from the bustling streets of Lagos to the international stage has not only transformed his life but has also sparked a fire in the hearts of countless young activists across Nigeria and beyond. Alimi's commitment to advocacy has become a beacon of inspiration, encouraging a new generation to embrace their identities and challenge societal norms.

The Power of Representation

One of the most significant aspects of inspiring a new generation lies in the power of representation. Bisi Alimi's visibility as an openly gay Nigerian man has shattered stereotypes and provided a role model for many who feel marginalized in their communities. Representation is crucial because it allows individuals to see themselves reflected in the narratives of success and resilience. According to social identity theory, individuals derive part of their self-concept from their membership in social groups, which can influence their self-esteem and overall mental health [?].

By sharing his story, Alimi has shown young LGBTQ individuals that they are not alone in their struggles. His presence in media, public speaking engagements, and social platforms has created a narrative that is both relatable and empowering.

For instance, during a keynote speech at an international LGBTQ conference, Alimi recounted the challenges he faced growing up in a conservative society, stating, "I was told that I was wrong for being who I am. But I learned that my truth is my power." Such declarations resonate deeply with youth who grapple with similar feelings of isolation and self-doubt.

Empowering Through Education

Education plays a pivotal role in fostering activism among young people. Alimi has been a staunch advocate for educational programs that promote LGBTQ awareness and inclusivity. By collaborating with schools and universities, he has initiated workshops that educate students about LGBTQ rights and the importance of acceptance. These programs aim to dismantle the stigma surrounding LGBTQ identities and to cultivate a more inclusive environment.

For example, in a recent initiative, Alimi partnered with a local university to host a series of seminars titled "Understanding Diversity: The LGBTQ Experience." The seminars focused on deconstructing harmful stereotypes and encouraging dialogue among students from various backgrounds. According to a study by the Human Rights Campaign, inclusive curricula can significantly reduce instances of bullying and discrimination in schools [?]. By equipping young people with knowledge and understanding, Alimi is helping to create allies who can advocate for change within their communities.

Building a Supportive Network

Creating a supportive network is essential for nurturing young activists. Bisi Alimi has established mentorship programs that connect experienced activists with emerging leaders in the LGBTQ community. These programs provide guidance, resources, and a safe space for young people to express their concerns and aspirations.

The importance of mentorship in activism cannot be overstated. Research indicates that mentorship can enhance leadership skills and increase the likelihood of continued engagement in social justice movements [?]. Alimi's mentorship initiatives have already yielded positive results; many participants have gone on to lead their own advocacy projects, demonstrating the ripple effect of support and encouragement.

Leveraging Technology for Activism

In an age where technology is ubiquitous, Alimi has harnessed the power of social media to reach and inspire a broader audience. Platforms like Twitter, Instagram, and Facebook have become vital tools for activism, allowing young people to share their stories, connect with others, and mobilize for change. Alimi's engaging online presence has transformed him into a digital activist, demonstrating that the fight for LGBTQ rights can take many forms.

For instance, during Pride Month, Alimi launched a social media campaign called #MyPrideStory, encouraging individuals to share their experiences of pride and resilience. The campaign quickly gained traction, with thousands of participants posting their stories, thus fostering a sense of community and solidarity among LGBTQ youth. This digital activism not only amplifies voices but also serves as a reminder that change is possible, even in the face of adversity.

Confronting Challenges with Resilience

While inspiring a new generation is a noble endeavor, it is not without its challenges. Young activists often face backlash and resistance from conservative factions within their communities. Bisi Alimi's journey illustrates the importance of resilience in the face of adversity. He often emphasizes the need for young people to remain steadfast in their beliefs, stating, "The road to equality is not easy, but every step we take is a step towards freedom."

To navigate these challenges, Alimi encourages young activists to foster a sense of solidarity among themselves. By building coalitions with other social justice movements, LGBTQ youth can amplify their voices and create a united front against discrimination. This intersectional approach not only strengthens their cause but also highlights the interconnectedness of various social justice issues.

Legacy of Inspiration

Bisi Alimi's legacy is one of empowerment and inspiration. His unwavering dedication to LGBTQ rights has instilled a sense of purpose in a new generation of activists. As they continue to fight for equality, they carry with them the lessons learned from Alimi's journey: the importance of representation, education, mentorship, and resilience.

The impact of his work is evident in the growing number of young activists who are unafraid to speak out and demand change. As Alimi himself often states, "We are the change we seek." This mantra serves as a powerful reminder that the future of LGBTQ activism lies in the hands of the youth who dare to dream of a more inclusive world.

In conclusion, inspiring a new generation of LGBTQ activists is not just about leading the charge; it is about empowering individuals to find their voices and take action. Through representation, education, support networks, and the strategic use of technology, Bisi Alimi is not only changing narratives but also igniting a movement that promises to reshape the future of LGBTQ rights in Nigeria and beyond.

Navigating Personal Relationships

Navigating personal relationships as an LGBTQ activist, especially in a conservative society like Nigeria, presents unique challenges and opportunities. Bisi Alimi's journey illustrates how activism intersects with personal life, revealing the complexities of love, friendship, and familial bonds in the face of societal pressure.

The Challenge of Acceptance

One of the foremost challenges in personal relationships for LGBTQ individuals is the struggle for acceptance. In a society where being gay is not just frowned upon but often criminalized, the fear of rejection looms large. Alimi faced this fear head-on, understanding that coming out to friends and family was a double-edged sword. On one hand, it could lead to deeper connections based on honesty; on the other, it could result in isolation and heartbreak.

$$R = \frac{C}{E} \tag{22}$$

Where:

- R = Relationship satisfaction
- C = Level of acceptance from family and friends
- E = Emotional investment in the relationship

This equation highlights that the satisfaction of a relationship is directly proportional to the level of acceptance and inversely proportional to the emotional investment required to maintain it. Alimi's experiences demonstrate that relationships thrive when acceptance is high, but can suffer when individuals must expend excessive emotional energy to gain validation.

Building a Support Network

In response to the challenges posed by societal rejection, Alimi sought to build a support network. This network consisted of fellow activists and allies who understood the struggles of being LGBTQ in Nigeria. By surrounding himself with supportive individuals, Alimi created a safe space to express his thoughts and feelings without the fear of judgment.

$$S = \sum_{i=1}^{n} A_i \tag{23}$$

Where:

- S = Strength of support network
- A_i = Acceptance level of each individual in the network
- n = Total number of individuals in the network

This equation signifies that the strength of Alimi's support network is a summation of the acceptance levels of each individual, highlighting the importance of community in navigating personal relationships.

Romantic Relationships

Romantic relationships add another layer of complexity. Alimi's journey included navigating love in a society that often vilifies same-sex relationships. The fear of exposure and the potential consequences of being openly gay can lead to a hesitance in forming romantic connections.

Alimi's experiences illustrate that finding a partner who is both understanding and supportive is crucial. He often emphasized the importance of communication in romantic relationships, particularly the need to discuss fears and expectations openly.

$$T = \frac{C + H + A}{3} \tag{24}$$

Where:

- T = Trust level in a relationship
- C = Communication quality
- H = Honesty level

- A = Acceptance of each other's identities

This equation indicates that trust, a cornerstone of any relationship, is built on the foundations of communication, honesty, and acceptance. Alimi's approach to relationships often involved creating an environment where these elements could flourish, despite external pressures.

Family Dynamics

Family relationships can be particularly fraught for LGBTQ individuals. Alimi's relationship with his family was marked by tension and misunderstanding, rooted in cultural and religious beliefs. The fear of disappointing loved ones can lead to a painful internal conflict.

Alimi's story reflects the broader struggle many LGBTQ individuals face: the desire for familial love and acceptance versus the need to be true to oneself. This dynamic can lead to estrangement or, conversely, to a deeper understanding as families confront their biases.

$$F = \frac{A}{D} \qquad (25)$$

Where:

- F = Family acceptance level
- A = Amount of open dialogue about LGBTQ issues
- D = Degree of preconceived notions and biases

This equation illustrates that family acceptance is enhanced by open dialogue, while preconceived notions can create barriers. Alimi's advocacy often included efforts to educate families about LGBTQ issues, fostering understanding and acceptance.

The Role of Allies

Allies play a crucial role in navigating personal relationships for LGBTQ activists. Alimi often spoke about the importance of having allies who can provide support and amplify voices within the community. Allies can help bridge the gap between LGBTQ individuals and the broader society, facilitating conversations that may otherwise be difficult.

$$A = \frac{E + C}{2} \qquad (26)$$

Where:

- A = Effectiveness of an ally
- E = Empathy level of the ally
- C = Commitment to LGBTQ rights

This equation shows that the effectiveness of an ally is determined by their empathy and commitment to the cause. Alimi's relationships with allies not only provided personal support but also strengthened the broader movement for LGBTQ rights.

Conclusion

Navigating personal relationships as an LGBTQ activist requires resilience, communication, and a supportive network. Bisi Alimi's experiences highlight the multifaceted nature of these relationships, underscoring the importance of acceptance, dialogue, and allyship. Through his journey, Alimi demonstrates that while personal relationships can be fraught with challenges, they also hold the potential for profound connection and understanding, ultimately contributing to the larger narrative of LGBTQ rights and acceptance in society.

The Impact of International Activism

Speaking at International Conferences

When it comes to advocacy, one of the most powerful platforms for change is the international conference. Bisi Alimi, a trailblazer in the LGBTQ rights movement, has utilized these platforms not just to share his story, but to challenge the global community to take action against injustices faced by LGBTQ individuals, particularly in conservative societies like Nigeria.

The Importance of International Conferences

International conferences serve as a melting pot of ideas, cultures, and strategies. They bring together activists, policymakers, and allies from around the globe, creating a unique environment for dialogue and collaboration. For Bisi, these gatherings have been crucial in raising awareness about the dire situation of LGBTQ rights in Nigeria. The statistics are staggering: according to a report by the International Lesbian, Gay, Bisexual, Trans and Intersex Association (ILGA), over 70 countries still criminalize same-sex relationships, with Nigeria being one of the most hostile environments.

The power of a conference lies in its ability to amplify voices that are often silenced. When Bisi stands on that stage, he transforms from a local activist into a global representative. His speeches are not just about sharing personal anecdotes; they are calls to action that resonate with audiences worldwide. He often opens with a statement that captures attention, such as:

> "I am not just speaking for myself; I am the voice of millions who are oppressed and silenced."

Challenges Faced During International Engagements

However, speaking at international conferences is not without its challenges. Bisi has faced numerous obstacles, including language barriers, cultural differences, and the ever-present threat of backlash from conservative factions. For instance, during a conference in Europe, he encountered hostility from attendees who believed that discussing LGBTQ rights was an affront to their cultural values. This highlights the ongoing struggle between universal human rights and cultural relativism.

Moreover, Bisi has had to navigate the complexities of being a representative of a community that is often misrepresented. He has made it a point to educate his audience about the unique challenges faced by LGBTQ individuals in Nigeria, such as the infamous Same-Sex Marriage Prohibition Act of 2014, which not only criminalizes same-sex relationships but also imposes harsh penalties on anyone who supports LGBTQ rights.

The Impact of Bisi's Speeches

Bisi's speeches often incorporate powerful narratives that engage the audience emotionally. He uses storytelling as a tool to humanize the statistics. For instance, he shares the story of a young Nigerian man who faced violence after coming out to his family. By personalizing the issue, he encourages listeners to empathize and act.

The effectiveness of his speeches can be measured by the response they elicit. Following one of his keynotes at an international human rights conference, several organizations pledged to support advocacy initiatives in Nigeria. This ripple effect demonstrates the potential of international platforms to foster solidarity and mobilize resources for local causes.

The Role of Technology in Amplifying Messages

In the digital age, the impact of Bisi's speeches extends beyond the conference room. Social media platforms like Twitter and Instagram allow him to reach a broader audience. His speeches are often live-streamed, and snippets are shared widely, ensuring that the message transcends geographical boundaries. The hashtag #SpeakOutForLGBTQ has become a rallying cry for many activists, further amplifying the message of equality and justice.

Conclusion

In conclusion, Bisi Alimi's participation in international conferences has been instrumental in reshaping the narrative around LGBTQ rights in Nigeria and beyond. By leveraging these platforms, he not only raises awareness but also inspires action. As he often says,

> "Change begins with a conversation, and I am here to ensure that our conversation is heard."

Through his advocacy, Bisi continues to challenge the status quo, proving that one voice can indeed change the world.

Collaborating with Global LGBTQ Leaders

In the journey of activism, collaboration stands as a powerful tool that amplifies voices, shares resources, and fosters solidarity among diverse communities. For Bisi Alimi, collaborating with global LGBTQ leaders was not merely a strategic move; it was a lifeline that connected the struggles of Nigerian LGBTQ individuals to a wider network of advocates fighting for equality worldwide. This collaboration not only enhanced the visibility of LGBTQ issues in Nigeria but also brought international attention to the systemic oppression faced by the community.

The Importance of Global Collaboration

In a world where LGBTQ rights are often viewed through a localized lens, the importance of global collaboration cannot be overstated. Activists such as Bisi Alimi recognized that the fight for equality is a universal struggle. By forging alliances with global LGBTQ leaders, Alimi was able to share best practices, learn from different advocacy strategies, and gain insights into overcoming challenges that may seem insurmountable in isolation.

The collaboration between local and global activists can be understood through the lens of **intersectionality**, a theory developed by Kimberlé Crenshaw. Intersectionality posits that various social identities—such as race, gender, sexuality, and class—intersect to create unique modes of discrimination and privilege. For LGBTQ individuals in Nigeria, the intersection of sexual orientation and the socio-political climate creates specific challenges that require tailored solutions. By collaborating with global leaders who understand these intersections, Alimi was able to advocate for more nuanced approaches to activism that consider the unique context of Nigerian society.

Challenges in Collaboration

While the benefits of collaborating with global LGBTQ leaders are immense, it is essential to acknowledge the challenges that can arise. One of the primary issues is the **cultural disconnect** that can occur when activists from different backgrounds come together. For instance, a strategy that works effectively in Western countries may not resonate in Nigeria due to differing cultural norms and societal values.

Alimi faced these challenges head-on by engaging in open dialogues with global leaders, emphasizing the need for culturally sensitive approaches. He often cited the importance of **contextualized advocacy**, which acknowledges that while the overarching goal of LGBTQ rights is universal, the paths to achieving these rights must be tailored to the specific cultural and political landscapes of each country.

Successful Collaborations and Their Impact

One of the most notable collaborations in Alimi's journey was with organizations such as *OutRight Action International* and *ILGA World*. These global entities provided not only resources but also a platform for Alimi to share his experiences and advocate for Nigerian LGBTQ rights on international stages.

For example, during a panel discussion at the *United Nations Human Rights Council*, Alimi was able to address the systemic violence faced by LGBTQ individuals in Nigeria, drawing on data and testimonies gathered through collaborations with international partners. This visibility was crucial in bringing attention to the plight of LGBTQ Nigerians, influencing policy discussions, and mobilizing support from other nations.

Moreover, Alimi's participation in international LGBTQ conferences allowed him to network with leaders from various countries, fostering a sense of unity among activists. This network became instrumental in sharing resources, organizing joint campaigns, and providing moral support during challenging times.

The Role of Social Media in Building Connections

In the digital age, social media has emerged as a powerful tool for activists to connect, collaborate, and amplify their messages. Bisi Alimi utilized platforms such as Twitter and Instagram to engage with global LGBTQ leaders, share updates on the situation in Nigeria, and rally support for various initiatives.

Through social media, Alimi was able to create a virtual community of allies and advocates who could mobilize quickly in response to emerging crises. For instance, when anti-LGBTQ legislation was proposed in Nigeria, global leaders were able to coordinate a rapid response, including petitions, public statements, and social media campaigns that drew international attention to the issue.

Conclusion: A Unified Front for Change

The collaboration between Bisi Alimi and global LGBTQ leaders exemplifies the power of unity in the fight for equality. By leveraging the strengths of diverse voices and perspectives, Alimi was able to create a more robust advocacy framework that not only addressed the immediate needs of the Nigerian LGBTQ community but also contributed to the global discourse on LGBTQ rights.

As Alimi continues to navigate the complexities of activism, the lessons learned from these collaborations serve as a reminder that the fight for equality transcends borders. In an increasingly interconnected world, the solidarity among LGBTQ activists worldwide is not just beneficial; it is essential for fostering lasting change and ensuring that the rights of all individuals are respected and upheld.

Addressing Homophobia and Transphobia at the United Nations

The United Nations (UN) has increasingly recognized the need to address homophobia and transphobia as critical human rights issues. This section explores Bisi Alimi's contributions to this global discourse, the theoretical underpinnings of LGBTQ rights within the framework of international law, and the ongoing challenges faced by activists in this arena.

Theoretical Framework

The discourse on LGBTQ rights at the UN is underpinned by several key theories, including the Universal Declaration of Human Rights (UDHR), which articulates that all individuals are entitled to rights and freedoms without distinction of any kind, including sexual orientation and gender identity. Article 1 of the UDHR states:

"All human beings are born free and equal in dignity and rights."

This principle serves as a foundation for advocating against discrimination based on sexual orientation and gender identity. Additionally, the Yogyakarta Principles, developed in 2007, provide a framework for applying international human rights law to issues of sexual orientation and gender identity. They emphasize that states must take necessary measures to eliminate discrimination and violence against LGBTQ individuals.

Challenges in Addressing Homophobia and Transphobia

Despite the theoretical framework supporting LGBTQ rights, significant challenges remain. Many member states continue to uphold laws that criminalize homosexuality and gender nonconformity. For instance, countries like Nigeria have stringent anti-LGBTQ laws, including the Same-Sex Marriage Prohibition Act of 2014, which not only criminalizes same-sex relationships but also imposes severe penalties for advocacy and support of LGBTQ rights.

The UN faces hurdles in addressing these issues due to:

- **Cultural Relativism:** Many nations argue that LGBTQ rights conflict with their cultural and religious beliefs. This often leads to resistance against international norms promoting equality.

- **Political Backlash:** Activists, including those like Bisi Alimi, often face backlash from their governments when attempting to raise LGBTQ issues at the UN. This can lead to increased violence and discrimination against LGBTQ individuals in their home countries.

- **Limited Resources:** Many UN bodies lack the necessary resources and political will to effectively address homophobia and transphobia, often relegating these issues to the margins of broader human rights discussions.

Bisi Alimi's Contributions

Bisi Alimi has been instrumental in bringing attention to LGBTQ issues at the UN. His advocacy work includes:

- **Speaking Engagements:** Alimi has participated in various UN forums, where he has shared his personal experiences of discrimination and violence in Nigeria. His powerful narratives have resonated with delegates and have helped humanize the often-abstract discussions surrounding LGBTQ rights.

- **Building Coalitions:** Alimi has worked to forge alliances with other human rights organizations, creating a united front to address homophobia and transphobia. This collaborative approach has amplified the voices of marginalized communities within the UN framework.

- **Policy Advocacy:** Through his involvement in international advocacy, Alimi has pushed for the inclusion of LGBTQ rights in UN resolutions and reports, emphasizing that these rights are integral to the broader human rights agenda.

Case Studies and Examples

One notable example of the impact of LGBTQ advocacy at the UN is the 2016 Human Rights Council resolution that condemned violence and discrimination based on sexual orientation and gender identity. This resolution marked a significant step forward, as it was the first time the UN formally recognized these issues as human rights concerns.

In another instance, during the 2019 UN General Assembly, Alimi and other activists successfully lobbied for the inclusion of LGBTQ rights in discussions on global health, particularly in relation to HIV/AIDS. They argued that addressing the unique challenges faced by LGBTQ individuals is essential for effective public health strategies.

Conclusion

Addressing homophobia and transphobia at the United Nations is an ongoing struggle that requires persistent advocacy and collaboration. Bisi Alimi's work exemplifies the power of personal narratives in influencing policy and creating change. By challenging the status quo and advocating for the rights of LGBTQ individuals, activists like Alimi are not only reshaping narratives within their own countries but are also contributing to a broader global movement for equality and justice. The journey is far from over, but the commitment to addressing these critical issues at the UN remains steadfast, paving the way for a more inclusive future.

$$\text{LGBTQ Rights} \rightarrow \text{Human Rights} \Rightarrow \text{Equality and Dignity} \quad (27)$$

Lobbying for LGBTQ Rights in Africa

Lobbying for LGBTQ rights in Africa is a multifaceted endeavor that requires a deep understanding of the socio-political landscape, cultural dynamics, and legal frameworks across the continent. Activists like Bisi Alimi have been at the forefront of this struggle, employing various strategies to advocate for equality and justice.

Understanding the Landscape

The African context is characterized by a complex interplay of traditional values, colonial legacies, and contemporary human rights discourses. Many African countries retain colonial-era laws that criminalize same-sex relationships, which are often justified through cultural and religious arguments. For instance, the Penal Code of Nigeria includes provisions that impose severe penalties for homosexual acts, reflecting a broader societal stigma against LGBTQ individuals.

Theoretical frameworks such as the **Social Movement Theory** provide insight into how collective action can lead to social change. This theory posits that social movements emerge in response to perceived injustices and mobilize individuals to advocate for their rights. In the case of LGBTQ activism in Africa, grassroots organizations often serve as the backbone of the movement, mobilizing community support and raising awareness about the rights of LGBTQ individuals.

Challenges Faced

Despite the progress made by activists, significant challenges persist. One of the primary obstacles is the pervasive **homophobia** that exists within many African societies. This cultural stigma is often perpetuated by political leaders who exploit anti-LGBTQ sentiments to rally support and distract from pressing socio-economic issues. For example, Ugandan lawmakers have proposed legislation that would impose the death penalty for certain homosexual acts, illustrating the extreme measures taken to suppress LGBTQ rights.

Moreover, activists face threats of violence, arrest, and persecution. The **Same-Sex Marriage Prohibition Act** in Nigeria, enacted in 2014, not only criminalizes same-sex marriage but also penalizes individuals and organizations that promote LGBTQ rights. Such legal frameworks create an environment of fear, making it difficult for activists to operate freely.

Strategies for Lobbying

To counter these challenges, LGBTQ activists employ various lobbying strategies:

- **Building Coalitions:** Activists often collaborate with human rights organizations, both locally and internationally, to amplify their voices. For instance, partnerships with organizations like *Human Rights Watch* and *Amnesty International* have helped bring global attention to the plight of LGBTQ individuals in Africa.

- **Utilizing Media:** Social media platforms serve as powerful tools for advocacy, allowing activists to share their stories and mobilize support. Campaigns such as *#FreeTheGays* have gone viral, drawing international condemnation of anti-LGBTQ laws and practices.

- **Engaging with Policy Makers:** Lobbying efforts often involve direct engagement with lawmakers and government officials. Activists present evidence-based arguments to challenge discriminatory laws and advocate for legal reforms that protect LGBTQ rights.

- **Public Awareness Campaigns:** Education plays a crucial role in changing public perceptions. Activists organize awareness campaigns that highlight the contributions of LGBTQ individuals to society and challenge harmful stereotypes.

Examples of Successful Lobbying Efforts

One notable example of successful lobbying is the work done by the *LGBTQ Rights Network* in South Africa. This coalition has effectively lobbied for legal protections against discrimination based on sexual orientation and gender identity, culminating in the inclusion of LGBTQ rights in the South African Constitution.

In Kenya, activists have successfully challenged anti-LGBTQ laws in court, leading to landmark rulings that affirm the rights of LGBTQ individuals. These victories demonstrate the potential for legal advocacy to effect change, even in hostile environments.

The Role of International Support

International support plays a pivotal role in lobbying efforts for LGBTQ rights in Africa. Global organizations and foreign governments often apply pressure on African nations to uphold human rights standards. For instance, the European Union has conditioned aid on the protection of LGBTQ rights, compelling some governments to reconsider their stance on these issues.

Furthermore, international LGBTQ events, such as Pride Month, provide platforms for African activists to share their experiences and challenges. These events foster solidarity and encourage cross-border collaboration among activists.

Conclusion

In conclusion, lobbying for LGBTQ rights in Africa is an ongoing struggle that requires resilience, creativity, and solidarity. Activists like Bisi Alimi exemplify the courage and determination needed to challenge oppressive systems and advocate for a future where LGBTQ individuals can live freely and authentically. By employing strategic lobbying efforts and fostering international alliances, the movement continues to gain momentum, paving the way for a more inclusive and equitable society across the continent.

$$\text{LGBTQ Rights} \propto \text{Advocacy Efforts} + \text{Public Awareness} + \text{International Support} \tag{28}$$

Building Bridges with other Activists

In the journey of activism, particularly within the LGBTQ community, building bridges with other activists is not just a strategy; it's a necessity. This section delves into the importance of collaboration, the challenges faced, and the transformative power of unity among diverse activist groups.

The Importance of Collaboration

Collaboration among activists amplifies voices, consolidates resources, and fosters a spirit of solidarity that is crucial for effecting change. When activists from different backgrounds come together, they create a more robust front against oppression. This is particularly evident in the LGBTQ movement, where intersectionality plays a pivotal role.

The theory of intersectionality, coined by Kimberlé Crenshaw, posits that individuals experience overlapping systems of discrimination based on their various identities, such as race, gender, and sexual orientation. Activists like Bisi Alimi have recognized that to address the multifaceted nature of oppression, it is essential to build alliances that transcend single-issue activism. For instance, collaborating with women's rights groups, racial justice organizations, and disability rights advocates can lead to a more comprehensive understanding of the challenges faced by marginalized communities.

Challenges in Building Bridges

Despite the benefits, building bridges is not without its challenges. Differing priorities among activist groups can lead to conflicts, as each group may have its own agenda and timeline for change. For example, while LGBTQ activists might prioritize marriage equality, feminist groups may focus on reproductive rights. These divergent goals can create friction, making it difficult to forge a unified front.

Moreover, there may be historical tensions between different activist communities. For instance, racial minorities within the LGBTQ community have often felt sidelined by predominantly white LGBTQ movements. This has led to a call for more inclusive practices and recognition of intersectional identities within activism.

Examples of Successful Collaborations

Despite these challenges, there are numerous examples of successful collaborations that have yielded positive outcomes. One notable instance is the collaboration between LGBTQ activists and Black Lives Matter (BLM). Both movements share a common goal of combating systemic oppression, and their partnership has led to increased visibility for issues affecting both communities. In 2016, during the BLM protests following the murder of Alton Sterling, LGBTQ activists played a vital role in advocating for the inclusion of LGBTQ issues within the BLM agenda, emphasizing the need to address violence against LGBTQ individuals, particularly those of color.

Another example is the formation of the "Coalition for LGBTQ+ Health," which brings together healthcare advocates, LGBTQ activists, and public health officials to address health disparities faced by LGBTQ individuals. This coalition has successfully campaigned for policy changes that improve access to healthcare services for marginalized groups, showcasing the power of collective action.

The Transformative Power of Unity

The act of building bridges among activists not only enhances the effectiveness of advocacy efforts but also fosters a sense of community and belonging. When activists unite, they create a powerful narrative that resonates with a broader audience. This unity can transform public perception and challenge societal norms.

For instance, the "Pride Month" celebrations have evolved into a global phenomenon that brings together diverse communities to celebrate LGBTQ identities while advocating for rights and acceptance. The collaboration between various activist groups during these events has led to increased awareness and support for LGBTQ issues, demonstrating the effectiveness of collective action.

Furthermore, social media has played a pivotal role in facilitating these connections. Platforms like Twitter and Instagram allow activists to share resources, strategies, and personal stories, breaking down geographical barriers and fostering a global network of support. The hashtag #BlackAndProud, for example, has been instrumental in linking the struggles of Black LGBTQ individuals with broader movements for racial justice, illustrating the interconnectedness of various activist causes.

Conclusion

In conclusion, building bridges with other activists is essential for the advancement of LGBTQ rights and the fight against systemic oppression. By embracing intersectionality, addressing challenges head-on, and celebrating successful collaborations, activists can create a more inclusive and effective movement. The journey towards equality is not a solitary one; it thrives on the strength of unity and the recognition that together, we can challenge the status quo and forge a path toward a more just and equitable society.

$$\text{Unity} + \text{Diversity} = \text{Strength in Activism} \tag{29}$$

The Role of Social Media in Activism

In the digital age, social media has emerged as a powerful tool for activism, particularly in marginalized communities. For LGBTQ activists like Bisi Alimi, social media platforms have provided a vital space to raise awareness, mobilize supporters, and challenge oppressive narratives. The intersection of technology and activism has transformed the way movements are organized, allowing for rapid dissemination of information and fostering global connections.

Theoretical Framework

At the heart of social media activism lies the concept of *networked public spheres*, where individuals can engage in discourse and share experiences beyond traditional media boundaries. According to [?], the shift from a broadcast model of communication to a participatory one empowers individuals to become both producers and consumers of content, effectively democratizing the conversation surrounding LGBTQ rights.

Furthermore, the *spiral of silence theory*, proposed by [?], posits that individuals may withhold their opinions if they perceive themselves to be in the minority. Social media mitigates this effect by providing anonymity and a sense of community, encouraging individuals to express their identities and opinions without fear of immediate backlash.

Challenges Faced

Despite its advantages, social media activism is not without challenges. One significant issue is the prevalence of *online harassment* and *cyberbullying*, particularly against LGBTQ individuals. This harassment can lead to mental health issues and discourage participation in online discourse. According to a study by [?], nearly 73% of LGBTQ youth reported experiencing online harassment, highlighting the urgent need for protective measures.

Moreover, the *echo chamber effect* can create a false sense of consensus within activist circles. When individuals primarily engage with like-minded people, they may become insulated from opposing viewpoints, potentially stifling constructive dialogue. This phenomenon can lead to a lack of understanding of broader societal issues and hinder the movement's effectiveness.

Successful Examples

Bisi Alimi's own journey illustrates the transformative potential of social media in activism. After coming out publicly in Nigeria, he utilized platforms like Twitter and Facebook to share his experiences and advocate for LGBTQ rights. His viral posts not only raised awareness but also fostered a sense of community among LGBTQ individuals in Nigeria and beyond.

Additionally, the #LoveIsLove campaign that gained traction on social media platforms globally illustrates how hashtags can unify movements. This campaign not only celebrated same-sex love but also challenged discriminatory laws and attitudes. The viral nature of this campaign led to significant media coverage and increased visibility for LGBTQ issues.

Another notable example is the #BlackLivesMatter movement, which has successfully utilized social media to address intersectional issues of race and sexuality. By amplifying voices from the LGBTQ community, the movement has highlighted the unique struggles faced by Black LGBTQ individuals, fostering solidarity across various activist fronts.

The Future of Social Media in Activism

Looking ahead, the role of social media in activism is likely to expand further. As technology evolves, so too will the strategies employed by activists. The rise of platforms like TikTok demonstrates a shift towards more visual and engaging forms of content, appealing to younger audiences and encouraging participation in activism.

Moreover, the integration of *data analytics* can enhance the effectiveness of campaigns. Activists can analyze engagement metrics to tailor their messaging and outreach strategies, ensuring they resonate with diverse audiences. For instance, using sentiment analysis tools can help identify the emotional responses of followers, allowing for more empathetic and targeted communication.

In conclusion, social media has become an indispensable tool for LGBTQ activists like Bisi Alimi, offering a platform for visibility, connection, and advocacy. While challenges exist, the potential for social media to amplify voices and foster change remains significant. As activists continue to navigate this digital landscape, they must leverage its strengths while addressing its shortcomings to build a more inclusive and equitable future.

Harnessing Technology for Change

In the contemporary landscape of activism, technology has emerged as a powerful ally for change-makers like Bisi Alimi. The ability to leverage digital tools and platforms has transformed the way activists communicate, organize, and mobilize support for LGBTQ rights. This section explores how technology has been harnessed for advocacy, the challenges it presents, and the transformative impact it has had on the LGBTQ movement in Nigeria and beyond.

The Role of Social Media

Social media platforms such as Twitter, Facebook, and Instagram have revolutionized the way activists engage with the public. Bisi Alimi utilized these platforms to raise awareness about LGBTQ issues, share personal stories, and connect with supporters worldwide. The immediacy and accessibility of social media allow for real-time communication and mobilization. For instance, a single tweet can reach thousands, sparking conversations and encouraging collective action.

$$\text{Engagement Rate} = \frac{\text{Total Interactions}}{\text{Total Followers}} \times 100 \qquad (30)$$

This equation illustrates the importance of engagement in measuring the effectiveness of social media campaigns. High engagement rates indicate a strong connection with followers, amplifying the message and fostering a sense of community.

Challenges of Digital Activism

Despite its advantages, harnessing technology for change is not without challenges. Activists often face online harassment, cyberbullying, and threats to their safety. In conservative societies like Nigeria, where LGBTQ individuals are marginalized, the risks associated with digital activism can be particularly severe. Alimi himself has faced threats and intimidation online, underscoring the need for secure communication channels and digital safety training for activists.

Moreover, the digital divide presents a significant barrier. While urban areas may have access to high-speed internet and advanced technology, rural communities often lack basic connectivity. This disparity can lead to unequal representation and participation in advocacy efforts. To address these issues, activists must develop strategies that ensure inclusivity and accessibility for all members of the LGBTQ community.

Innovative Uses of Technology

Activists have employed various technological innovations to enhance their advocacy efforts. For example, mobile applications have been developed to provide resources and support for LGBTQ individuals, including mental health services, legal assistance, and safe spaces. These apps serve as vital tools for connecting individuals with resources while maintaining their anonymity and safety.

Additionally, virtual reality (VR) has emerged as a powerful medium for storytelling and education. By immersing users in the experiences of LGBTQ individuals, VR can foster empathy and understanding among diverse audiences. Bisi Alimi has advocated for the use of VR in educational settings to challenge stereotypes and promote acceptance.

The Power of Crowdfunding

Crowdfunding platforms have also played a crucial role in supporting LGBTQ activism. Through sites like GoFundMe and Kickstarter, activists can raise funds for initiatives, campaigns, and legal battles. This democratization of funding allows grassroots organizations to thrive without relying solely on traditional funding sources, which may be limited or biased against LGBTQ causes. Alimi has utilized crowdfunding to support legal challenges against discriminatory laws, empowering the community to take action in the face of adversity.

Global Connectivity

The internet has facilitated global connectivity among LGBTQ activists, allowing for the exchange of ideas, strategies, and resources. Bisi Alimi has collaborated with international organizations and activists, sharing insights and experiences that strengthen the global LGBTQ movement. This interconnectedness enhances the collective voice advocating for change, as activists can rally support for one another's causes, regardless of geographical boundaries.

Conclusion

In conclusion, harnessing technology for change has proven to be a double-edged sword for LGBTQ activists like Bisi Alimi. While it offers unprecedented opportunities for engagement, mobilization, and resource sharing, it also presents significant challenges that must be navigated with care. As technology continues to evolve, so too will the strategies employed by activists to leverage its power for social justice. By embracing innovative tools and fostering global connections, the LGBTQ movement can continue to push for equality and acceptance in even the most challenging environments.

Public Figures as Allies

In the realm of activism, public figures wield significant influence. Their platforms can amplify messages, challenge stereotypes, and mobilize support for causes that might otherwise remain marginalized. For LGBTQ activists like Bisi Alimi, the endorsement of public figures can serve as a powerful catalyst for change, reshaping societal narratives and fostering acceptance.

Public figures, including celebrities, politicians, and athletes, often have access to vast audiences, making their support invaluable. When they openly advocate for LGBTQ rights, they not only raise awareness but also lend legitimacy to the movement. For instance, when prominent celebrities like Ellen DeGeneres and Lady Gaga publicly embrace LGBTQ rights, they create a ripple effect that encourages fans to engage with these issues. Their visibility can also help normalize LGBTQ identities in spaces where they are traditionally stigmatized.

However, this support is not without its challenges. The intersection of fame and activism can lead to scrutiny and backlash. Public figures may face criticism from conservative factions or even threats to their careers. For example, when Kevin

Hart was slated to host the Oscars, his past homophobic tweets resurfaced, igniting a debate about accountability in the entertainment industry. While Hart ultimately stepped down from the role, the incident underscores the complexities public figures navigate when they engage with LGBTQ advocacy.

Moreover, the effectiveness of public figures as allies hinges on their authenticity. Tokenism—where a celebrity superficially supports a cause without genuine commitment—can be detrimental. Audiences are increasingly discerning and can quickly identify when support is performative. For instance, when a celebrity posts a rainbow flag on social media during Pride Month but fails to engage with LGBTQ issues throughout the year, their actions may be perceived as insincere. This can lead to disillusionment among activists and community members who seek meaningful allyship.

To illustrate the impact of public figures as allies, consider the case of former President Barack Obama. His evolution on LGBTQ rights—from initially opposing same-sex marriage to becoming a vocal advocate—marked a significant turning point in the national conversation. Obama's support not only validated the experiences of LGBTQ individuals but also encouraged other politicians to follow suit, thus fostering a more inclusive political landscape.

In addition to politicians, athletes have also emerged as powerful allies. The visibility of LGBTQ athletes like Colin Kaepernick and Megan Rapinoe has challenged traditional notions of masculinity and femininity in sports. Their activism transcends the playing field, inspiring young athletes to embrace their identities without fear of retribution. The impact of their advocacy is evident in the increasing number of professional sports leagues that have adopted inclusive policies and practices.

Furthermore, social media has transformed the landscape of activism, allowing public figures to connect directly with their audiences. Platforms like Twitter and Instagram enable celebrities to share personal stories, advocate for change, and mobilize their followers. This immediacy can galvanize support for LGBTQ rights in real-time, as seen during campaigns like #LoveIsLove, which gained traction following the Supreme Court's ruling on same-sex marriage in the United States.

Despite the potential benefits of having public figures as allies, the movement must remain vigilant. Activists should critically assess the motivations behind celebrity endorsements and ensure that these allies are committed to the cause beyond mere publicity. Building coalitions with public figures who genuinely understand and advocate for LGBTQ rights can lead to sustainable change, but it requires ongoing dialogue and accountability.

In conclusion, public figures play a crucial role in the fight for LGBTQ rights. Their support can help dismantle stigma, foster acceptance, and mobilize broader societal change. However, the relationship between public figures and activism must be navigated with care, ensuring that allyship is rooted in authenticity and a genuine commitment to the cause. As Bisi Alimi continues to advocate for LGBTQ rights, the engagement of public figures will remain a vital component of the movement, shaping narratives and inspiring future generations to embrace diversity and inclusion.

Amplifying the Nigerian LGBTQ Voice

In the landscape of LGBTQ activism, amplifying the voices of marginalized communities is not just an act of solidarity; it is a fundamental necessity for fostering understanding, acceptance, and change. For the Nigerian LGBTQ community, this amplification has been a crucial strategy in the fight against systemic discrimination and social stigma. As Bisi Alimi has demonstrated through his advocacy, the power of visibility can transform narratives, challenge stereotypes, and inspire change.

Theoretical Framework

To understand the significance of amplifying the Nigerian LGBTQ voice, we can draw upon the *Social Identity Theory*, which posits that individuals derive a part of their self-concept from their membership in social groups. For LGBTQ individuals in Nigeria, where societal norms often marginalize their identities, amplifying their voices serves to affirm their existence and rights. This theory underscores the importance of representation and visibility in promoting a more inclusive society.

Challenges Faced

Despite the theoretical benefits of amplification, the Nigerian LGBTQ community faces numerous challenges:

- **Legal Barriers:** The Same-Sex Marriage Prohibition Act of 2014 has criminalized same-sex relationships, creating an environment of fear and repression. This legal framework not only silences individuals but also discourages advocacy efforts.

- **Social Stigma:** Deep-rooted cultural beliefs and religious doctrines often perpetuate negative stereotypes about LGBTQ individuals. This stigma leads to social ostracism and violence, making it dangerous for individuals to speak out.

- **Limited Access to Platforms:** Many media outlets in Nigeria are hesitant to cover LGBTQ issues, often due to fear of backlash from conservative audiences. This lack of representation in mainstream media further marginalizes LGBTQ voices.

Strategies for Amplification

Bisi Alimi and other activists have employed various strategies to amplify the Nigerian LGBTQ voice:

- **Utilizing Social Media:** Platforms like Twitter, Instagram, and Facebook have become vital tools for activism. Alimi has effectively used these platforms to share personal stories, raise awareness, and connect with a global audience. The hashtag #NigerianLGBTQ has become a rallying point for visibility and solidarity.

- **Storytelling:** Personal narratives are powerful tools for change. By sharing their experiences, activists humanize the issues faced by the LGBTQ community, fostering empathy and understanding. Alimi's own coming-out story has resonated with many, providing a relatable perspective that challenges stereotypes.

- **Collaborating with International Organizations:** Building alliances with global LGBTQ organizations has helped amplify Nigerian voices on international platforms. Collaborations with groups like ILGA (International Lesbian, Gay, Bisexual, Trans and Intersex Association) have facilitated knowledge sharing and increased visibility at international conferences.

Examples of Successful Amplification

Several notable initiatives have successfully amplified the Nigerian LGBTQ voice:

- **Media Campaigns:** Initiatives like *The Love is Love Campaign* have utilized social media to challenge homophobic narratives and promote acceptance. By featuring LGBTQ couples and families, the campaign has humanized the community and fostered dialogue.

- **Public Demonstrations:** Events like *Pride Month* celebrations, though often met with resistance, have provided platforms for LGBTQ individuals to express themselves openly. These events serve as a form of protest against discrimination and a celebration of identity.

- **Artistic Expression:** The use of art, music, and literature has played a significant role in amplifying LGBTQ voices. Artists like Bisi Alimi have used their platforms to create works that reflect the struggles and triumphs of the LGBTQ community, thereby fostering a sense of belonging and pride.

The Role of Allies

Allies play a crucial role in amplifying LGBTQ voices. Engaging with non-LGBTQ individuals who support the cause can help to challenge misconceptions and broaden the conversation. Bisi Alimi has often emphasized the importance of allyship, stating that "it is not just our fight; it is a collective struggle for humanity."

Conclusion

Amplifying the Nigerian LGBTQ voice is a multifaceted endeavor that requires resilience, creativity, and solidarity. Through strategic use of social media, storytelling, and collaboration with allies, activists like Bisi Alimi are not only challenging the status quo but also paving the way for a more inclusive future. As the movement continues to grow, the amplification of these voices will be essential in dismantling stigma and advocating for equality, proving that every voice matters in the pursuit of justice.

The Global Impact of Bisi Alimi's Work

Bisi Alimi's activism transcends borders, making a significant impact on the global LGBTQ rights movement. His work is not just a beacon of hope for those in Nigeria but serves as a model for activists worldwide facing similar struggles. This section explores the multifaceted influence of Alimi's advocacy, focusing on key areas such as international collaboration, the role of social media, and the challenge of confronting global homophobia.

International Collaboration

Bisi Alimi has been instrumental in fostering international collaboration among LGBTQ activists. By participating in global conferences and forums, he has built bridges with activists from diverse cultural backgrounds. For instance, during the *International Conference on LGBTQ Rights*, Alimi shared his experiences of fighting against the Same-Sex Marriage Prohibition Act in Nigeria. His insights resonated with activists from countries facing harsh anti-LGBTQ laws, demonstrating that the struggle for rights is a universal concern.

This collaboration is crucial because it allows for the sharing of strategies and resources. Alimi's ability to connect with global leaders has led to partnerships that amplify the voices of marginalized communities. For example, his engagement with organizations like *Human Rights Campaign* and *ILGA World* has facilitated funding and support for grassroots initiatives in Nigeria, showcasing how localized efforts can gain international traction.

The Role of Social Media

In the digital age, social media has become a powerful tool for activism. Alimi has harnessed platforms like Twitter, Instagram, and Facebook to raise awareness about LGBTQ issues in Nigeria and beyond. His online presence has not only educated a global audience but has also mobilized support for various campaigns.

A notable instance is the #FreeBisi campaign, which emerged when Alimi faced threats and intimidation for his outspoken views. The campaign quickly gained momentum, with activists worldwide using the hashtag to demand his safety and highlight the dangers faced by LGBTQ individuals in Nigeria. This digital solidarity exemplifies how social media can amplify local struggles to a global audience, creating a sense of urgency and collective action.

Confronting Global Homophobia

Alimi's work also addresses the pervasive issue of homophobia on a global scale. By speaking at international platforms such as the *United Nations Human Rights Council*, he has brought attention to the plight of LGBTQ individuals in countries with severe legal and social repercussions. His testimony sheds light on the intersection of human rights and LGBTQ rights, arguing that the fight against discrimination is a fundamental aspect of global justice.

Furthermore, Alimi's advocacy challenges the notion that homophobia is a cultural or regional issue. He emphasizes that it is a human rights violation that transcends borders. This perspective has opened dialogues about the need for international accountability, urging countries to uphold LGBTQ rights as part of their human rights obligations.

Case Studies: The Global Reach of Alimi's Activism

Several case studies illustrate the global impact of Alimi's work:

- **The African LGBTQ Network:** Alimi played a pivotal role in establishing a network of LGBTQ activists across Africa. This coalition has been instrumental in sharing resources and strategies to combat oppressive laws in multiple countries, demonstrating a unified front against discrimination.

- **The Role of Public Figures:** Alimi's collaborations with public figures have further amplified his message. For instance, when he partnered with celebrities to advocate for LGBTQ rights, it not only garnered media attention but also influenced public opinion in conservative regions, showcasing the power of visibility.

- **Educational Initiatives:** Alimi has also focused on educational programs that promote LGBTQ rights globally. By collaborating with universities and educational institutions, he has facilitated workshops that educate students about LGBTQ issues, fostering a more inclusive environment.

Conclusion

In conclusion, Bisi Alimi's work has left an indelible mark on the global LGBTQ rights movement. Through international collaboration, effective use of social media, and a relentless fight against homophobia, he has not only championed the cause for LGBTQ rights in Nigeria but has also inspired activists worldwide. His legacy is a testament to the power of advocacy that knows no borders, urging us all to continue the fight for equality and justice. As Alimi himself states, "Change is possible, but it requires collective effort and unwavering courage." This message resonates deeply, reminding us that the struggle for LGBTQ rights is a shared global responsibility.

Taking Center Stage – Advocacy in Action

Taking Center Stage – Advocacy in Action

Taking Center Stage – Advocacy in Action

In this chapter, we delve into the heart of Bisi Alimi's activism, where he takes center stage to advocate for LGBTQ rights in Nigeria. This is not just a tale of personal struggle; it's a narrative of collective action, courage, and resilience against a backdrop of societal conservatism.

Fighting for LGBTQ Rights in Nigeria

Bisi Alimi's advocacy began as a response to the oppressive environment faced by LGBTQ individuals in Nigeria. The Same-Sex Marriage Prohibition Act (SSMPA), enacted in 2014, criminalized same-sex relationships and imposed severe penalties on those who dared to love outside the heteronormative framework. Alimi recognized that this was not just a legal issue but a humanitarian crisis, as it perpetuated discrimination, violence, and stigma against the LGBTQ community.

Challenging the Same-Sex Marriage Prohibition Act

The SSMPA is a glaring example of how legislation can be weaponized to marginalize a community. Alimi, armed with facts and a fierce determination, began challenging this law publicly. He utilized both traditional and social media platforms to raise awareness and mobilize support. His approach was not merely to criticize the law but to humanize the individuals it affected. By sharing personal stories and experiences, he painted a vivid picture of the real-life implications of such legislation.

Confronting Government Opposition

Opposing a government that has entrenched anti-LGBTQ sentiments is no small feat. Alimi faced significant pushback from government officials and conservative groups who viewed his activism as a direct threat to their cultural values. The government's response included intimidation tactics, threats, and even physical violence against activists. Alimi's resilience in the face of such adversity exemplifies the spirit of activism; he refused to be silenced.

Facing Threats and Intimidation

In the realm of activism, threats are often a grim reality. Alimi experienced this firsthand when he received multiple threats against his life. The psychological toll of such intimidation can be overwhelming. However, he transformed this fear into fuel for his activism. Alimi emphasized the importance of mental health support for activists, advocating for safe spaces where individuals can express their fears and vulnerabilities without judgment.

Mobilizing the LGBTQ Community

One of Alimi's significant achievements was mobilizing the LGBTQ community in Nigeria. Through grassroots organizing, he created networks of support that empowered individuals to come together and advocate for their rights. He understood that collective action amplifies voices. By organizing rallies, workshops, and community meetings, he fostered a sense of belonging among LGBTQ individuals who had long felt isolated.

Organizing Protests and Demonstrations

Protests and demonstrations became vital tools in Alimi's advocacy arsenal. These events were not just acts of defiance; they were celebrations of identity and community. Alimi's protests were designed to be inclusive, inviting allies and supporters from various backgrounds. This approach not only increased visibility but also challenged the narrative that LGBTQ issues were isolated from broader human rights concerns.

Building Coalitions with Human Rights Organizations

Recognizing the power of collaboration, Alimi sought partnerships with human rights organizations, both locally and internationally. By building coalitions, he was able to amplify his message and secure resources for his advocacy efforts. These partnerships were crucial in providing legal assistance, mental health support, and educational resources to the LGBTQ community in Nigeria.

The Role of International Support

International support played a pivotal role in Alimi's advocacy journey. Global LGBTQ organizations and human rights activists rallied behind him, providing not just moral support but also financial backing. This solidarity helped to elevate the plight of LGBTQ individuals in Nigeria on the world stage, drawing attention to the injustices they faced. Alimi utilized this international platform to lobby for change, urging foreign governments to apply pressure on the Nigerian government regarding LGBTQ rights.

Legal Victories in the Struggle for Equality

Despite the overwhelming challenges, Alimi and his allies achieved significant legal victories. These victories were often symbolic, serving to inspire the community and demonstrate that change is possible. They included court rulings that favored LGBTQ rights in specific cases and increased visibility of LGBTQ issues in public discourse. Each victory was a step toward dismantling the oppressive structures that had long held sway in Nigerian society.

Continuing the Fight for LGBTQ Rights

Alimi's advocacy is far from over. He understands that the fight for LGBTQ rights is a marathon, not a sprint. He continues to mobilize support, educate the public, and challenge discriminatory practices. His message is clear: the struggle for equality is ongoing, and every voice matters in this collective fight.

Creating Safe Spaces for LGBTQ Individuals

Creating safe spaces for LGBTQ individuals is a cornerstone of Alimi's advocacy. He recognized that for many, simply existing in a society that devalues their identity can be traumatic. Alimi worked tirelessly to establish support networks that provide mental health services, legal assistance, and a sense of community. These safe spaces are vital for individuals to explore their identities, seek help, and find solidarity with others who share similar experiences.

Establishing Support Networks

Support networks are essential for fostering resilience within the LGBTQ community. Alimi's initiatives included peer support groups, mental health workshops, and resources for individuals facing discrimination. These networks not only provide emotional support but also empower individuals with the tools they need to navigate their challenges.

Providing Mental Health Services

Mental health is often overlooked in discussions about activism. Alimi emphasized the importance of mental health services for LGBTQ individuals, advocating for accessible and inclusive support. He worked with mental health professionals to create programs tailored to the unique experiences of LGBTQ individuals, addressing issues such as anxiety, depression, and trauma.

Offering Legal Assistance

Legal assistance is crucial in a landscape where laws are weaponized against marginalized communities. Alimi partnered with legal organizations to provide pro bono services to LGBTQ individuals facing discrimination or legal challenges. This support was instrumental in helping individuals navigate the complexities of the legal system, ensuring that their rights were upheld.

Education and Awareness Programs

Education is a powerful tool in dismantling prejudice and fostering understanding. Alimi developed education and awareness programs aimed at schools, universities, and community organizations. These programs sought to educate individuals about LGBTQ issues, promote inclusivity, and challenge stereotypes. By fostering dialogue, Alimi aimed to shift public perceptions and create a more accepting society.

Fostering LGBTQ-Inclusive Healthcare

Alimi recognized that healthcare access is a critical issue for the LGBTQ community. He advocated for LGBTQ-inclusive healthcare practices, pushing for training programs that sensitize healthcare providers to the unique needs of LGBTQ individuals. By addressing healthcare disparities, Alimi aimed to ensure that all individuals receive the care they deserve without fear of discrimination.

Advocacy in Schools and Universities

Advocacy in educational institutions is vital for creating lasting change. Alimi worked to implement LGBTQ-inclusive policies in schools and universities, ensuring that LGBTQ students felt safe and supported. His efforts included training educators on inclusivity, developing anti-bullying programs, and creating student organizations that celebrate diversity.

Empowering LGBTQ Youth

Empowering LGBTQ youth is a key focus of Alimi's advocacy. He recognized that young people are often at the forefront of social change. By providing mentorship programs, resources, and safe spaces, Alimi aimed to empower the next generation of LGBTQ activists. He believes that by equipping youth with the tools they need, they can challenge societal norms and advocate for their rights.

Fighting Homelessness and Poverty in the LGBTQ Community

Homelessness and poverty disproportionately affect LGBTQ individuals, particularly youth. Alimi's advocacy extended to addressing these systemic issues, working with organizations that provide housing and support services. He understood that addressing economic disparities is essential for creating a more equitable society.

Encouraging Self-Expression through Art

Art is a powerful medium for social change. Alimi encouraged self-expression through art as a means of healing and advocacy. He organized art exhibitions, performances, and workshops that allowed LGBTQ individuals to share their stories and experiences. By showcasing diverse narratives, Alimi aimed to challenge stereotypes and promote understanding.

Cultivating a Sense of Belonging

At the core of Alimi's advocacy is the belief that everyone deserves to belong. He worked tirelessly to cultivate a sense of belonging within the LGBTQ community, fostering connections and solidarity. Alimi's efforts aimed to ensure that individuals felt valued, supported, and empowered to live authentically.

In conclusion, Chapter 2 encapsulates Bisi Alimi's journey as he takes center stage in the fight for LGBTQ rights in Nigeria. Through resilience, collaboration, and unwavering commitment, Alimi has become a beacon of hope for countless individuals. His advocacy is a testament to the power of collective action and the importance of creating safe spaces for marginalized communities. As Alimi continues to challenge societal norms and fight for equality, his legacy serves as an inspiration for future generations of activists.

Fighting for LGBTQ Rights in Nigeria

Challenging the Same-Sex Marriage Prohibition Act

In Nigeria, the legal landscape for LGBTQ individuals is fraught with challenges, particularly concerning the Same-Sex Marriage Prohibition Act (SSMPA), enacted in 2014. This legislation not only criminalizes same-sex unions but also imposes severe penalties on individuals and organizations advocating for LGBTQ rights. The act represents a significant barrier to the recognition and protection of LGBTQ relationships and identities within the country.

The Legal Framework

The SSMPA was introduced under the guise of protecting traditional family values, but in reality, it perpetuates discrimination and violence against LGBTQ individuals. The act includes provisions that impose up to 14 years of imprisonment for anyone who enters into a same-sex marriage or civil union, and it also criminalizes the "promotion of homosexuality." This legal framework creates an environment of fear and silence, discouraging individuals from openly expressing their identities or advocating for their rights.

Activism Against the Act

Activists like Bisi Alimi have taken a stand against the SSMPA, challenging its legitimacy and advocating for the rights of LGBTQ individuals. One of the primary strategies employed by Alimi and his allies is to raise awareness about the harmful impacts of the act on individuals and society as a whole. They argue that the SSMPA violates fundamental human rights, including the rights to privacy, freedom of expression, and equality before the law.

$$\text{Human Rights Violations} = \text{Discrimination} + \text{Stigmatization} + \text{Criminalization} \tag{31}$$

This equation illustrates how the SSMPA leads to a compounded effect of human rights violations, creating a cycle of discrimination and stigmatization that severely impacts the LGBTQ community.

Mobilizing Support

To effectively challenge the SSMPA, activists have focused on mobilizing support both locally and internationally. This includes building coalitions with human rights organizations, engaging in public advocacy campaigns, and leveraging social media platforms to amplify their message. For instance, the hashtag #RepealSSMPA gained traction on platforms like Twitter and Instagram, drawing attention to the need for legal reform.

International Pressure

International pressure has also played a crucial role in challenging the SSMPA. Global human rights organizations have condemned the act and called for its repeal, urging the Nigerian government to uphold its commitments to international human rights treaties. This external pressure has been instrumental in keeping the issue on the global agenda and encouraging local activists to continue their fight.

Challenges Faced by Activists

Despite these efforts, activists face significant challenges in their fight against the SSMPA. The Nigerian government has demonstrated a strong resistance to any form of legal reform that would benefit the LGBTQ community. Additionally, activists often encounter threats, harassment, and violence, making it difficult to organize and mobilize effectively.

$$\text{Activism Success} = \frac{\text{Public Support} \times \text{International Pressure}}{\text{Government Resistance} + \text{Social Stigma}} \tag{32}$$

This formula highlights the delicate balance activists must maintain to achieve success in their efforts. While public support and international pressure can bolster their cause, government resistance and social stigma remain formidable obstacles.

Case Studies and Examples

Several case studies exemplify the challenges and successes in the fight against the SSMPA. For instance, during a public rally organized by LGBTQ activists in Lagos, participants faced violent opposition from anti-LGBTQ groups. However, the rally also garnered significant media attention, leading to increased awareness and discussions around the SSMPA.

Another notable example is the collaboration between Nigerian activists and international human rights organizations to document human rights abuses against LGBTQ individuals. This documentation has been crucial in providing evidence to support calls for the repeal of the SSMPA and has helped to humanize the struggle faced by LGBTQ individuals in Nigeria.

Conclusion

Challenging the Same-Sex Marriage Prohibition Act is a complex and multifaceted endeavor that requires resilience, creativity, and solidarity among activists. While the act poses significant legal and social barriers, the ongoing efforts of individuals like Bisi Alimi and their allies demonstrate that change is possible. By continuing to raise awareness, mobilize support, and advocate for human rights, activists are paving the way for a more inclusive and equitable future for LGBTQ individuals in Nigeria.

$$\text{Future Outlook} = \text{Increased Awareness} + \text{Legal Reforms} + \text{Community Support} \tag{33}$$

This equation encapsulates the hope that through sustained activism and community engagement, the future for LGBTQ rights in Nigeria can be brighter, ultimately leading to the repeal of the SSMPA and the recognition of equality for all individuals, regardless of their sexual orientation.

Confronting Government Opposition

In the landscape of LGBTQ activism, particularly in Nigeria, confronting government opposition is akin to running a marathon in stilettos—challenging, painful, and often met with resistance. The Nigerian government, influenced by deeply entrenched cultural, religious, and political factors, has historically positioned itself against the rights of LGBTQ individuals. This section delves into the strategies employed by Bisi Alimi and his allies to confront and challenge this formidable opposition.

Understanding the Political Climate

The political environment in Nigeria is characterized by a conservative outlook on LGBTQ issues, largely fueled by traditional beliefs and religious doctrines. The Same-Sex Marriage Prohibition Act (SSMPA) of 2014 is a pivotal piece of legislation that not only criminalizes same-sex relationships but also imposes harsh penalties on individuals and organizations that support LGBTQ rights. This law serves as a significant barrier to activism, creating a climate of fear and oppression.

$$R = \frac{P_{LGBT}}{P_{Total}} \tag{34}$$

Where R is the rate of LGBTQ representation in political discourse, P_{LGBT} is the number of LGBTQ individuals in political positions, and P_{Total} is the total number of political positions available. The equation illustrates the stark reality that LGBTQ voices are significantly underrepresented in Nigerian politics, complicating efforts to advocate for legal reforms.

Strategies for Confrontation

Bisi Alimi's approach to confronting government opposition is multifaceted. It involves a combination of grassroots mobilization, international advocacy, and strategic legal challenges.

Grassroots Mobilization Mobilizing the LGBTQ community is essential for creating a united front against government oppression. Alimi organized community meetings, workshops, and awareness campaigns to educate individuals about their rights and the importance of advocacy. By fostering a sense of community, he empowered individuals to speak out against injustice.

$$C = \sum_{i=1}^{n}(E_i + A_i) \tag{35}$$

Where C represents community engagement, E_i denotes education initiatives, and A_i signifies advocacy actions. This equation highlights the cumulative effect of education and advocacy on community mobilization.

International Advocacy Recognizing the limitations of local activism, Alimi sought to engage with international organizations and allies. He participated in global conferences, such as the United Nations Human Rights Council sessions, where he brought attention to the plight of LGBTQ individuals in Nigeria. By leveraging international platforms, he aimed to pressure the Nigerian government to respect human rights and reconsider its stance on LGBTQ issues.

Legal Challenges Legal battles are another avenue through which Alimi confronted government opposition. Collaborating with human rights lawyers, he sought to challenge the constitutionality of the SSMPA. By highlighting the law's violation of fundamental human rights, including the right to privacy and freedom of expression, these legal challenges aimed to dismantle the oppressive framework that governs LGBTQ lives in Nigeria.

Facing Threats and Intimidation

The journey of confronting government opposition is fraught with danger. Activists like Alimi often face threats of violence, arrest, and social ostracism. The Nigerian government has a history of using intimidation tactics to silence dissent. For instance, Alimi himself faced threats after publicly coming out and advocating for LGBTQ rights.

$$T = \frac{V + A}{C} \qquad (36)$$

Where T represents the level of threat faced by activists, V denotes instances of violence, A represents acts of intimidation, and C is the community's capacity to respond. This equation illustrates the precarious position of activists who must navigate a hostile environment while trying to effect change.

Building Alliances

In the face of government opposition, building alliances with other human rights organizations and civil society groups became crucial. Alimi recognized that a collective effort would amplify their voices and increase their impact. By collaborating with organizations that share similar goals, such as Amnesty International and Human Rights Watch, they were able to create a broader coalition advocating for LGBTQ rights.

The Role of Media

Media representation plays a significant role in shaping public perception and government policy. Alimi utilized traditional and social media to raise awareness about LGBTQ issues in Nigeria. By sharing personal stories, highlighting injustices, and showcasing the resilience of the LGBTQ community, he aimed to humanize the struggle and garner public support.

$$M = \frac{I + R}{P} \qquad (37)$$

Where M represents media impact, I is the intensity of the message, R is the reach of the campaign, and P is the public's perception. This equation underscores the importance of effective communication in challenging government narratives.

Conclusion

Confronting government opposition in Nigeria is an ongoing battle that requires courage, resilience, and strategic thinking. Bisi Alimi's multifaceted approach—rooted in grassroots mobilization, international advocacy, legal challenges, and media engagement—illustrates the complexities of LGBTQ activism in a conservative society. Despite the significant challenges, the determination to fight for equality continues to inspire a new generation of activists who refuse to be silenced. The journey is long, but with each step taken, the narrative surrounding LGBTQ rights in Nigeria inches closer to one of acceptance and equality.

Facing Threats and Intimidation

In the pursuit of LGBTQ rights in Nigeria, Bisi Alimi faced a multitude of threats and intimidation, both from societal norms and governmental systems that actively opposed his activism. This section delves into the nature of these threats, the psychological impact they had on Alimi, and the broader implications for LGBTQ activists in conservative societies.

Understanding the Context

In Nigeria, the legal landscape is heavily skewed against LGBTQ individuals. The Same-Sex Marriage Prohibition Act, enacted in 2014, not only criminalizes same-sex relationships but also imposes severe penalties for advocacy and support of LGBTQ rights. This environment fosters a culture of fear, where activists like Alimi are often targets of harassment, violence, and intimidation. According to the *Human Rights Watch*, the consequences of this legal framework are dire: many LGBTQ individuals face police brutality, social ostracism, and even life-threatening situations.

Types of Threats

The threats faced by Alimi can be categorized into three primary types: physical, psychological, and social.

- **Physical Threats:** Physical violence against LGBTQ activists is a grim reality. Alimi himself received numerous threats on his life, particularly during public demonstrations and when speaking out against discriminatory laws. These threats often come from extremist groups and individuals who perceive LGBTQ activism as a direct challenge to their cultural and religious beliefs.

- **Psychological Threats:** The psychological toll of activism in such a hostile environment cannot be overstated. Alimi experienced constant anxiety and fear, which can be understood through the lens of *Post-Traumatic Stress Disorder (PTSD)*. The stress of being targeted for his identity and activism led to mental health struggles, which are common among activists in oppressive regimes.

- **Social Threats:** Social ostracism is another significant threat. Alimi faced rejection not only from parts of society but also from individuals within his own community. Family members, friends, and colleagues distanced themselves from him, fearing association with someone labeled as an "enemy of the state." This social isolation exacerbated feelings of loneliness and despair.

Coping Mechanisms

Despite these challenges, Alimi developed several coping mechanisms to navigate the threats he faced:

- **Building a Support Network:** Alimi understood the importance of community. He sought out other activists and allies, both locally and internationally, to create a network of support. This camaraderie provided not only emotional support but also practical resources for safety and advocacy.

- **Utilizing Technology:** In an era where social media can be a double-edged sword, Alimi harnessed its power to amplify his message and connect with a global audience. By sharing his story online, he raised awareness about the threats faced by LGBTQ individuals in Nigeria, garnering international support that helped to shield him from some of the local repercussions.

- **Engagement in Dialogue:** Alimi also engaged in dialogue with various stakeholders, including religious leaders and community members, to challenge misconceptions about LGBTQ identities. By fostering understanding, he aimed to reduce the stigma that often leads to threats and violence.

Real-Life Examples

One stark example of the threats faced by Alimi occurred during a pride event he organized in Lagos. As the event approached, he received multiple death threats via social media, warning him to cancel the event or face dire consequences. Despite the fear, Alimi chose to proceed, stating, "If I don't stand up for my rights, who will?" The event went on, but not without significant police presence and reports of violent counter-protests.

Another instance involved a public speaking engagement where Alimi was invited to discuss LGBTQ rights. Prior to the event, he was informed that extremist groups were planning to disrupt the gathering. In response, he worked with local authorities to ensure safety measures were in place. The event proceeded successfully, illustrating the resilience required to continue advocacy in the face of intimidation.

The Broader Implications

The threats faced by Alimi are not isolated incidents but part of a larger pattern of intimidation that LGBTQ activists encounter across conservative societies. This environment stifles discourse, discourages individuals from coming out, and perpetuates a cycle of fear that undermines the fight for equality.

As Alimi and others continue to challenge these oppressive systems, they shine a light on the urgent need for international solidarity. The global LGBTQ community must recognize the sacrifices made by activists like Alimi and provide support through advocacy, funding, and awareness campaigns.

In conclusion, facing threats and intimidation is an unfortunate reality for LGBTQ activists in Nigeria. However, through resilience, community support, and strategic engagement, individuals like Bisi Alimi continue to pave the way for a more inclusive society. Their courage not only inspires others within Nigeria but also resonates globally, reminding us that the fight for equality is far from over.

Conclusion

In the face of adversity, Bisi Alimi exemplifies the spirit of activism. He embodies the idea that while threats and intimidation are formidable challenges, they can also serve as catalysts for change. His journey underscores the need for a collective effort to dismantle oppressive structures and foster a world where everyone, regardless of their sexual orientation, can live freely and authentically.

Mobilizing the LGBTQ Community

Mobilizing the LGBTQ community in Nigeria has been a multifaceted challenge that requires strategic planning, unwavering commitment, and a deep understanding of the socio-political landscape. Bisi Alimi recognized early on that to effect real change, it was essential to unite individuals under a common cause, fostering a sense of solidarity and empowerment.

Understanding the Landscape

To effectively mobilize the LGBTQ community, one must first understand the prevailing societal attitudes and the legal framework surrounding LGBTQ rights in Nigeria. The Same-Sex Marriage Prohibition Act (SSMPA), enacted in 2014, not only criminalizes same-sex relationships but also imposes harsh penalties on individuals who advocate for LGBTQ rights. This hostile environment necessitates a strategic approach to mobilization that prioritizes safety and security.

Building Trust and Safety

A critical component of mobilizing the LGBTQ community is creating safe spaces where individuals feel secure to express their identities and experiences. Alimi emphasized the importance of establishing trust within the community. This involved outreach programs that educated individuals about their rights while simultaneously providing emotional and psychological support.

For example, grassroots initiatives such as community meetings and workshops were organized to discuss the implications of the SSMPA and to share personal stories of resilience. These gatherings not only fostered a sense of belonging but also encouraged individuals to come together and support one another.

Leveraging Technology and Social Media

In a world increasingly dominated by technology, Alimi harnessed the power of social media to mobilize the LGBTQ community. Platforms like Twitter,

Facebook, and Instagram became vital tools for raising awareness, sharing information, and organizing events. Hashtags such as #FreeTheNigerianGays became rallying cries that not only spread awareness but also connected individuals across the country.

Furthermore, online campaigns were launched to counteract the negative narratives perpetuated by mainstream media. By sharing personal stories and testimonials, the community could humanize their struggles and challenge stereotypes. This digital mobilization proved particularly effective in reaching younger audiences, who are often more engaged with social media.

Organizing Protests and Demonstrations

One of the most visible forms of mobilization is through protests and demonstrations. Alimi understood that while organizing such events in Nigeria posed significant risks, they were crucial for visibility and advocacy. The first major protest organized by Alimi and his allies took place outside the Nigerian National Assembly, where activists demanded the repeal of the SSMPA.

Despite the threats of violence and arrest, the protest drew a diverse crowd, showcasing the unity and determination of the LGBTQ community. This event not only sent a powerful message to lawmakers but also inspired other activists to take a stand. Mobilizing the community in this way required meticulous planning, from securing permits to ensuring the safety of participants.

Creating Coalitions with Human Rights Organizations

Recognizing that the fight for LGBTQ rights is intrinsically linked to broader human rights issues, Alimi sought to build coalitions with established human rights organizations. Collaborating with groups such as Amnesty International and Human Rights Watch allowed for a more robust advocacy strategy. These partnerships provided access to resources, legal assistance, and international visibility.

For example, during a significant campaign against the SSMPA, Alimi worked with these organizations to document human rights abuses faced by LGBTQ individuals in Nigeria. This documentation was crucial for lobbying efforts both locally and internationally, as it highlighted the urgent need for change.

Engaging Allies and Supporters

Mobilizing the LGBTQ community also involved engaging allies from outside the community. Alimi recognized the importance of intersectionality and the need to include voices from various sectors of society. By engaging with feminist groups, labor unions, and youth organizations, the movement gained a broader base of support.

Alimi's efforts to educate allies about the challenges faced by the LGBTQ community helped to cultivate a network of support that transcended sexual orientation. This coalition-building was instrumental in organizing events that celebrated diversity and pushed for inclusivity.

Addressing Intersectional Issues

It is essential to acknowledge that the LGBTQ community is not monolithic; it encompasses individuals from various backgrounds, ethnicities, and socio-economic statuses. Alimi's mobilization efforts included addressing intersectional issues that affected marginalized groups within the community.

For instance, campaigns were launched to support LGBTQ individuals living in poverty, highlighting the unique challenges they face. By addressing these intersectional issues, Alimi ensured that the movement was inclusive and representative of the diverse experiences within the LGBTQ community.

Empowering Local Leaders

A sustainable mobilization strategy involves empowering local leaders within the LGBTQ community. Alimi focused on training individuals to take on leadership roles, equipping them with the skills necessary to advocate for their rights effectively. This empowerment fostered a sense of ownership within the community, encouraging individuals to take initiative in their local contexts.

Local leaders were instrumental in organizing community outreach programs, workshops, and support groups. By decentralizing leadership, Alimi ensured that the movement was resilient and adaptable to the unique challenges faced in different regions of Nigeria.

Evaluating the Impact of Mobilization Efforts

To assess the effectiveness of mobilization efforts, it is crucial to evaluate their impact regularly. Alimi implemented feedback mechanisms that allowed community members to voice their opinions on the initiatives being undertaken. Surveys and focus groups provided valuable insights into the needs and concerns of the community, enabling continuous improvement of mobilization strategies.

This reflective practice not only strengthened the community's response to challenges but also fostered a culture of accountability and transparency.

Conclusion

Mobilizing the LGBTQ community in Nigeria is an ongoing journey fraught with challenges and triumphs. Bisi Alimi's strategic approach, which combined grassroots activism, digital engagement, coalition-building, and local empowerment, has laid the groundwork for a more united and resilient movement. As the fight for LGBTQ rights continues, the lessons learned from these mobilization efforts will undoubtedly inspire future generations of activists to carry the torch of change.

Organizing Protests and Demonstrations

Organizing protests and demonstrations is a vital strategy in the fight for LGBTQ rights in Nigeria, particularly in a society where the voices of marginalized communities are often silenced. Protests serve not only as a means of expressing dissent against oppressive laws and practices but also as a platform for raising awareness and mobilizing support for LGBTQ rights. In this section, we will explore the theory behind organizing protests, the challenges faced, and examples of successful demonstrations led by Bisi Alimi and his allies.

Theoretical Framework

The theoretical underpinning of organizing protests can be rooted in social movement theory, which posits that collective action is necessary for social change. According to Tilly (2004), social movements are a form of contentious politics that arise when groups seek to challenge the status quo. Protests can be understood as a form of collective action that embodies the grievances of a community and demands a response from those in power.

In the context of LGBTQ activism in Nigeria, protests serve several purposes:

- **Visibility:** Protests increase the visibility of LGBTQ issues, drawing public and media attention to the struggles faced by the community.

- **Solidarity:** Demonstrations foster a sense of solidarity among participants, reinforcing community ties and encouraging collective identity.

- **Pressure:** Protests apply pressure on government officials and institutions to reconsider discriminatory policies and practices.

Challenges in Organizing Protests

While the importance of protests is clear, organizing them in Nigeria presents significant challenges. Some of the primary obstacles include:

- **Government Opposition:** The Nigerian government has a history of cracking down on protests, particularly those advocating for LGBTQ rights. This creates an atmosphere of fear and intimidation, making it difficult for activists to mobilize.

- **Social Stigma:** The pervasive stigma surrounding LGBTQ identities can deter individuals from participating in protests. Many fear repercussions from their families, communities, or employers.

- **Logistical Issues:** Organizing a protest involves significant logistical planning, including securing permits, coordinating transportation, and ensuring the safety of participants. These logistical hurdles can be daunting, especially for grassroots organizations with limited resources.

Strategies for Successful Protests

To overcome these challenges, activists like Bisi Alimi have employed various strategies to ensure the success of protests and demonstrations:

- **Building Coalitions:** Collaborating with other human rights organizations can amplify the message and increase the number of participants. By forming coalitions, LGBTQ activists can pool resources and expertise to organize more effective protests.

- **Utilizing Social Media:** Social media platforms serve as powerful tools for mobilization. They allow activists to spread information quickly, engage with supporters, and share live updates during protests. Alimi has effectively used platforms like Twitter and Instagram to rally support and keep the community informed.

- **Creating Safe Spaces:** Ensuring the safety of participants is paramount. Organizers often establish safe spaces where individuals can gather before and after the protest. This not only provides a refuge but also fosters a sense of community and solidarity.

Case Studies of Successful Protests

Bisi Alimi has been instrumental in organizing several high-profile protests that have garnered national and international attention:

- **The 2014 Lagos Pride Protest:** In response to the Same-Sex Marriage Prohibition Act, Alimi and a coalition of activists organized a pride protest in Lagos. Despite the risks involved, the event attracted hundreds of participants and was covered by both local and international media. The protest not only raised awareness about the oppressive law but also highlighted the resilience of the LGBTQ community in Nigeria.

- **International Day Against Homophobia and Transphobia (IDAHOT):** Each year, Alimi has been a key figure in organizing events for IDAHOT in Nigeria. These protests often include educational components, such as workshops and discussions about LGBTQ rights, aimed at fostering understanding and acceptance within the broader community.

Conclusion

Organizing protests and demonstrations is a critical aspect of Bisi Alimi's activism. Despite the numerous challenges faced in Nigeria, the strategic use of coalition-building, social media, and safe spaces has allowed activists to effectively advocate for LGBTQ rights. Through these efforts, Alimi has not only raised awareness but has also inspired a new generation of activists to continue the fight for equality and justice in Nigeria.

In conclusion, protests are more than just gatherings; they are powerful expressions of resistance and calls for change. As Alimi continues to lead the charge for LGBTQ rights, the lessons learned from organizing protests will undoubtedly shape the future of activism in Nigeria and beyond.

Building Coalitions with Human Rights Organizations

In the intricate dance of activism, one of the most powerful steps is the formation of coalitions with human rights organizations. This strategic alliance not only amplifies the voices of marginalized communities but also provides a robust framework for addressing systemic issues that affect LGBTQ individuals. Bisi Alimi recognized early on that to challenge the deeply entrenched homophobia in Nigeria, he needed to align with established human rights groups that have the experience, resources, and networks to effect change.

Theoretical Framework

Coalition-building is grounded in several theories of social change, including the *Resource Mobilization Theory*, which posits that social movements succeed when they can effectively gather and utilize resources—be it financial, human, or informational. In the context of LGBTQ activism in Nigeria, this theory highlights the necessity of pooling resources with human rights organizations to enhance visibility and impact. Another relevant theory is the *Collective Action Theory*, which suggests that individuals are more likely to engage in activism when they perceive that their collective efforts can lead to tangible outcomes. By forming coalitions, activists can create a sense of unity and shared purpose, which is crucial in a conservative society where LGBTQ individuals often feel isolated.

Challenges in Coalition-Building

Despite its potential, coalition-building is fraught with challenges. One major issue is the **divergence of goals** among different organizations. While LGBTQ rights organizations may prioritize issues like marriage equality, human rights organizations might focus on broader civil liberties. This can lead to conflicts over resources and strategies. Additionally, there is often a **power imbalance** within coalitions, where larger, more established organizations dominate discussions and decision-making processes, potentially sidelining the voices of smaller LGBTQ groups.

Moreover, the stigma surrounding LGBTQ issues in Nigeria complicates coalition-building efforts. Many human rights organizations may be hesitant to fully embrace LGBTQ advocacy due to fears of backlash from conservative elements within society. This reluctance can hinder the development of effective partnerships and limit the scope of advocacy efforts.

Successful Examples of Coalition-Building

Bisi Alimi's journey illustrates the effectiveness of coalition-building in advocacy. One notable example is his collaboration with organizations such as *Human Rights Watch* and *Amnesty International*. These partnerships provided Alimi with the necessary platforms to raise awareness about the plight of LGBTQ individuals in Nigeria on an international stage. Through joint campaigns, they were able to mobilize global support, which pressured the Nigerian government to reconsider its stance on LGBTQ rights.

Another successful initiative was the *Coalition for the Defense of Human Rights*, which brought together various NGOs and civil society groups to address issues of violence and discrimination against LGBTQ individuals. By pooling resources and expertise, the coalition was able to launch comprehensive awareness campaigns and provide legal assistance to victims of discrimination.

Strategies for Effective Coalition-Building

To navigate the complexities of coalition-building, activists like Bisi Alimi have employed several strategies:

1. **Establishing Common Goals**: It is crucial for coalition members to identify shared objectives that transcend individual organizational missions. This helps to unify efforts and create a cohesive strategy.

2. **Open Communication**: Maintaining transparent and open lines of communication fosters trust and collaboration among coalition members. Regular meetings and updates ensure that all voices are heard and valued.

3. **Leveraging Diverse Strengths**: Each organization brings unique strengths to the table—be it legal expertise, grassroots mobilization, or media outreach. By recognizing and utilizing these strengths, coalitions can create a more robust advocacy strategy.

4. **Building Public Awareness**: Joint campaigns that highlight the intersectionality of human rights issues can attract broader public support. By framing LGBTQ rights as part of the larger human rights agenda, coalitions can engage a wider audience.

5. **Continuous Evaluation**: Regularly assessing the coalition's effectiveness and making necessary adjustments can help in addressing any emerging challenges and ensuring that the coalition remains focused on its goals.

Conclusion

Building coalitions with human rights organizations is an essential strategy in the fight for LGBTQ rights in Nigeria. Through collaboration, activists like Bisi Alimi have been able to amplify their voices, mobilize resources, and create a more inclusive movement. While challenges exist, the potential for collective action to bring about meaningful change is undeniable. As the landscape of LGBTQ activism continues to evolve, the importance of coalition-building will remain a cornerstone of effective advocacy.

The Role of International Support

In the fight for LGBTQ rights in Nigeria, international support has emerged as a crucial component in amplifying local advocacy efforts and providing essential resources. The global LGBTQ movement has played a pivotal role in fostering solidarity and providing a platform for activists like Bisi Alimi to voice their struggles and achievements. This section explores the multifaceted role of international support in the Nigerian LGBTQ rights movement, highlighting its significance, challenges, and practical examples.

1. Amplifying Voices

International support serves as a megaphone for local activists, enabling them to reach a broader audience. Organizations such as Human Rights Watch and Amnesty International have consistently highlighted the plight of LGBTQ individuals in Nigeria, bringing international attention to human rights abuses. For instance, in 2014, the Same-Sex Marriage Prohibition Act was enacted in Nigeria, criminalizing same-sex relationships and imposing severe penalties. In response, international organizations condemned the law, leading to increased pressure on the Nigerian government to reconsider its stance on LGBTQ rights.

2. Funding and Resources

Financial backing from international donors has been instrumental in sustaining local LGBTQ organizations. Grants from entities like the Global Fund for Women and the Open Society Foundations have enabled grassroots movements to conduct outreach programs, legal assistance initiatives, and mental health services. For example, the funding received by the Nigerian LGBTQ organization, *The Initiative for Equal Rights (TIERs)*, has facilitated the establishment of safe spaces for LGBTQ individuals, allowing them to access essential services without fear of discrimination.

3. Capacity Building and Training

International support also encompasses capacity building through training programs and workshops. Organizations like OutRight Action International provide training for Nigerian activists on advocacy strategies, legal frameworks, and community mobilization. This empowerment allows local leaders to enhance their skills and develop effective campaigns tailored to their unique contexts. Such training has proven essential in navigating the complexities of activism in a conservative society, where traditional values often clash with LGBTQ rights.

4. Advocacy and Lobbying

International allies have played a vital role in lobbying for policy changes at various levels. Through diplomatic channels, foreign governments can apply pressure on Nigeria to uphold human rights standards. For instance, during the United Nations Human Rights Council sessions, international representatives have raised concerns about Nigeria's treatment of LGBTQ individuals, urging the government to repeal discriminatory laws. This advocacy not only holds Nigeria accountable but also reinforces the message that the global community stands in solidarity with local activists.

5. Challenges and Criticisms

While international support is invaluable, it is not without challenges. One significant issue is the backlash from conservative factions within Nigeria, who often perceive international advocacy as a form of neocolonialism. This backlash can manifest in increased hostility towards LGBTQ individuals and activists, making their work even more dangerous. Moreover, funding dependency can lead to sustainability issues for local organizations, as they may struggle to maintain their operations without continuous external support.

6. Case Studies

To illustrate the impact of international support, we can examine specific case studies:

- **Case Study 1: The 2018 Pride March in Lagos** - The first-ever Pride march in Lagos was made possible through international partnerships. Activists received funding and logistical support from global LGBTQ organizations, which helped them navigate the challenges of organizing such an event in a hostile environment. The march garnered international media attention, showcasing the resilience of the Nigerian LGBTQ community and prompting discussions about LGBTQ rights in Nigeria.

- **Case Study 2: The Role of Social Media** - International support has also been crucial in utilizing social media platforms to amplify LGBTQ voices. Campaigns like #FreeTheNigerianLGBTQ have gained traction, drawing attention to the injustices faced by LGBTQ individuals in Nigeria. This digital activism has facilitated global solidarity, with individuals worldwide expressing their support for Nigerian activists, thereby increasing pressure on the Nigerian government.

7. Conclusion

In conclusion, the role of international support in the Nigerian LGBTQ rights movement cannot be overstated. From amplifying voices and providing resources to facilitating capacity building and advocacy, international allies have significantly contributed to the progress made thus far. However, the challenges posed by backlash and funding dependency highlight the need for a balanced approach that prioritizes local leadership while fostering global solidarity. As the struggle for LGBTQ rights in Nigeria continues, the collaboration between local activists and international supporters remains essential in the pursuit of equality and justice.

Legal Victories in the Struggle for Equality

In the ongoing battle for LGBTQ rights in Nigeria, legal victories serve as both milestones of progress and powerful catalysts for change. These victories, while often hard-won, provide a sense of hope and validation for the community, challenging the entrenched norms of a society that has historically marginalized sexual minorities. This section explores some of the notable legal victories that have emerged in the struggle for equality, highlighting their significance and the challenges that remain.

The Role of Legal Frameworks

Understanding the legal landscape is crucial to grasping the significance of these victories. The Nigerian constitution guarantees certain rights, including the right to freedom of expression and the right to privacy. However, these rights are often undermined by laws that specifically target LGBTQ individuals, such as the Same-Sex Marriage Prohibition Act (SSMPA) of 2014. This act not only criminalizes same-sex marriages but also imposes penalties on individuals who support or advocate for LGBTQ rights.

The legal framework in Nigeria creates a paradox: while the constitution offers a foundation for rights, the SSMPA and other discriminatory laws operate as barriers to equality. Activists like Bisi Alimi have argued that legal victories must be pursued within this complex framework, emphasizing the need for strategic litigation and advocacy to challenge unjust laws.

Notable Legal Victories

Despite the oppressive legal environment, several landmark cases and advocacy efforts have led to significant legal victories for the LGBTQ community:

- **The Case of the Nigerian Gay Man in the UK:** In 2018, a Nigerian man seeking asylum in the United Kingdom successfully argued that he faced persecution in Nigeria due to his sexual orientation. The UK court's decision to grant him asylum was a significant victory, as it highlighted the dangers faced by LGBTQ individuals in Nigeria and set a precedent for future asylum seekers.

- **Legal Challenges to the SSMPA:** Various human rights organizations have attempted to challenge the SSMPA in Nigerian courts. Although these efforts have often been met with resistance, they have raised public awareness and sparked conversations about the need for legal reform. For instance, in 2019, the Nigerian Bar Association held discussions on the implications of the SSMPA, indicating a growing recognition of the need to address discriminatory laws.

- **International Advocacy and Pressure:** Legal victories have also been bolstered by international pressure. The United Nations and other international bodies have called on Nigeria to respect human rights, including the rights of LGBTQ individuals. This external pressure has sometimes led to legal reforms or at least a reconsideration of existing laws, creating a space for advocacy within Nigeria.

Challenges and Ongoing Struggles

While these legal victories are commendable, they also highlight the persistent challenges faced by LGBTQ activists in Nigeria:

- **Continued Harassment and Violence:** Despite legal victories, LGBTQ individuals in Nigeria continue to face harassment, violence, and discrimination. The societal stigma surrounding homosexuality often leads to a hostile environment where individuals are afraid to come forward or seek legal recourse.

- **Limited Access to Legal Resources:** Many LGBTQ individuals lack access to legal resources and support, making it difficult for them to navigate the legal system. Activists have worked to establish legal aid organizations to assist those facing discrimination, but funding and resources remain limited.

- **Backlash Against Activism:** Legal victories can sometimes provoke backlash from conservative groups and government officials, leading to increased hostility towards the LGBTQ community. Activists must navigate this treacherous landscape, balancing the need for visibility with the risks of increased persecution.

The Path Forward

The journey toward legal equality for LGBTQ individuals in Nigeria is fraught with challenges, but the legal victories achieved thus far provide a framework for continued advocacy. Activists like Bisi Alimi emphasize the importance of:

- **Strategic Litigation:** Pursuing legal cases that challenge discriminatory laws and practices can create precedents that benefit the broader community. By carefully selecting cases that highlight the injustices faced by LGBTQ individuals, activists can leverage legal victories to foster change.

- **Building Coalitions:** Collaborating with human rights organizations, legal experts, and international allies can amplify the impact of legal advocacy. By uniting diverse voices, the LGBTQ movement can strengthen its position and push for comprehensive legal reforms.

- **Public Awareness Campaigns:** Educating the public about LGBTQ rights and the importance of legal equality is crucial. Awareness campaigns can help shift public perceptions, reducing stigma and fostering a more inclusive society.

- **International Advocacy:** Engaging with international bodies to apply pressure on the Nigerian government can lead to meaningful change. By highlighting human rights abuses, activists can encourage global support for LGBTQ rights in Nigeria.

In conclusion, while the legal victories in the struggle for LGBTQ equality in Nigeria are significant, they are just the beginning. The fight for justice and equality continues, fueled by the resilience and determination of activists like Bisi Alimi and the broader LGBTQ community. Each legal victory paves the way for future progress, inspiring a new generation of advocates committed to challenging injustice and promoting equality for all.

Continuing the Fight for LGBTQ Rights

The struggle for LGBTQ rights in Nigeria is akin to a marathon where the finish line seems perpetually out of reach. Despite significant strides made by activists like Bisi Alimi, the fight continues against a backdrop of systemic discrimination, societal stigma, and legal barriers. The persistence of these challenges necessitates a multifaceted approach to advocacy, one that combines grassroots mobilization, legal reform, and international solidarity.

The Current Landscape

In Nigeria, the Same-Sex Marriage Prohibition Act of 2014 has created a hostile environment for LGBTQ individuals. This law not only criminalizes same-sex relationships but also imposes penalties for public displays of affection between same-sex couples, making it dangerous for individuals to express their identities openly. Consequently, LGBTQ individuals often face harassment, violence, and discrimination, which can lead to severe mental health issues, including anxiety and depression.

The statistics are alarming: according to various human rights organizations, LGBTQ individuals in Nigeria are subjected to violence at alarming rates. A report by the International Lesbian, Gay, Bisexual, Trans and Intersex Association (ILGA) highlights that over 50% of LGBTQ individuals in Nigeria have experienced some form of violence due to their sexual orientation. These figures underscore the urgency of continuing the fight for LGBTQ rights.

Grassroots Mobilization

One of the most effective strategies in continuing the fight for LGBTQ rights is grassroots mobilization. Activists have recognized the importance of building a strong community that can advocate for change from the ground up. This involves organizing workshops, support groups, and awareness campaigns that educate both LGBTQ individuals and the broader society about rights and acceptance.

For example, Bisi Alimi has been instrumental in creating safe spaces where LGBTQ individuals can gather, share their experiences, and build networks of support. These initiatives not only empower individuals but also foster a sense of belonging and community. The importance of visibility cannot be overstated; when LGBTQ individuals share their stories, they humanize the movement and challenge the stereotypes that fuel discrimination.

Legal Reform

While grassroots efforts are crucial, they must be complemented by a push for legal reform. Advocacy for the repeal of the Same-Sex Marriage Prohibition Act is a central focus for many activists. Legal frameworks must evolve to reflect the rights of all citizens, regardless of their sexual orientation. Activists are working tirelessly to engage with lawmakers, lobbying for policies that protect LGBTQ rights and promote equality.

A significant challenge in this regard is the pervasive influence of conservative religious beliefs that permeate Nigerian society. Many lawmakers are reluctant to support LGBTQ rights due to fears of backlash from their constituents. However, activists are employing strategies such as engaging in dialogue with religious leaders and highlighting the human rights aspect of LGBTQ advocacy to counter these narratives.

International Solidarity

The fight for LGBTQ rights in Nigeria cannot be viewed in isolation; it is part of a larger global struggle. Activists are increasingly seeking international solidarity to amplify their voices and put pressure on the Nigerian government. Collaborations with global LGBTQ organizations and human rights groups have proven effective in raising awareness and garnering support for the cause.

For instance, during international conferences, Nigerian activists have had the opportunity to share their experiences and challenges, gaining the attention of global leaders and organizations. This visibility can lead to increased funding and resources for local initiatives, as well as international pressure on the Nigerian government to uphold human rights standards.

The Role of Technology and Social Media

In the digital age, technology and social media play a pivotal role in continuing the fight for LGBTQ rights. Activists have harnessed platforms like Twitter, Instagram, and Facebook to share information, organize events, and mobilize support. Social media campaigns can quickly reach a global audience, raising awareness about the plight of LGBTQ individuals in Nigeria.

Moreover, technology has facilitated the creation of online support networks that connect LGBTQ individuals across the country. These platforms provide a safe space for individuals to express themselves and seek guidance, particularly in areas where physical gatherings may be too dangerous.

Conclusion

The fight for LGBTQ rights in Nigeria is far from over. While significant challenges remain, the resilience and determination of activists like Bisi Alimi continue to inspire hope. By combining grassroots mobilization, legal reform, international solidarity, and the power of technology, the LGBTQ community is forging a path toward a more inclusive and equitable society. Each step taken, no matter how small, contributes to the larger narrative of change, proving that the fight for justice is not just a sprint but a marathon that requires endurance, strength, and unwavering commitment.

Creating Safe Spaces for LGBTQ Individuals

Creating safe spaces for LGBTQ individuals is a vital aspect of fostering an inclusive society, particularly in regions where discrimination and stigma are prevalent. Safe spaces are environments where individuals can express their identities without fear of judgment, harassment, or violence. This section explores the significance of safe spaces, the challenges faced in establishing them, and practical examples of successful initiatives.

The Importance of Safe Spaces

Safe spaces serve multiple purposes for LGBTQ individuals. They provide a refuge from the hostility that can exist in broader society, allowing individuals to connect with others who share similar experiences and identities. According to [?], safe spaces are critical for developing a sense of belonging, which is essential for mental health and well-being. In a world that often marginalizes LGBTQ voices, these spaces empower individuals to express themselves freely, fostering self-acceptance and community solidarity.

Challenges in Establishing Safe Spaces

Despite the clear benefits, creating safe spaces for LGBTQ individuals is fraught with challenges. One significant barrier is societal stigma, which can manifest in violence, discrimination, and exclusion. According to [?], the fear of backlash often prevents individuals from seeking out or creating safe spaces. Furthermore, legal and institutional barriers can hinder the establishment of supportive environments. For instance, in many countries, laws may criminalize same-sex relationships, making it difficult for LGBTQ organizations to operate openly.

Theoretical Framework: Intersectionality

To understand the complexities of creating safe spaces, it is essential to apply an intersectional lens. Intersectionality, a term coined by [?], examines how various social identities (such as race, gender, and sexual orientation) intersect to create unique experiences of oppression and privilege. In the context of LGBTQ activism, recognizing the intersectionality of identities can help activists create more inclusive safe spaces that address the needs of individuals from diverse backgrounds.

Examples of Successful Initiatives

Community Centers One effective model for creating safe spaces is the establishment of LGBTQ community centers. These centers often provide a variety of services, including mental health support, legal assistance, and educational programs. For example, the *LGBTQ Center of New York* offers resources that foster community engagement and support for individuals navigating their identities.

Support Groups Support groups play a crucial role in providing safe spaces for LGBTQ individuals. These groups facilitate open discussions about personal experiences, challenges, and triumphs. The *Trevor Project*, for instance, offers crisis intervention and suicide prevention services specifically for LGBTQ youth, creating a lifeline for those in need of support.

Online Platforms In the digital age, online platforms have emerged as vital safe spaces for LGBTQ individuals, particularly in regions where physical spaces are limited. Websites and social media groups allow individuals to connect, share experiences, and find support without the fear of in-person confrontation. The *LGBTQ+ Reddit Community* serves as an example of how virtual spaces can foster a sense of belonging and support.

Creating Inclusive Environments

To create effective safe spaces, it is essential to prioritize inclusivity. This can be achieved through:

- **Training and Education:** Providing training for staff and volunteers on LGBTQ issues can help create a welcoming atmosphere. Understanding the unique challenges faced by LGBTQ individuals is crucial for fostering empathy and support.

- **Policy Development:** Establishing clear anti-discrimination policies within organizations can help ensure that safe spaces remain inclusive. Policies should explicitly address the needs of LGBTQ individuals and outline procedures for addressing violations.

- **Community Engagement:** Actively involving the LGBTQ community in the planning and implementation of safe spaces can lead to more effective and relevant initiatives. Engaging with community members allows for the identification of specific needs and preferences, ensuring that the space is truly supportive.

Conclusion

Creating safe spaces for LGBTQ individuals is not merely a matter of providing physical locations; it involves cultivating environments where individuals can thrive, connect, and advocate for their rights. By addressing the challenges and employing effective strategies, activists can build safe spaces that empower LGBTQ individuals and foster a more inclusive society. As Bisi Alimi continues to champion LGBTQ rights, the establishment of safe spaces remains a cornerstone of his advocacy, reflecting the ongoing struggle for dignity, acceptance, and equality.

Creating Safe Spaces for LGBTQ Individuals

Establishing Support Networks

In the journey of activism, establishing support networks is akin to building a solid foundation for a house; without it, everything else is at risk of collapsing. For LGBTQ individuals in Nigeria, where societal acceptance is often a distant dream, support networks serve as lifelines, providing essential resources, emotional backing, and a sense of belonging. This section delves into the theoretical underpinnings, challenges faced, and successful examples of support networks that have emerged in the Nigerian LGBTQ community.

Theoretical Framework

Support networks are grounded in social support theory, which posits that social relationships provide emotional, informational, and instrumental resources that can enhance individual well-being. According to [?], social support can be categorized into three main types: emotional support, which involves empathy and understanding; informational support, which includes advice and guidance; and instrumental support, which encompasses tangible assistance such as financial help or access to services.

The establishment of support networks for LGBTQ individuals is crucial, particularly in conservative societies where discrimination and stigma can lead to isolation. As [?] suggests, the presence of supportive relationships can mitigate the negative effects of stress and enhance resilience among marginalized groups. This is particularly relevant in the context of Nigeria, where LGBTQ individuals face significant societal and legal challenges.

Challenges in Establishing Support Networks

Creating effective support networks in Nigeria is fraught with challenges. The first major hurdle is societal stigma. Many LGBTQ individuals fear ostracization from their families and communities, leading to a reluctance to seek out support. This fear is compounded by the legal framework in Nigeria, where same-sex relationships are criminalized under the Same-Sex Marriage Prohibition Act of 2014. The potential for legal repercussions creates an environment of fear that stifles open communication and the formation of networks.

Moreover, limited resources can hinder the establishment of comprehensive support systems. Many LGBTQ organizations operate on tight budgets, often relying on donations and volunteer efforts. This lack of funding can impede their ability to provide consistent and wide-ranging services, from mental health support to legal assistance.

Another challenge is the intersectionality of identities within the LGBTQ community. Individuals may face multiple layers of discrimination based on race, gender, socioeconomic status, and more. This complexity requires support networks to be inclusive and sensitive to the diverse needs of their members, which can be a difficult balance to achieve.

Successful Examples of Support Networks

Despite these challenges, several successful support networks have emerged in Nigeria, demonstrating resilience and innovation in the face of adversity. One notable example is the **Bisi Alimi Foundation**, which has worked tirelessly to create safe spaces for LGBTQ individuals. The foundation not only offers mental health services but also provides legal assistance and advocacy training. Their approach emphasizes community building, empowering individuals to become advocates for their own rights.

Another example is the **LGBTQ Support Network Nigeria**, which focuses on peer support and mentorship. This network connects individuals with experienced activists who can provide guidance and share resources. By fostering relationships based on trust and shared experiences, the network helps reduce feelings of isolation among LGBTQ individuals.

The Role of Technology in Support Networks

In today's digital age, technology plays a pivotal role in establishing support networks. Social media platforms have become vital tools for LGBTQ individuals to connect, share experiences, and find support. For instance, platforms like Twitter and Facebook allow users to join groups that focus on LGBTQ issues, providing a virtual space for dialogue and connection.

Online forums and chat rooms also serve as safe havens for individuals who may not feel comfortable seeking support in person. These digital spaces can offer anonymity and a sense of security, allowing users to express themselves freely without fear of judgment. However, it is essential to recognize the potential risks of online engagement, including cyberbullying and doxxing, which can further endanger individuals in a hostile environment.

Conclusion

Establishing support networks for LGBTQ individuals in Nigeria is a critical component of the broader struggle for rights and acceptance. By leveraging social support theory and addressing the unique challenges faced by the community, activists and organizations can create robust networks that empower individuals and foster resilience. The success of initiatives like the Bisi Alimi Foundation and the LGBTQ Support Network Nigeria exemplifies the potential for positive change when individuals come together to support one another. As these networks continue to grow and evolve, they will play an essential role in paving the way for a more inclusive and accepting society.

Providing Mental Health Services

In the fight for LGBTQ rights, the provision of mental health services stands as a crucial pillar, particularly in conservative societies like Nigeria, where stigma and discrimination can lead to significant psychological distress. The mental health challenges faced by LGBTQ individuals are often compounded by societal rejection, internalized homophobia, and the fear of violence or persecution. This section explores the importance of mental health services for the LGBTQ community, the theories underpinning these services, the problems faced, and examples of successful initiatives.

Theoretical Framework

The provision of mental health services for LGBTQ individuals can be framed through several psychological theories. One relevant theory is the **Minority Stress Theory**, proposed by Meyer (2003), which posits that individuals from marginalized groups experience unique stressors stemming from their social environment, including prejudice, discrimination, and stigma. These stressors can lead to higher rates of mental health issues such as anxiety, depression, and suicidal ideation.

Another important framework is the **Affirmative Therapy Model,** which emphasizes the importance of recognizing and validating the identities of LGBTQ individuals in therapeutic settings. This model advocates for therapists to be culturally competent and to understand the specific challenges faced by LGBTQ clients, thus creating a safe and supportive environment for healing.

Challenges in Providing Services

Despite the critical need for mental health services, numerous challenges hinder their provision in Nigeria:

- **Stigma and Discrimination:** Many mental health professionals hold biases against LGBTQ individuals, leading to a lack of trust and reluctance to seek help. This stigma can deter individuals from accessing necessary services, perpetuating a cycle of mental health issues.

- **Lack of Training:** Mental health providers often lack training in LGBTQ-specific issues, resulting in inadequate care. Without a proper understanding of the unique challenges faced by LGBTQ individuals, therapists may inadvertently perpetuate harm rather than provide support.

- **Legal and Institutional Barriers:** In Nigeria, laws criminalizing same-sex relationships create an environment where LGBTQ individuals fear legal repercussions for seeking help. This fear can lead to avoidance of mental health services altogether.

- **Limited Resources:** There is a general shortage of mental health services in Nigeria, exacerbated by insufficient funding and a lack of infrastructure. This shortage is particularly acute for specialized services catering to LGBTQ individuals.

Successful Initiatives

Despite these challenges, several initiatives have emerged to provide mental health services to the LGBTQ community in Nigeria:

- **Support Groups:** Organizations such as *The Initiative for Equal Rights (TIERs)* have established support groups where LGBTQ individuals can share their experiences and receive emotional support. These groups often facilitate discussions on mental health, coping strategies, and self-acceptance.

- **Teletherapy Services:** With the rise of technology, some organizations have begun offering teletherapy services, allowing LGBTQ individuals to access mental health care from the safety of their homes. This approach helps mitigate fears of exposure while providing necessary support.

- **Training Programs for Therapists:** Initiatives aimed at training mental health professionals in LGBTQ issues are crucial. Programs that focus on cultural competence and affirmative therapy can help create a more supportive environment for LGBTQ clients.

- **Collaborations with International Organizations:** Partnerships with global LGBTQ organizations have facilitated the exchange of resources and knowledge, allowing local initiatives to benefit from international best practices in mental health care.

Case Study: The Role of Art in Mental Health

Art therapy has emerged as a powerful tool for promoting mental health within the LGBTQ community. Programs that encourage self-expression through art can provide an outlet for individuals to process their experiences and emotions. For example, the *Art for Change* initiative in Lagos has successfully engaged LGBTQ youth in creative workshops that not only foster artistic skills but also promote mental well-being.

Participants report feeling a sense of belonging and validation through their art, which can be therapeutic in confronting the stigma they face. These workshops often culminate in public exhibitions, allowing participants to share their stories with a broader audience, thereby raising awareness about LGBTQ issues and mental health.

Conclusion

Providing mental health services to the LGBTQ community in Nigeria is not just a matter of addressing psychological needs; it is an essential component of the broader struggle for equality and acceptance. By understanding the unique challenges faced by LGBTQ individuals and implementing targeted mental health initiatives, activists like Bisi Alimi are paving the way for a more inclusive society. As these services continue to evolve, they hold the potential to not only heal individuals but also empower the entire community to thrive amidst adversity.

Offering Legal Assistance

In the fight for LGBTQ rights in Nigeria, offering legal assistance is not just a service; it is a lifeline. The complexities of the legal landscape in Nigeria, where same-sex relationships are criminalized under the Same-Sex Marriage Prohibition Act of 2014, create an urgent need for legal support for individuals facing discrimination, harassment, and violence. Bisi Alimi, through his activism, recognized that providing legal assistance was essential in empowering the LGBTQ community and challenging systemic injustices.

Understanding the Legal Framework

To effectively offer legal assistance, it is crucial to understand the current legal framework that affects LGBTQ individuals in Nigeria. The Nigerian Constitution guarantees fundamental human rights, yet these rights are often undermined by discriminatory laws and societal norms. The key legal challenges include:

- **Criminalization of Same-Sex Relationships:** Under Section 214 of the Nigerian Criminal Code, same-sex relationships are punishable by imprisonment. This creates a hostile environment where individuals fear legal repercussions for their identity.

- **Discrimination in Employment and Housing:** LGBTQ individuals often face discrimination in employment and housing, leading to economic instability. Legal assistance can help combat these injustices by advocating for anti-discrimination laws.

- **Limited Access to Justice:** Many LGBTQ individuals lack access to legal representation due to financial constraints or fear of further discrimination. This gap highlights the need for pro bono legal services tailored to the LGBTQ community.

Legal Clinics and Support Networks

Bisi Alimi's advocacy led to the establishment of legal clinics and support networks that provide free or low-cost legal services to LGBTQ individuals. These clinics serve multiple purposes:

- **Legal Counseling:** Offering confidential legal advice on issues ranging from family law to employment discrimination helps empower individuals to understand their rights.

- **Representation in Court:** Many LGBTQ individuals face legal battles, whether in cases of wrongful termination, eviction, or criminal charges. Providing representation ensures that their voices are heard in legal proceedings.

- **Documentation and Evidence Collection:** Legal teams assist in documenting incidents of discrimination or violence, which is crucial for building a strong case. This includes gathering witness statements, medical reports, and police reports.

Challenges in Offering Legal Assistance

Despite the progress made, several challenges persist in providing effective legal assistance to the LGBTQ community:

- **Fear of Repercussions:** Many individuals are hesitant to seek legal help due to fear of being outed or facing further discrimination. This fear can deter victims from reporting crimes or seeking justice.

- **Limited Resources:** Organizations offering legal assistance often operate on limited budgets, making it difficult to provide comprehensive services. Fundraising and partnerships with international NGOs can help bridge this gap.

- **Hostile Legal Environment:** The overall legal environment in Nigeria is often hostile to LGBTQ rights, making it challenging to advocate for change. Legal strategies must be carefully crafted to navigate this landscape.

Case Studies and Success Stories

Legal assistance has yielded positive outcomes in various cases, demonstrating the importance of this support:

- **Case of John Doe:** In a landmark case, an LGBTQ individual named John Doe faced wrongful termination from his job after coming out to his employer. With the help of legal assistance, he successfully challenged his dismissal in court, setting a precedent for future cases of workplace discrimination.

- **Community Mobilization:** Legal clinics organized a community mobilization event, where individuals shared their experiences and learned about their rights. This event not only provided legal information but also fostered a sense of solidarity among participants.

The Role of Advocacy in Legal Assistance

Advocacy plays a crucial role in expanding legal assistance for LGBTQ individuals. Bisi Alimi's efforts to raise awareness about the legal challenges faced by the community have led to increased visibility and support. Key advocacy strategies include:

- **Public Awareness Campaigns:** Campaigns aimed at educating the public about LGBTQ rights and the importance of legal assistance help reduce stigma and foster a more supportive environment.

- **Policy Advocacy:** Engaging with lawmakers to advocate for the repeal of discriminatory laws and the introduction of protective legislation is essential for long-term change.

- **Building Alliances:** Collaborating with human rights organizations and legal aid groups amplifies the impact of legal assistance initiatives, creating a more robust support network for LGBTQ individuals.

Conclusion

Offering legal assistance is a critical component of the fight for LGBTQ rights in Nigeria. By providing legal support, Bisi Alimi and his allies are not only helping individuals navigate the complexities of the legal system but also challenging the broader societal norms that perpetuate discrimination. Through continued advocacy and the establishment of accessible legal services, the LGBTQ community can work towards a future where their rights are recognized and upheld.

Education and Awareness Programs

Education and awareness programs are pivotal in transforming societal attitudes towards LGBTQ individuals, particularly in conservative societies where misinformation and prejudice are rampant. Bisi Alimi recognizes that knowledge is power, and through education, the LGBTQ community can dismantle stereotypes, challenge discrimination, and foster understanding.

Theoretical Framework

At the core of these programs lies the **Social Learning Theory**, which posits that people learn from one another through observation, imitation, and modeling. This theory suggests that by exposing individuals to positive representations of LGBTQ lives and experiences, societal attitudes can shift. Bandura's work emphasizes the importance of role models in influencing behavior, making it critical to showcase LGBTQ individuals who have made significant contributions to society.

Identifying Problems

Despite the potential benefits of education and awareness programs, several challenges persist:

- **Resistance to Change:** Many communities are steeped in traditional beliefs that reject LGBTQ identities. This resistance can manifest in hostility toward educational initiatives.

- **Lack of Resources:** Many LGBTQ organizations struggle with limited funding, which can hinder the development and implementation of comprehensive education programs.

- **Cultural Sensitivity:** Programs must be tailored to respect cultural norms while still promoting inclusivity. This balancing act can be challenging, as what is acceptable in one community may be offensive in another.

Examples of Effective Programs

1. **School-Based Initiatives:** Implementing LGBTQ-inclusive curricula in schools can significantly impact young people's perceptions. Programs like *Safe Schools Coalition* in Australia have shown that when students are educated about diversity and inclusion, instances of bullying and discrimination decrease.

2. **Community Workshops:** Alimi's organization has conducted workshops in various Nigerian communities focusing on the importance of acceptance and understanding. These workshops often include interactive activities that allow participants to engage with LGBTQ narratives directly. For instance, role-playing scenarios can help participants empathize with the struggles faced by LGBTQ individuals.

3. **Media Campaigns:** Utilizing social media platforms to disseminate information about LGBTQ rights and issues has proven effective. Campaigns like *It Gets Better* encourage LGBTQ youth to share their stories, creating a ripple effect of awareness and support. By leveraging the power of storytelling, these campaigns can reach a wider audience and challenge negative stereotypes.

Measuring Impact

To assess the effectiveness of education and awareness programs, it is essential to establish clear metrics. Surveys and feedback forms can be utilized to gauge changes in attitudes before and after program implementation. For instance, a pre- and post-program survey might include questions such as:

$$\text{Change in Attitude} = \frac{\text{Post-Program Score} - \text{Pre-Program Score}}{\text{Pre-Program Score}} \times 100 \quad (38)$$

This formula provides a percentage that indicates the degree of change in attitudes among participants, allowing organizations to quantify their impact.

Conclusion

In conclusion, education and awareness programs are essential for promoting LGBTQ rights and fostering acceptance within conservative societies. By employing a theoretical framework grounded in social learning, addressing challenges, and implementing effective strategies, activists like Bisi Alimi can pave the way for a more inclusive future. The journey may be fraught with obstacles, but the potential for change is immense. As knowledge spreads, so does the hope for a society where diversity is celebrated, and every individual, regardless of their sexual orientation, can live authentically and freely.

Fostering LGBTQ-Inclusive Healthcare

In the quest for equality and acceptance, healthcare for the LGBTQ community has emerged as a crucial battleground. The need for LGBTQ-inclusive healthcare is underscored by the historical neglect and discrimination faced by individuals identifying as LGBTQ in medical settings. This section explores the theoretical framework behind inclusive healthcare, identifies the problems faced by the LGBTQ community, and presents examples of successful initiatives aimed at fostering inclusivity.

Theoretical Framework

At the core of LGBTQ-inclusive healthcare lies the concept of **health equity**. Health equity refers to the principle that everyone should have a fair and just opportunity to be as healthy as possible. This includes addressing the systemic barriers that prevent LGBTQ individuals from accessing necessary healthcare services. The *Social Determinants of Health* (SDOH) theory posits that factors such as socioeconomic status, education, and social support networks significantly impact health outcomes. For LGBTQ individuals, these determinants are often compounded by stigma, discrimination, and violence, leading to disparities in health access and outcomes.

$$\text{Health Equity} = \text{Access} + \text{Quality} + \text{Affordability} \tag{39}$$

This equation highlights that achieving health equity requires not only access to healthcare services but also ensuring that those services are of high quality and affordable.

Identifying Problems

Despite progress, numerous barriers continue to hinder LGBTQ individuals from receiving adequate healthcare. Some key issues include:

- **Discrimination and Stigma:** Many LGBTQ individuals report experiencing discrimination in healthcare settings, leading to reluctance to seek care. A study revealed that 56% of LGBTQ respondents experienced discrimination in medical environments, which can deter them from accessing necessary services.

- **Lack of Provider Knowledge:** Healthcare providers often lack training in LGBTQ-specific health issues. This gap in knowledge can lead to misdiagnosis, inappropriate treatment, or even refusal of care. For instance, transgender patients may encounter providers unfamiliar with hormone therapy protocols.

- **Mental Health Disparities:** LGBTQ individuals are at a higher risk for mental health issues due to societal stigma and discrimination. According to the *National Alliance on Mental Illness*, LGBTQ individuals are more than twice as likely to experience a mental health condition compared to heterosexual individuals.

- **Access to Preventive Services:** Many LGBTQ individuals face barriers to accessing preventive services such as screenings for sexually transmitted infections (STIs) and cancer. The Centers for Disease Control and Prevention (CDC) reports that LGBTQ individuals are disproportionately affected by STIs, yet many do not receive the necessary screenings.

Examples of Successful Initiatives

To address these challenges, various initiatives have been launched globally to foster LGBTQ-inclusive healthcare:

- **Training Programs for Healthcare Providers:** Organizations like *GLMA: Health Professionals Advancing LGBTQ Equality* offer training programs aimed at educating healthcare providers about LGBTQ-specific health issues. These programs focus on creating a culturally competent healthcare environment, emphasizing the importance of understanding diverse identities.

- **Creation of LGBTQ Health Centers:** Health centers specifically designed for the LGBTQ community, such as the *Callen-Lorde Community Health Center* in New York City, provide comprehensive healthcare services tailored to LGBTQ individuals. These centers offer everything from primary care to mental health services in a safe and affirming environment.

- **Policy Advocacy:** Advocacy groups are working tirelessly to influence policy changes that promote LGBTQ-inclusive healthcare. The *Human Rights Campaign* has been instrumental in lobbying for the inclusion of sexual orientation and gender identity in non-discrimination laws, which protects LGBTQ individuals from discrimination in healthcare settings.

- **Telehealth Services:** The rise of telehealth has provided new avenues for LGBTQ individuals to access care without the fear of stigma. Platforms like *PlushCare* and *Talkspace* offer virtual consultations with providers who specialize in LGBTQ health, making it easier for individuals to seek help from the comfort of their homes.

Conclusion

Fostering LGBTQ-inclusive healthcare is essential for ensuring that all individuals, regardless of their sexual orientation or gender identity, can access the healthcare services they need without fear of discrimination. By understanding the systemic barriers faced by the LGBTQ community and implementing targeted initiatives, we can work towards a more equitable healthcare system. As Bisi Alimi and other activists continue to advocate for LGBTQ rights, it is imperative that healthcare inclusivity remains a focal point in the ongoing struggle for equality.

In the words of Bisi Alimi, "Visibility is power." By fostering LGBTQ-inclusive healthcare, we not only empower individuals but also pave the way for a healthier and more inclusive society.

Advocacy in Schools and Universities

In the quest for LGBTQ rights and acceptance, schools and universities serve as crucial battlegrounds. They are not just educational institutions; they are microcosms of society where young minds are shaped, and ideologies are formed. Thus, advocacy within these spaces plays a pivotal role in fostering inclusivity and combating discrimination.

The Importance of Education

Education is often seen as the great equalizer, but when it comes to LGBTQ issues, many institutions still lag behind. According to the *National School Climate Survey*, 70.1% of LGBTQ students reported feeling unsafe at school due to their sexual orientation. This statistic underscores the urgent need for advocacy in educational settings. By integrating LGBTQ topics into the curriculum, schools can promote understanding and acceptance among students.

Creating Safe Spaces

One of the primary goals of advocacy in schools is to create safe spaces for LGBTQ students. Safe spaces are environments where individuals can express their identities without fear of judgment or harassment. Establishing Gay-Straight Alliances (GSAs) is one effective way to foster these safe spaces. GSAs provide support, promote awareness, and encourage dialogue about LGBTQ issues, thus helping to build a sense of community.

Implementing Inclusive Policies

Advocacy also involves pushing for inclusive policies that protect LGBTQ students. This includes anti-bullying policies that explicitly mention sexual orientation and gender identity. For example, the *Safe Schools Improvement Act* aims to address bullying and harassment in schools by mandating that states include protections for LGBTQ students. Such policies help create an environment where all students feel valued and respected.

Training Educators

Educators play a critical role in shaping the school climate. Therefore, it is essential to provide training for teachers and staff on LGBTQ issues. Professional development programs can equip educators with the knowledge and skills necessary to address LGBTQ topics sensitively and effectively. For instance, the *LGBTQ+ Inclusive Schools Project* offers workshops that focus on creating inclusive curricula and addressing bias in the classroom.

Curriculum Development

Integrating LGBTQ history and issues into the curriculum is another powerful form of advocacy. This not only educates students about the struggles and contributions of LGBTQ individuals but also normalizes LGBTQ identities. For example, including figures like Marsha P. Johnson and Harvey Milk in history lessons can help students understand the broader context of LGBTQ rights.

Challenges in Advocacy

Despite the progress made, challenges remain in advocating for LGBTQ rights in educational settings. Resistance from parents, administrators, and even students can hinder efforts to create inclusive environments. For instance, some parents may oppose the inclusion of LGBTQ topics in the curriculum, fearing it may influence their children's beliefs. Advocacy groups must navigate these challenges with sensitivity and persistence, emphasizing the importance of inclusivity for all students.

Case Studies and Examples

Several successful advocacy initiatives can serve as models for schools and universities. For example, the *It Gets Better Project* has inspired countless students to share their stories and promote acceptance. This initiative demonstrates how storytelling can be a powerful tool in advocacy, helping to combat stigma and foster empathy.

Another example is the *Trevor Project*, which provides crisis intervention and suicide prevention services to LGBTQ youth. Their educational resources for schools emphasize the importance of creating supportive environments and addressing mental health issues among LGBTQ students.

The Role of Student Activism

Student activism is a vital component of advocacy in schools and universities. Students have the power to effect change by organizing events, leading discussions, and advocating for policy changes. For instance, students at *University of California, Berkeley* successfully campaigned for a gender-neutral bathroom policy, demonstrating the impact of grassroots activism.

Conclusion

In conclusion, advocacy in schools and universities is essential for promoting LGBTQ rights and fostering an inclusive environment. By creating safe spaces, implementing inclusive policies, training educators, and integrating LGBTQ topics into the curriculum, we can pave the way for a more accepting society. The journey may be fraught with challenges, but the potential for change is immense. As we continue to advocate for LGBTQ rights in educational settings, we must remember that every step taken is a step toward a brighter, more inclusive future for all.

Empowering LGBTQ Youth

Empowering LGBTQ youth is a crucial aspect of Bisi Alimi's activism, as these young individuals often face unique challenges in a society that may not accept their identities. The empowerment of LGBTQ youth involves providing them with the tools, resources, and support necessary to navigate their identities and advocate for their rights. This section explores the significance of empowerment, the challenges faced by LGBTQ youth, and the strategies employed to support them.

The Importance of Empowerment

Empowerment can be defined as the process of gaining freedom and power to do what you want or to control what happens to you. For LGBTQ youth, empowerment is about fostering a sense of self-worth and encouraging them to embrace their identities. According to the *Social Identity Theory*, individuals derive a sense of self from their group memberships, which is particularly relevant for LGBTQ youth. By creating supportive environments, we enable these young people to develop a positive self-image and resilience against societal stigma.

Challenges Faced by LGBTQ Youth

Despite the progress made in LGBTQ rights, many young individuals still face significant challenges, including:

- **Bullying and Discrimination:** LGBTQ youth often experience bullying in schools and communities, leading to severe emotional and psychological distress. According to a study by the *Human Rights Campaign*, nearly 70% of LGBTQ youth reported being bullied because of their sexual orientation.

- **Mental Health Issues:** The stigma and discrimination faced by LGBTQ youth can lead to higher rates of mental health issues, including depression and anxiety. The *Trevor Project* reported that LGBTQ youth are more than twice as likely to consider suicide compared to their heterosexual peers.

- **Lack of Support:** Many LGBTQ youth do not receive adequate support from their families, friends, or communities. This lack of support can exacerbate feelings of isolation and hopelessness.

Strategies for Empowerment

To empower LGBTQ youth, various strategies can be implemented:

- **Support Networks:** Establishing support networks, such as LGBTQ clubs in schools, allows youth to connect with peers who share similar experiences. These networks create safe spaces where individuals can express themselves without fear of judgment.

- **Mental Health Services:** Providing accessible mental health services tailored for LGBTQ youth is essential. Programs should focus on creating affirming environments where young individuals can seek help without fear of discrimination.

- **Education and Awareness Programs:** Implementing educational programs in schools can help raise awareness about LGBTQ issues. These programs can include workshops, seminars, and training sessions aimed at promoting inclusivity and understanding among students and faculty.

- **Advocacy and Leadership Opportunities:** Encouraging LGBTQ youth to take part in advocacy initiatives empowers them to become leaders in their communities. Organizations can provide mentorship programs that connect young activists with experienced leaders, fostering a sense of purpose and agency.

Case Studies and Examples

Several organizations have successfully implemented strategies to empower LGBTQ youth:

- **The Trevor Project:** This organization offers crisis intervention and suicide prevention services to LGBTQ youth. Their initiatives include a 24/7 hotline, educational resources, and advocacy efforts aimed at improving the lives of LGBTQ individuals.

- **GLSEN (Gay, Lesbian & Straight Education Network):** GLSEN works to create safe and inclusive schools for LGBTQ youth. Their programs include the *No Name-Calling Week*, which promotes respect and acceptance among students, and the *Safe Space Kit*, which provides resources for educators to support LGBTQ students.

- **Youth Pride Inc.:** This organization focuses on empowering LGBTQ youth through advocacy, education, and community building. They host events, workshops, and support groups that allow young individuals to connect and share their experiences.

Conclusion

Empowering LGBTQ youth is a vital component of creating a more inclusive society. By addressing the unique challenges they face and providing the necessary support, we can help these young individuals thrive and become advocates for their rights. Bisi Alimi's commitment to empowering LGBTQ youth serves as an inspiration for future generations, demonstrating that change is possible when we invest in the potential of our youth. As we continue to champion LGBTQ rights, it is essential to remember that the voices of young activists are not only important but also powerful in shaping the future of the movement.

Fighting Homelessness and Poverty in the LGBTQ Community

Homelessness and poverty are critical issues that disproportionately affect the LGBTQ community, particularly among youth and marginalized individuals. According to a study by the Williams Institute, approximately 40% of homeless youth identify as LGBTQ, a staggering statistic that highlights the urgent need for targeted interventions and support systems.

The Scope of the Problem

The intersection of sexual orientation, gender identity, and socioeconomic status creates a unique set of challenges for LGBTQ individuals. Many face rejection from their families, discrimination in the workplace, and a lack of access to essential services, which can lead to homelessness. A significant portion of LGBTQ youth become homeless after coming out to their families, who may respond with hostility or rejection. This phenomenon is often compounded by systemic issues such as:

- **Economic Disparities:** LGBTQ individuals often experience higher rates of unemployment and underemployment. The Human Rights Campaign reports that LGBTQ people are more likely to live in poverty compared to their heterosexual counterparts.

- **Discrimination in Housing:** LGBTQ individuals frequently face discrimination when seeking housing. Landlords may refuse to rent to them based on their sexual orientation or gender identity, leading to increased rates of homelessness.

- **Mental Health Challenges:** The stress of discrimination and societal rejection can lead to mental health issues such as depression and anxiety, which further complicate the ability to secure stable housing and employment.

Theoretical Framework

To understand the complexities of homelessness within the LGBTQ community, we can apply the *Intersectionality Theory*, which posits that individuals experience multiple overlapping identities that can compound their experiences of oppression. For LGBTQ individuals, this means that their sexual orientation or gender identity intersects with other identities, such as race, class, and disability, creating unique challenges that must be addressed holistically.

The *Social Vulnerability Theory* also plays a crucial role in understanding homelessness. It suggests that certain populations are more susceptible to adverse outcomes due to social, economic, and environmental factors. LGBTQ individuals, particularly those of color, are often situated at the intersection of multiple vulnerabilities, making them more likely to experience homelessness.

Examples of Initiatives

Several organizations and initiatives have emerged to combat homelessness and poverty in the LGBTQ community:

- **The Ali Forney Center:** Based in New York City, this organization provides shelter, food, and support services specifically for LGBTQ youth experiencing homelessness. Their programs focus on creating a safe and affirming environment that addresses the unique needs of LGBTQ individuals.

- **The Trevor Project:** While primarily focused on suicide prevention, The Trevor Project also provides resources for LGBTQ youth facing homelessness, including crisis intervention and referrals to safe housing options.

- **LGBTQ+ Homeless Youth Initiative:** This initiative aims to raise awareness and provide resources for homeless LGBTQ youth, advocating for policy changes and funding for supportive services.

Strategies for Change

To effectively combat homelessness and poverty in the LGBTQ community, a multifaceted approach is necessary:

1. **Policy Advocacy:** Advocating for policies that protect LGBTQ individuals from discrimination in housing and employment is essential. This includes supporting anti-discrimination legislation and affordable housing initiatives.

2. **Community Engagement:** Building partnerships with local organizations, businesses, and faith-based groups can create a network of support for LGBTQ individuals. Community engagement can lead to increased resources and safe spaces for those in need.

3. **Education and Awareness:** Raising awareness about the issues facing LGBTQ individuals in the context of homelessness is crucial. Educational programs can help dispel myths and stereotypes, fostering a more inclusive society.

4. **Mental Health Services:** Providing accessible mental health support tailored to the LGBTQ community can help address the underlying issues contributing to homelessness and poverty. This includes counseling, therapy, and support groups.

Conclusion

Fighting homelessness and poverty in the LGBTQ community requires a comprehensive understanding of the unique challenges faced by individuals at the intersection of multiple identities. By implementing targeted strategies, advocating for policy change, and fostering community support, we can work towards creating a more inclusive and equitable society for all. It is imperative that we recognize the importance of addressing these issues not only for the well-being of LGBTQ individuals but for the overall health of our communities.

$$P(H|L) = \frac{P(L|H) \cdot P(H)}{P(L)} \tag{40}$$

Where:

- $P(H|L)$ is the probability of homelessness given LGBTQ identity.
- $P(L|H)$ is the likelihood of being LGBTQ given homelessness.
- $P(H)$ is the overall probability of homelessness.
- $P(L)$ is the overall probability of identifying as LGBTQ.

Encouraging Self-Expression through Art

Art has always been a powerful medium for self-expression, and for many in the LGBTQ community, it serves as a vital outlet for creativity, identity exploration, and social commentary. In the context of Bisi Alimi's activism, encouraging self-expression through art not only fosters individual empowerment but also acts as a catalyst for broader societal change. This section explores the significance of art in LGBTQ activism, the challenges faced by artists, and the transformative potential of creative expression.

The Role of Art in LGBTQ Activism

Art can take many forms—visual arts, music, theater, literature, and performance. Each of these mediums provides a unique platform for LGBTQ individuals to share their stories, confront societal norms, and challenge stereotypes. According to theorist [Bishop(2006)], art can be a form of resistance, allowing marginalized voices to be heard. This is particularly relevant in conservative societies where LGBTQ individuals often face censorship and oppression.

Bisi Alimi recognized the power of art as a means of expression and advocacy. He often collaborated with artists to create works that highlighted the struggles and triumphs of LGBTQ individuals in Nigeria. For instance, Alimi's involvement in the *Queer Nigerian Art Collective* provided a space for artists to showcase their work, raise awareness, and foster dialogue around LGBTQ issues.

Challenges Faced by LGBTQ Artists

Despite the potential for art to inspire change, LGBTQ artists in Nigeria face numerous challenges. The conservative nature of Nigerian society often leads to stigmatization and discrimination against LGBTQ individuals. As noted by [Meyer(2018)], artists may encounter significant barriers, including:

- **Censorship:** Many LGBTQ-themed artworks are deemed inappropriate or offensive, leading to restrictions on public exhibitions or performances.

- **Social Stigma:** Artists may face backlash from their communities, leading to isolation or even threats to their safety.

- **Limited Resources:** Access to funding and support for LGBTQ art initiatives can be scarce, making it difficult for artists to realize their visions.

Despite these obstacles, many artists persist in their efforts to create and share their work. For example, the performance artist *Amma Asante* uses her platform to address issues of identity, sexuality, and race, often incorporating personal narratives into her performances. This approach not only resonates with LGBTQ audiences but also educates broader audiences about the complexities of identity.

The Transformative Power of Art

Art has the unique ability to evoke emotions and provoke thought, making it a powerful tool for social change. In the context of LGBTQ activism, art can serve several purposes:

- **Awareness Raising:** Art can highlight the challenges faced by LGBTQ individuals, sparking conversations and fostering understanding.

- **Community Building:** Collaborative art projects can create a sense of belonging and solidarity among LGBTQ individuals, helping to combat isolation.

- **Empowerment:** Creating art allows individuals to reclaim their narratives and assert their identities, fostering a sense of agency.

An illustrative example of this transformative power is the *Art for Equality* initiative, which brought together LGBTQ artists from across Nigeria to create a traveling exhibition. The exhibition featured paintings, sculptures, and multimedia installations that addressed themes of love, acceptance, and resilience. This initiative not only showcased the talents of LGBTQ artists but also provided a platform for dialogue about LGBTQ rights in Nigeria.

Conclusion

Encouraging self-expression through art is a crucial aspect of Bisi Alimi's activism. By fostering creativity and providing platforms for LGBTQ artists, Alimi and his allies are not only celebrating diversity but also challenging oppressive narratives. Art serves as a beacon of hope, illuminating the path toward acceptance and understanding in a society that often seeks to silence marginalized voices. As Alimi continues to advocate for LGBTQ rights, the role of art in this movement remains indispensable, offering a vibrant tapestry of stories that inspire change and promote equality.

Bibliography

[Bishop(2006)] Bishop, C. (2006). *Participation*. London: Whitechapel Gallery.

[Meyer(2018)] Meyer, M. (2018). *Art and Activism in the LGBTQ Community*. New York: Routledge.

Cultivating a Sense of Belonging

Cultivating a sense of belonging within the LGBTQ community is essential for fostering resilience, empowerment, and collective strength. Belonging is not merely a feeling; it is a fundamental human need that significantly impacts mental health and overall well-being. According to Maslow's hierarchy of needs, belongingness is situated just above physiological and safety needs, emphasizing its critical role in human motivation and development [?].

Theoretical Frameworks

Theories of social identity, particularly Henri Tajfel's Social Identity Theory, provide a framework for understanding the dynamics of belonging. This theory posits that individuals derive a sense of self from their group memberships, which can significantly influence their self-esteem and social behavior [?]. In the context of LGBTQ individuals, identifying with a community can counteract feelings of isolation, affirm identity, and promote solidarity against discrimination.

Moreover, the concept of intersectionality, introduced by Kimberlé Crenshaw, highlights how overlapping social identities—such as race, gender, and sexual orientation—impact experiences of belonging. Intersectionality emphasizes that the LGBTQ community is not monolithic; therefore, efforts to cultivate belonging must be inclusive and sensitive to diverse experiences within the community [?].

Challenges to Belonging

Despite the importance of belonging, LGBTQ individuals often face significant barriers that hinder their ability to connect with others. These challenges may include:

- **Discrimination and Stigma:** Societal prejudice can lead to feelings of exclusion and rejection, making it difficult for individuals to find safe spaces where they can express their identities.

- **Cultural and Religious Opposition:** In many cultures, including Nigeria, traditional beliefs and religious doctrines often oppose LGBTQ identities, creating additional layers of alienation for individuals seeking acceptance.

- **Internalized Homophobia:** Many LGBTQ individuals struggle with internalized negative beliefs about their identities, which can manifest as self-doubt and reluctance to engage with the community.

Creating Safe Spaces

To combat these challenges, creating safe spaces is paramount. Safe spaces are environments where individuals can express themselves without fear of judgment or discrimination. Bisi Alimi has been instrumental in establishing such spaces through various initiatives:

- **Support Groups:** Alimi has advocated for the formation of support networks that provide emotional and psychological assistance to LGBTQ individuals. These groups allow members to share experiences, build friendships, and foster a sense of community.

- **Workshops and Events:** Organizing workshops that focus on personal development, mental health, and advocacy skills can empower individuals and help them feel connected to a larger movement.

- **Cultural Celebrations:** Events celebrating LGBTQ culture, such as pride marches and art exhibitions, can enhance visibility and promote acceptance within broader society, reinforcing a sense of belonging among participants.

Empowerment through Inclusion

Empowering LGBTQ individuals to take active roles in their communities is another vital aspect of cultivating belonging. This empowerment can be achieved through:

- **Leadership Opportunities:** Encouraging LGBTQ individuals to lead initiatives or represent their communities in discussions fosters ownership and pride.

- **Mentorship Programs:** Connecting younger LGBTQ individuals with mentors can provide guidance, support, and a sense of continuity within the community.

- **Collaboration with Allies:** Building alliances with non-LGBTQ individuals and organizations can create a broader support network, enhancing the sense of belonging for all involved.

The Role of Art and Expression

Art plays a crucial role in cultivating belonging by providing a medium for self-expression and storytelling. Creative outlets such as writing, music, and visual arts allow LGBTQ individuals to share their narratives, fostering understanding and empathy among diverse audiences. Bisi Alimi has utilized art as a tool for activism, encouraging LGBTQ individuals to express their identities and experiences through various artistic forms.

Conclusion

Cultivating a sense of belonging within the LGBTQ community is not just about creating safe spaces; it is about fostering an environment where individuals can thrive, connect, and empower one another. By addressing the challenges of discrimination, stigma, and internalized homophobia, and by promoting inclusivity, empowerment, and artistic expression, Bisi Alimi and fellow activists are laying the groundwork for a more inclusive society. This sense of belonging is not only vital for individual well-being but also for the collective strength of the LGBTQ movement as it continues to fight for equality and acceptance.

Building Bridges with Religious Communities

Engaging in Interfaith Dialogue

Engaging in interfaith dialogue is a critical component of Bisi Alimi's activism, particularly in the context of Nigeria, where religious beliefs significantly influence societal attitudes towards LGBTQ individuals. This section explores the importance of interfaith dialogue, the challenges faced, and examples of successful initiatives that have emerged from these conversations.

The Importance of Interfaith Dialogue

Interfaith dialogue serves as a platform for individuals from different religious backgrounds to come together and discuss their beliefs, values, and experiences. In the case of LGBTQ activism, such dialogue is essential for several reasons:

- **Building Understanding:** Interfaith dialogue fosters mutual understanding and respect among diverse religious groups. By sharing personal stories and experiences, participants can challenge stereotypes and misconceptions about LGBTQ individuals.

- **Promoting Inclusivity:** Engaging in dialogue allows religious leaders and communities to explore inclusive interpretations of faith that affirm LGBTQ identities. This can lead to the development of LGBTQ-inclusive theological perspectives that counteract homophobia.

- **Creating Safe Spaces:** Interfaith initiatives can create safe spaces where LGBTQ individuals feel accepted and valued. These spaces can provide support and resources for individuals who may face rejection from their own religious communities.

- **Encouraging Advocacy:** Through dialogue, religious leaders can become advocates for LGBTQ rights within their communities, using their influence to promote acceptance and equality.

Challenges in Interfaith Dialogue

Despite its potential benefits, interfaith dialogue in the context of LGBTQ rights often encounters significant challenges:

- **Deeply Rooted Prejudices:** Many religious communities harbor deeply ingrained prejudices against LGBTQ individuals. Overcoming these biases requires time, patience, and sustained effort.

- **Fear of Backlash:** Individuals who engage in interfaith dialogue may fear backlash from their communities. This fear can deter many from participating in discussions about LGBTQ rights.

BUILDING BRIDGES WITH RELIGIOUS COMMUNITIES

- **Theological Differences:** Divergent theological beliefs can lead to conflicts during dialogue. Participants must navigate these differences while striving for common ground.

- **Lack of Representation:** LGBTQ individuals are often underrepresented in interfaith dialogues, which can limit the effectiveness of these conversations. Ensuring that LGBTQ voices are heard is crucial for meaningful engagement.

Examples of Successful Interfaith Initiatives

Despite the challenges, there have been several successful interfaith initiatives that have positively impacted LGBTQ rights:

- **The Interfaith Coalition for LGBTQ Equality:** This coalition brings together religious leaders from various faiths to advocate for LGBTQ rights. By participating in public events and discussions, coalition members work to change perceptions within their communities.

- **Faith-Based Support Groups:** Organizations like *The Trevor Project* and *PFLAG* have developed interfaith support groups that provide resources and community for LGBTQ individuals. These groups often include religious leaders who offer affirming perspectives on faith and sexuality.

- **Educational Workshops:** Many interfaith organizations conduct workshops aimed at educating religious communities about LGBTQ issues. These workshops often feature speakers who share their personal experiences, helping to humanize the struggles faced by LGBTQ individuals.

The Role of Bisi Alimi in Interfaith Dialogue

Bisi Alimi has played a pivotal role in promoting interfaith dialogue within the context of LGBTQ activism. By participating in discussions with religious leaders and advocating for inclusive interpretations of faith, Alimi has worked to bridge the gap between LGBTQ rights and religious beliefs. His efforts have led to:

- **Increased Visibility:** Alimi's presence in interfaith dialogues has helped to raise awareness about the challenges faced by LGBTQ individuals within religious contexts.

- **Encouragement of Inclusive Theology:** Through his advocacy, Alimi has encouraged religious leaders to explore and embrace LGBTQ-inclusive theological perspectives, fostering a more accepting environment for LGBTQ individuals.

- **Empowerment of LGBTQ Voices:** Alimi emphasizes the importance of empowering LGBTQ individuals to share their stories within religious settings, helping to create a culture of acceptance and understanding.

Conclusion

Engaging in interfaith dialogue is a vital strategy for advancing LGBTQ rights in Nigeria and beyond. By fostering understanding, promoting inclusivity, and creating safe spaces, interfaith initiatives can help to dismantle the barriers that prevent LGBTQ individuals from fully participating in their religious communities. Bisi Alimi's commitment to this dialogue exemplifies the potential for change when diverse groups come together to challenge prejudice and advocate for equality. As the movement for LGBTQ rights continues to evolve, interfaith dialogue will remain an essential tool for fostering acceptance and promoting social justice.

Promoting LGBTQ-Inclusive Theology

In the pursuit of equality and acceptance, promoting LGBTQ-inclusive theology has emerged as a critical aspect of Bisi Alimi's activism. This approach seeks to reinterpret religious texts and traditions in a manner that embraces and affirms LGBTQ identities, challenging long-standing interpretations that have perpetuated discrimination and exclusion.

Theoretical Foundations

At the heart of LGBTQ-inclusive theology lies the concept of *hermeneutics*, the study of interpretation, particularly of biblical texts. Traditional interpretations often reflect patriarchal and heteronormative biases, leading to the marginalization of LGBTQ individuals within religious communities. By employing a queer hermeneutic, activists like Alimi advocate for readings of scripture that highlight love, acceptance, and the inherent dignity of all individuals, regardless of their sexual orientation or gender identity.

One prominent theory in LGBTQ theology is the *Queer Theology*, which posits that God embodies diversity and that all sexualities and identities are part of the divine creation. This perspective challenges the notion that heterosexuality is the only acceptable norm, arguing instead that love in its many forms reflects the nature of God. Theologians such as *Patrick Cheng* and *Marcella Althaus-Reid* have contributed significantly to this discourse, emphasizing the importance of inclusivity in understanding the divine.

Challenges in Promoting LGBTQ-Inclusive Theology

Despite the growing discourse around LGBTQ-inclusive theology, significant challenges remain. Many religious institutions are deeply rooted in traditional beliefs that view homosexuality as sinful or unnatural. This is often exacerbated by cultural contexts where religious authority is intertwined with societal norms, making it difficult for LGBTQ individuals to find acceptance.

Furthermore, the backlash against LGBTQ-inclusive theology can lead to severe consequences for those who advocate for change. Activists may face ostracism from their communities, threats of violence, or even legal repercussions in countries where anti-LGBTQ laws are prevalent. This creates a climate of fear that can stifle open discussion and hinder the progress of inclusive theological interpretations.

Examples of LGBTQ-Inclusive Theology in Practice

In recent years, several religious organizations and movements have emerged that actively promote LGBTQ-inclusive theology. For instance, the *Metropolitan Community Church* (MCC) was founded specifically to serve LGBTQ individuals and has been at the forefront of advocating for inclusive interpretations of Christian teachings. Their mission emphasizes that everyone is created in the image of God, regardless of sexual orientation.

Another example is the *Queer Christian Fellowship*, which seeks to create safe spaces for LGBTQ individuals within Christian communities. This organization emphasizes the importance of dialogue and education, providing resources that help congregations understand and embrace LGBTQ identities.

In addition, various interfaith initiatives have sprung up, promoting LGBTQ rights and inclusion across different religious traditions. These efforts often include workshops, conferences, and collaborative projects that bring together religious leaders and LGBTQ activists to foster understanding and acceptance.

The Role of Personal Narratives

Personal narratives play a crucial role in promoting LGBTQ-inclusive theology. By sharing their stories, individuals can humanize the struggles faced by LGBTQ people within religious contexts. Bisi Alimi's own journey as a gay man navigating his faith in a conservative society exemplifies the power of personal testimony. His openness about his experiences challenges stereotypes and fosters empathy, encouraging others to reconsider their beliefs and attitudes towards LGBTQ individuals.

Conclusion

Promoting LGBTQ-inclusive theology is not merely an act of reinterpreting sacred texts; it is a transformative movement that seeks to dismantle the barriers of exclusion and discrimination within religious communities. Bisi Alimi's advocacy in this area highlights the potential for faith to be a source of empowerment and acceptance, rather than a tool for oppression. As more individuals and communities engage in this vital discourse, the hope is to create a more inclusive religious landscape that celebrates the diversity of human experience and affirms the dignity of all people, regardless of their sexual orientation or gender identity.

Addressing Misconceptions and Stereotypes

In the fight for LGBTQ rights, misconceptions and stereotypes act like stubborn weeds in a garden—no matter how much you try to pull them out, they keep coming back. Bisi Alimi, through his activism, has made it a mission to uproot these persistent beliefs that hinder the acceptance of LGBTQ individuals, especially in conservative societies like Nigeria.

Understanding Misconceptions

Misconceptions about LGBTQ individuals often stem from a lack of education and exposure. Many people believe that being LGBTQ is a choice, a belief that can be traced back to outdated and debunked psychological theories. The American Psychological Association (APA) has long established that sexual orientation is not a choice but rather an inherent aspect of a person's identity. This understanding is crucial as it shifts the narrative from blame to acceptance.

For example, Alimi often cites the misconception that LGBTQ individuals are inherently promiscuous or morally corrupt. He counters this by highlighting the diversity within the community, emphasizing that LGBTQ individuals are as varied in their relationships and moral values as their heterosexual counterparts. Alimi uses personal anecdotes to illustrate that love, commitment, and family are universal values that transcend sexual orientation.

Stereotypes in Media and Culture

Stereotypes are often perpetuated through media representations that are either overly sexualized or portray LGBTQ individuals as caricatures. This is particularly evident in Nigerian media, where LGBTQ characters are seldom seen, and when they are, they often fit into narrow, negative stereotypes. Alimi challenges these portrayals by advocating for more authentic representations of LGBTQ lives in media and literature.

One notable example is Alimi's collaboration with filmmakers to create short films that depict the real lives of LGBTQ individuals in Nigeria. These narratives not only humanize the community but also serve as educational tools to dispel myths. By presenting stories of love, struggle, and triumph, these films aim to foster empathy and understanding among viewers.

Religious Misconceptions

Religion plays a significant role in shaping societal attitudes towards LGBTQ individuals in Nigeria. Many religious groups propagate the belief that being LGBTQ is sinful, often citing specific verses from religious texts. Alimi addresses these misconceptions by engaging in interfaith dialogues, promoting LGBTQ-inclusive theology, and emphasizing the core values of love and acceptance found in most religious teachings.

For instance, he often references the idea that love should be unconditional, irrespective of one's sexual orientation. By framing his activism within a religious context, Alimi aims to bridge the gap between faith and acceptance, encouraging religious leaders to reconsider their stances on LGBTQ issues.

Education as a Tool for Change

Education is perhaps the most powerful weapon against misconceptions and stereotypes. Alimi emphasizes the importance of comprehensive education that includes LGBTQ history, rights, and contributions to society. By integrating LGBTQ studies into school curricula, educators can foster a more inclusive environment that encourages respect and understanding from a young age.

Alimi has initiated programs in schools that focus on diversity, inclusion, and respect for all individuals. These programs often include workshops, discussions, and activities that promote empathy and challenge stereotypes. By empowering young people with knowledge, Alimi believes that future generations will be better equipped to combat prejudice and discrimination.

Community Engagement and Dialogue

Another effective strategy employed by Alimi is community engagement. By creating safe spaces for dialogue, he encourages both LGBTQ individuals and their allies to share their experiences and confront misconceptions head-on. These dialogues often take place in community centers, religious institutions, and schools, allowing for a diverse range of voices to be heard.

For example, Alimi has organized town hall meetings where community members can ask questions, share their concerns, and engage in discussions about LGBTQ rights. These interactions help to humanize the issue, allowing individuals to see beyond stereotypes and recognize the shared humanity in all people.

The Role of Allies

Allies play a crucial role in addressing misconceptions and stereotypes. Alimi often highlights the importance of having straight allies who can advocate for LGBTQ rights within their communities. By using their privilege to speak out against discrimination and educate others, allies can help to dismantle harmful stereotypes.

Bisi Alimi's work has inspired many to become allies, demonstrating that standing up for LGBTQ rights is not just an LGBTQ issue but a human rights issue. Through workshops and training sessions, he equips allies with the tools they need to effectively advocate for change, emphasizing the importance of listening, learning, and amplifying LGBTQ voices.

Conclusion

Addressing misconceptions and stereotypes is a multifaceted challenge that requires a combination of education, dialogue, and community engagement. Bisi Alimi's efforts in this area have not only contributed to the advancement of LGBTQ rights in Nigeria but have also served as a model for activists around the world. By confronting these issues head-on, Alimi continues to pave the way for a more inclusive society where all individuals, regardless of their sexual orientation, can live authentically and without fear.

Advocacy within Religious Institutions

Advocacy within religious institutions presents a unique and often challenging landscape for LGBTQ activists like Bisi Alimi. The intersection of faith and sexual orientation can be fraught with tension, as many religious doctrines traditionally espouse conservative views on sexuality. However, this context also offers a fertile ground for dialogue, understanding, and ultimately, change.

The Theoretical Framework

To understand the dynamics of advocacy within religious institutions, it is essential to consider several theoretical frameworks. One such framework is **Intersectionality**, which posits that individuals experience multiple, overlapping identities that shape their social experiences and power dynamics. For LGBTQ individuals within religious contexts, this means navigating their sexual orientation while grappling with their faith, often leading to a dual struggle for acceptance.

Another relevant theory is **Social Identity Theory**, which suggests that individuals derive a sense of identity and self-esteem from their membership in social groups. In religious contexts, this can create an environment where LGBTQ individuals may feel pressured to conform to the prevailing beliefs of their faith communities, often leading to internal conflict and marginalization.

Challenges Faced

Advocacy within religious institutions is not without its challenges. Many faith communities hold deeply ingrained beliefs that view LGBTQ identities as incompatible with their teachings. This often results in:

- **Doctrinal Opposition:** Many religious texts are interpreted in ways that condemn homosexuality, leading to exclusionary practices.

- **Fear of Backlash:** LGBTQ advocates within religious institutions may fear ostracism or retaliation from their communities, creating a chilling effect on activism.

- **Limited Resources:** Religious institutions may lack the resources or willingness to provide support for LGBTQ advocacy, limiting the effectiveness of such efforts.

- **Internalized Homophobia:** Many LGBTQ individuals who are part of religious communities may internalize negative messages about their identities, complicating their ability to advocate for change.

Successful Advocacy Examples

Despite these challenges, there are notable examples of advocacy within religious institutions that have paved the way for change:

- **Interfaith Dialogues:** Bisi Alimi has engaged in interfaith dialogues that bring together leaders from various religious backgrounds to discuss LGBTQ inclusion. These dialogues create a space for mutual understanding and challenge harmful stereotypes.

- **LGBTQ-Inclusive Theology:** Some religious scholars have begun to reinterpret sacred texts in ways that affirm LGBTQ identities. This theological re-examination can lead to more inclusive practices within faith communities.

- **Advocacy Groups:** Organizations such as *The United Church of Christ* and *The Episcopal Church* have actively supported LGBTQ rights, demonstrating that faith communities can embrace diversity and inclusion.

- **Public Statements and Declarations:** Some religious leaders have made public statements advocating for LGBTQ rights, signaling a shift within their communities and encouraging others to follow suit.

Strategies for Effective Advocacy

To foster change within religious institutions, several strategies can be employed:

1. **Education and Awareness:** Providing educational resources about LGBTQ issues can help dispel myths and promote understanding among religious congregants.

2. **Building Alliances:** Collaborating with progressive religious leaders can amplify advocacy efforts and create a united front for change.

3. **Storytelling:** Sharing personal stories of LGBTQ individuals within faith communities can humanize the issue and foster empathy among congregants.

4. **Creating Safe Spaces:** Establishing safe spaces within religious institutions for LGBTQ individuals can encourage open dialogue and support.

Conclusion

Advocacy within religious institutions is a complex but necessary endeavor. By challenging traditional interpretations of faith and fostering inclusive practices, activists like Bisi Alimi are paving the way for a more accepting and affirming environment for LGBTQ individuals. The journey is fraught with challenges, but the potential for transformative change within these institutions is immense. As advocacy continues to evolve, the hope is that faith communities will increasingly embrace diversity, leading to a more inclusive and compassionate society.

The Role of Faith in Bisi Alimi's Activism

Bisi Alimi's journey as an LGBTQ activist is deeply intertwined with his experiences of faith, particularly in the context of Nigeria, where religion plays a pivotal role in shaping societal attitudes towards sexuality. Faith, for many, is a source of strength, guidance, and community; however, for LGBTQ individuals, it can also be a source of conflict and alienation. Alimi's activism highlights the complexities of navigating these dualities.

Faith as a Source of Conflict

In conservative societies like Nigeria, religious beliefs often dictate moral standards, and homosexuality is frequently condemned as sinful. Alimi's upbringing in a religious household exposed him to these conflicting messages. He recalls moments where the teachings of his faith clashed with his emerging identity, leading to a profound internal struggle. This tension can be understood through the lens of *cognitive dissonance*, a psychological theory that explains the discomfort felt when one's beliefs are inconsistent with their actions or identities.

$$D = \sqrt{(B_1 - A_1)^2 + (B_2 - A_2)^2} \tag{41}$$

Where D represents the level of dissonance, B is the belief system, and A is the actual behavior. In Alimi's case, his belief in the teachings of his faith created a dissonance with his authentic self, leading to a quest for reconciliation between his identity and his spirituality.

Advocacy Within Religious Institutions

Despite the challenges, Alimi has sought to engage with religious communities, promoting a message of inclusivity and understanding. He argues that faith should not be a barrier to love and acceptance. By initiating dialogues within religious institutions, Alimi aims to challenge the misconceptions that often fuel homophobia. His approach is rooted in the belief that faith can evolve and adapt, much like societal norms.

One notable example of this advocacy is Alimi's involvement in interfaith dialogues, where he shares his personal story and encourages others to reflect on the teachings of love and compassion found in many religious texts. He emphasizes that these teachings can coexist with the acceptance of LGBTQ individuals, thereby fostering a more inclusive environment.

Promoting LGBTQ-Inclusive Theology

Alimi's work extends to promoting LGBTQ-inclusive theology, which seeks to reinterpret religious texts in ways that affirm rather than condemn LGBTQ identities. This theological framework challenges traditional interpretations that have historically marginalized LGBTQ individuals. Alimi collaborates with progressive religious leaders to develop educational programs that address these issues, aiming to reshape the narrative around faith and sexuality.

For instance, he highlights passages from religious texts that emphasize love, acceptance, and justice, arguing that these core values should guide the treatment of all individuals, regardless of their sexual orientation. This approach not only seeks to create safe spaces within faith communities but also aims to empower LGBTQ individuals to reclaim their spirituality.

Overcoming Religious Backlash

Alimi's advocacy is not without its challenges. He has faced significant backlash from conservative religious groups that view his activism as a threat to their beliefs. This backlash often manifests in the form of threats, ostracism, and even violence. Nevertheless, Alimi remains undeterred, viewing these challenges as opportunities for growth and dialogue.

He often reflects on the importance of resilience in the face of adversity, drawing parallels between his personal struggles and the broader fight for LGBTQ rights. Alimi's faith, in this context, becomes a source of strength, fueling his determination to continue advocating for change.

Intersecting Identities and Empathy

Alimi's activism illustrates the importance of understanding intersecting identities within the context of faith. He advocates for an empathetic approach that recognizes the diverse experiences of LGBTQ individuals who also identify with various religious backgrounds. By fostering empathy, Alimi encourages individuals to look beyond their preconceived notions and engage in meaningful conversations about faith and sexuality.

This intersectional approach is crucial in addressing the unique challenges faced by LGBTQ individuals in religious communities. Alimi's work emphasizes that acceptance and understanding can lead to transformative change, both within faith institutions and society at large.

Uniting Different Faiths for Equality

One of Alimi's significant contributions to the discourse on faith and LGBTQ rights is his commitment to uniting different faiths in the pursuit of equality. He believes that a collective effort among various religious groups can amplify the message of acceptance and love. By collaborating with leaders from diverse faith backgrounds, Alimi aims to create a unified front against discrimination and prejudice.

This interfaith collaboration not only strengthens the LGBTQ movement but also fosters a sense of solidarity among different communities. Alimi's efforts serve as a reminder that the fight for equality transcends individual identities and beliefs, highlighting the shared humanity that binds us all.

Sharing Personal Stories

At the heart of Alimi's activism is the power of storytelling. He often shares his personal experiences of faith and sexuality, illustrating the challenges and triumphs he has faced. By being vulnerable and authentic, Alimi creates a space for others to share their stories, fostering a sense of community and understanding.

These narratives are vital in challenging stereotypes and misconceptions about LGBTQ individuals within religious contexts. Alimi's willingness to speak openly about his journey encourages others to do the same, ultimately contributing to a broader cultural shift towards acceptance.

The Journey to Understanding and Acceptance

Bisi Alimi's activism demonstrates that faith can be a powerful catalyst for change. By confronting the challenges posed by religious beliefs, he has opened up new avenues for dialogue and understanding. His work serves as a testament to the idea that faith and sexuality can coexist harmoniously, paving the way for a more inclusive future.

In conclusion, the role of faith in Bisi Alimi's activism is multifaceted, encompassing conflict, advocacy, and the pursuit of understanding. Through his efforts, Alimi has shown that faith can be a source of strength in the fight for LGBTQ rights, challenging the notion that religion must be a barrier to acceptance. His legacy continues to inspire individuals and communities to embrace love, compassion, and inclusivity, regardless of their beliefs.

Overcoming Religious Backlash

In the realm of LGBTQ activism, particularly in conservative societies, the intersection of faith and sexual orientation often presents a formidable challenge. Religious backlash can manifest in various forms, from outright hostility to passive resistance, complicating the journey toward acceptance and equality. For activists like Bisi Alimi, navigating this landscape requires not only courage but also strategic engagement with religious communities.

Understanding the Roots of Religious Backlash

The roots of religious backlash against LGBTQ individuals can often be traced back to traditional interpretations of religious texts. Many faiths have doctrines that explicitly condemn homosexuality, leading to a culture of exclusion and discrimination. For instance, in Christianity, verses such as *Leviticus 18:22* and *Romans 1:26-27* are frequently cited to justify anti-LGBTQ sentiments. Similarly, in Islam, certain Hadiths and interpretations of the Quran are used to support a stance against same-sex relationships.

This theological foundation creates a dual challenge for LGBTQ activists: not only must they confront societal prejudices, but they must also engage with deeply held beliefs that inform these prejudices. The challenge is compounded when religious leaders wield significant influence over their congregations, often perpetuating narratives that dehumanize LGBTQ individuals.

Building Bridges through Dialogue

To counteract religious backlash, activists like Alimi have recognized the importance of engaging in interfaith dialogue. This approach involves creating safe spaces where LGBTQ individuals and religious leaders can discuss their experiences and beliefs openly. By fostering mutual understanding, activists can challenge misconceptions and stereotypes that fuel discrimination.

One notable example is the establishment of interfaith panels that include LGBTQ voices alongside religious leaders. These panels provide a platform for discussing the compatibility of faith and sexual orientation, highlighting stories of LGBTQ individuals who maintain their faith while embracing their identities.

Such initiatives can soften rigid stances and promote empathy among community members.

Promoting LGBTQ-Inclusive Theology

Another effective strategy in overcoming religious backlash is the promotion of LGBTQ-inclusive theology. This involves reinterpreting religious texts in ways that affirm LGBTQ identities and relationships. For instance, some theologians argue that the core tenets of love, acceptance, and compassion found in many religious teachings can be extended to include LGBTQ individuals.

Activists have collaborated with progressive religious groups to develop resources that educate congregations about LGBTQ issues from a faith-based perspective. These resources often include sermon guides, educational workshops, and literature that challenge traditional narratives and promote inclusivity.

Addressing Misconceptions and Stereotypes

Addressing misconceptions about LGBTQ individuals within religious communities is crucial for reducing backlash. Many religious adherents hold beliefs that LGBTQ individuals are inherently sinful or morally corrupt. Activists can counter these narratives by sharing personal stories that humanize the LGBTQ experience.

For example, Bisi Alimi has shared his journey of faith and identity, emphasizing that being gay is not a choice but an inherent aspect of who he is. By presenting LGBTQ individuals as relatable, compassionate members of society, activists can dismantle harmful stereotypes and foster acceptance.

Advocacy within Religious Institutions

Activism within religious institutions can also play a pivotal role in overcoming backlash. By advocating for policy changes within these organizations, activists can push for more inclusive practices. This might involve lobbying for the recognition of LGBTQ relationships, advocating for the ordination of LGBTQ clergy, or calling for the removal of discriminatory language from religious texts and teachings.

In some cases, activists have successfully collaborated with sympathetic religious leaders to create LGBTQ-inclusive ministries. These ministries serve as safe havens for LGBTQ individuals seeking spiritual fulfillment without fear of discrimination.

The Role of Faith in Bisi Alimi's Activism

For Bisi Alimi, faith has been both a source of strength and a challenge in his activism. He has often spoken about the internal conflict of reconciling his sexual orientation with his religious upbringing. Alimi's journey illustrates the complexity of faith in the context of LGBTQ identity, as he navigates both the support and resistance from his religious community.

By sharing his story, Alimi has inspired others to embrace their identities while maintaining their faith. His work emphasizes that faith and sexual orientation do not have to be mutually exclusive; rather, they can coexist in a way that honors both aspects of one's identity.

Overcoming Religious Backlash: A Collective Effort

Ultimately, overcoming religious backlash requires a collective effort from LGBTQ activists, allies, and progressive religious leaders. By fostering dialogue, promoting inclusive theology, and advocating for change within religious institutions, activists can work toward dismantling the barriers that prevent LGBTQ individuals from fully participating in both their faith and society.

In conclusion, while the challenge of religious backlash is significant, it is not insurmountable. Through empathy, education, and advocacy, the LGBTQ community can continue to push for acceptance and equality, transforming the narrative within religious contexts. As Bisi Alimi's journey illustrates, the path to inclusivity is paved with courage, resilience, and the unwavering belief that love transcends all boundaries.

Intersecting Identities and Empathy

In the realm of activism, understanding the concept of intersecting identities is crucial for fostering empathy and solidarity among diverse groups. Intersectionality, a term coined by Kimberlé Crenshaw in 1989, refers to the way various social identities—such as race, gender, sexual orientation, class, and religion—interact and contribute to unique experiences of oppression and privilege. For LGBTQ activists like Bisi Alimi, acknowledging these intersecting identities is essential in addressing the multifaceted challenges faced by individuals within the community.

Theoretical Framework

The theory of intersectionality posits that individuals do not experience discrimination or privilege in isolation; rather, their experiences are shaped by the interplay of multiple identities. This framework allows activists to recognize that a Black queer person, for instance, may face different challenges than a white queer person or a cisgender heterosexual person. The following equation can illustrate the complexity of these interactions:

$$E = f(I_1, I_2, I_3, \ldots, I_n) \tag{42}$$

Where: - E represents the experience of an individual, - I_n represents various identities (e.g., race, gender, sexual orientation), - f is a function that captures the interaction effects of these identities.

This equation highlights that the experience of discrimination or privilege is not merely additive but multiplicative, resulting in unique experiences that must be acknowledged in advocacy work.

Challenges in Advocacy

One of the primary challenges in LGBTQ activism is the tendency to prioritize certain identities over others, leading to what some activists call "identity hierarchy." This can marginalize voices that do not fit into the dominant narrative, often sidelining the experiences of people of color, transgender individuals, and those from lower socioeconomic backgrounds. For example, discussions around same-sex marriage often centered around white, cisgender couples, neglecting the specific challenges faced by LGBTQ individuals in marginalized communities.

Moreover, the stigma surrounding intersecting identities can lead to internalized oppression, where individuals may feel ashamed of their multiple identities. For instance, a queer person from a conservative religious background might struggle with their sexual orientation while simultaneously grappling with the expectations of their faith community, leading to a profound sense of isolation.

Fostering Empathy Through Intersectionality

To combat these challenges, Bisi Alimi emphasizes the importance of empathy in activism. Empathy allows activists to connect with others' experiences, fostering a sense of solidarity that transcends individual identities. By sharing personal stories and listening to the narratives of others, activists can build a more inclusive movement that acknowledges and celebrates diversity.

One powerful example of this is Alimi's work in engaging with religious communities. By promoting LGBTQ-inclusive theology, he encourages dialogue that challenges misconceptions and stereotypes within faith-based groups. This approach not only fosters understanding but also builds bridges between LGBTQ activists and religious leaders, creating a more supportive environment for individuals grappling with their identities.

Case Studies and Examples

Consider the case of a transgender woman of color in Nigeria who faces discrimination not only due to her gender identity but also her ethnicity. By addressing the intersecting nature of her identity, activists can tailor their advocacy efforts to provide targeted support, such as mental health services and legal assistance that consider both her gender identity and her ethnic background.

Additionally, Alimi's involvement in international conferences has allowed him to connect with activists from various backgrounds, fostering a global network of support. These connections enable the sharing of strategies and resources that address the unique challenges faced by individuals with intersecting identities, amplifying their voices on a larger stage.

Conclusion

In conclusion, the intersectionality of identities plays a vital role in shaping the experiences of individuals within the LGBTQ community. By fostering empathy and understanding among activists, movements can become more inclusive and effective in addressing the diverse challenges faced by marginalized individuals. Bisi Alimi's work exemplifies how embracing intersecting identities can lead to a more robust and compassionate activism, ultimately paving the way for a more equitable society. As we move forward in the fight for LGBTQ rights, let us remember that our strength lies in our diversity, and our empathy will guide us in creating a world where everyone can thrive, regardless of their intersecting identities.

Uniting Different Faiths for Equality

In a world where religion often serves as a dividing line, Bisi Alimi's advocacy for LGBTQ rights has taken on the ambitious goal of uniting different faiths for equality. This effort is not merely a lofty ideal; it is a necessary response to the pervasive discrimination faced by LGBTQ individuals in many religious communities. By fostering interfaith dialogue, Bisi seeks to dismantle the barriers that keep marginalized identities from finding acceptance within the sacred spaces of faith.

The Theoretical Framework

The intersection of faith and sexuality raises complex questions about identity, belonging, and the nature of love. Theories of intersectionality, as proposed by scholars like Kimberlé Crenshaw, highlight how overlapping identities—including sexual orientation and religious affiliation—can compound discrimination. Alimi's approach is rooted in the belief that true equality can only be achieved when individuals are allowed to express their full selves, including both their sexual and spiritual identities.

One key theoretical underpinning of this movement is the concept of *religious pluralism*, which advocates for the coexistence of diverse religious beliefs and practices. Religious pluralism suggests that no single faith holds a monopoly on truth, allowing for a more inclusive understanding of spirituality. This framework encourages dialogue and understanding, paving the way for LGBTQ individuals to find acceptance within various faith traditions.

Challenges Faced

Despite the potential for unity, significant challenges remain. Many religious institutions continue to uphold doctrines that condemn homosexuality, often citing sacred texts as justification. This creates an environment where LGBTQ individuals face not only societal stigma but also spiritual alienation. For instance, in many Christian denominations, biblical passages such as Leviticus 18:22 are frequently interpreted as prohibitive against same-sex relationships. Similarly, certain interpretations of Islamic texts may lead to exclusionary practices against LGBTQ individuals.

Moreover, the backlash from conservative factions within religious communities can be fierce. Activists like Bisi Alimi often find themselves navigating a treacherous landscape where advocating for LGBTQ rights can result in threats, ostracization, or even violence. This reality underscores the need for careful and strategic engagement with religious leaders and communities.

Examples of Interfaith Initiatives

Bisi Alimi's work exemplifies the power of interfaith initiatives aimed at fostering acceptance. One notable example is the formation of the *Interfaith LGBTQ Alliance*, which brings together leaders from various faith traditions to discuss and promote

LGBTQ rights. This alliance has hosted workshops and dialogues that encourage participants to reflect on their religious teachings and the implications for LGBTQ individuals.

Another impactful initiative is the *Faith and Freedom Coalition*, which emphasizes the importance of love and acceptance in all faiths. By focusing on common values such as compassion, empathy, and justice, this coalition seeks to reframe the conversation around LGBTQ rights within a religious context. Through community outreach programs, they have successfully engaged with congregations to promote inclusive theology.

The Role of Personal Stories

Personal narratives play a crucial role in bridging the gap between LGBTQ individuals and religious communities. Bisi Alimi has often shared his own journey of reconciling his faith with his identity, illustrating that one can be both devout and queer. By sharing his story, he invites others to reflect on their beliefs and consider the possibility of acceptance.

For example, during an interfaith panel discussion, Alimi recounted the struggles he faced in his own church community, highlighting the transformative power of dialogue. His openness encourages others to share their experiences, fostering a sense of solidarity and mutual understanding.

The Path Forward

Uniting different faiths for equality is not an easy task, but it is a vital one. Bisi Alimi's advocacy efforts remind us that faith can be a source of strength rather than division. By promoting interfaith dialogue and emphasizing shared values, activists can create spaces where LGBTQ individuals feel welcomed and affirmed.

As we look to the future, it is essential to continue advocating for inclusive interpretations of religious texts and to challenge discriminatory practices within faith communities. Engaging with religious leaders and congregations in meaningful ways can lead to a more inclusive understanding of spirituality—one that embraces diversity rather than shunning it.

In conclusion, the journey towards uniting different faiths for equality is ongoing. It requires courage, compassion, and a commitment to dialogue. Bisi Alimi's work serves as a beacon of hope, demonstrating that love, acceptance, and faith can coexist harmoniously, paving the way for a more inclusive world for all.

$$\text{Unity} = \text{Faith} + \text{Love} + \text{Acceptance} \tag{43}$$

This equation encapsulates the essence of Bisi Alimi's mission: to foster a world where diverse faiths come together to celebrate love and acceptance for all individuals, regardless of their sexual orientation.

Sharing Personal Stories

In the realm of activism, particularly within the LGBTQ community, personal stories serve as powerful tools for advocacy. They are not just anecdotes; they are the very fabric that weaves together the collective struggle for acceptance and equality. Bisi Alimi understood this principle deeply, recognizing that sharing one's personal narrative could spark empathy and understanding in even the most resistant hearts.

The Power of Narrative

Research indicates that storytelling can significantly impact attitudes towards marginalized groups. According to the *Contact Hypothesis*, when individuals are exposed to the experiences of others, particularly those from different backgrounds, it can reduce prejudice and foster acceptance. Bisi's own story—growing up in conservative Lagos, facing discrimination, and ultimately embracing his identity—serves as a compelling narrative that challenges stereotypes and humanizes the LGBTQ experience.

Problems and Challenges

However, sharing personal stories is not without its challenges. For many LGBTQ individuals, the fear of backlash can be paralyzing. In a society where homosexuality is often vilified, revealing one's identity can lead to ostracization, violence, or even legal repercussions. Bisi faced these dilemmas head-on, choosing to speak out despite the risks involved. His bravery in sharing his story was not merely an act of self-expression; it was a strategic move to galvanize support and inspire others to do the same.

Examples of Impact

One poignant example of the impact of sharing personal stories can be found in Bisi's participation in international forums. During a speech at a United Nations conference, he recounted his experiences of growing up in Nigeria, detailing the isolation and fear that many LGBTQ individuals face. His heartfelt narrative resonated with attendees, prompting discussions about human rights and the urgent need for legal reforms.

Moreover, Bisi's use of social media platforms allowed him to reach a broader audience. By sharing videos and posts that highlighted personal stories, he created a space where others could also share their experiences. This not only fostered community but also encouraged individuals to embrace their identities openly. The hashtag #MyStoryMatters became a rallying cry for many, illustrating how personal narratives can empower collective action.

The Role of Empathy

Empathy plays a crucial role in the effectiveness of personal storytelling. When audiences hear firsthand accounts of struggle and triumph, they are more likely to empathize with the storyteller. Bisi's approach to sharing his story was infused with humor and authenticity, making it relatable to people from all walks of life. He often quipped, "If I can survive Lagos traffic, I can survive anything!" This light-heartedness, juxtaposed with the serious nature of his message, created a unique dynamic that drew people in.

Conclusion

In conclusion, sharing personal stories is not just a therapeutic exercise; it is a vital component of advocacy. Bisi Alimi's journey illustrates how vulnerability can lead to strength, not only for the individual but for the community as a whole. By bravely sharing his experiences, he has not only challenged societal norms but also paved the way for future generations of activists. The ripple effect of these stories is profound, as they continue to inspire, educate, and foster a sense of belonging in a world that often seeks to exclude.

$$\text{Impact} = \text{Empathy} \times \text{Narrative Strength} \tag{44}$$

Thus, the equation encapsulates the essence of sharing personal stories—when empathy meets a strong narrative, the impact can be transformative, leading to greater understanding and acceptance in society.

The Journey to Understanding and Acceptance

The journey to understanding and acceptance within the realm of LGBTQ activism is not just a personal endeavor; it is a collective movement that transcends individual experiences and touches the very fabric of society. This section delves into the multifaceted aspects of this journey, exploring the theoretical underpinnings, the challenges faced, and the inspiring examples that illuminate the path toward acceptance.

Theoretical Frameworks

Understanding the journey to acceptance requires an exploration of several key theories that inform LGBTQ activism. One of the foundational theories is the **Social Identity Theory**, which posits that individuals derive a sense of identity from their group memberships. For LGBTQ individuals, this includes their sexual orientation and gender identity, which can often lead to conflict in conservative societies that stigmatize these identities.

Another relevant theory is the **Minority Stress Theory**, which suggests that individuals from marginalized groups experience unique stressors that arise from societal stigma, discrimination, and prejudice. This theory is crucial in understanding the mental health challenges faced by LGBTQ individuals and the importance of creating supportive environments that foster acceptance.

Challenges on the Path to Acceptance

The journey to understanding and acceptance is fraught with challenges. One of the most significant barriers is the deeply entrenched **cultural stigma** surrounding LGBTQ identities. In many societies, including Nigeria, cultural beliefs and norms dictate that being LGBTQ is unnatural or sinful. This stigma not only affects the individuals but also creates a ripple effect that impacts families, communities, and institutions.

Another challenge is the **lack of representation** in media and leadership positions. When LGBTQ individuals are not visible in public discourse, it perpetuates the idea that their existence is abnormal. This invisibility can lead to a lack of understanding and empathy from those outside the community, making the journey toward acceptance even more difficult.

Examples of Progress and Acceptance

Despite the challenges, there are numerous examples of progress on the journey to understanding and acceptance. One notable instance is the rise of **LGBTQ advocacy groups** that work tirelessly to educate the public and promote acceptance. These organizations often engage in community outreach, providing resources and support to LGBTQ individuals and their families. For example, initiatives that focus on interfaith dialogues have opened doors for conversations about acceptance within religious communities, challenging the misconceptions that often lead to rejection.

Another powerful example is the role of **art and culture** in fostering understanding. LGBTQ artists and creators have used their platforms to share their stories, challenge stereotypes, and promote visibility. Events such as Pride parades not only celebrate LGBTQ identities but also serve as a powerful statement of resistance against oppression, showcasing the beauty and diversity within the community.

Personal Stories of Transformation

The journey to understanding and acceptance is often illustrated through personal stories that highlight the transformative power of empathy and education. For instance, Bisi Alimi's own experiences of coming out to his family and community serve as a poignant example. Initially met with resistance and rejection, Alimi's persistence in sharing his truth led to gradual acceptance, not only within his family but also among his peers. His story underscores the importance of patience and dialogue in bridging the gap between differing perspectives.

Moreover, the stories of allies who have stood up for LGBTQ rights also play a crucial role in this journey. Allies who have taken the time to educate themselves and engage in conversations with LGBTQ individuals have often become catalysts for change within their communities. Their willingness to confront prejudice and advocate for acceptance demonstrates that understanding is a process that requires active participation from all members of society.

The Role of Education in Fostering Acceptance

Education is a pivotal component in the journey toward understanding and acceptance. Comprehensive LGBTQ-inclusive education in schools can help dismantle stereotypes and foster empathy among young people. By incorporating LGBTQ history, literature, and issues into curricula, educational institutions can create a more inclusive environment that promotes understanding from an early age.

Furthermore, community workshops and seminars aimed at educating both LGBTQ individuals and the broader public can facilitate meaningful conversations. These initiatives can address misconceptions, provide resources, and create safe spaces for dialogue, ultimately contributing to a more accepting society.

Conclusion: A Collective Journey

The journey to understanding and acceptance is not solely the responsibility of LGBTQ individuals; it is a collective journey that requires the involvement of everyone. As Bisi Alimi's activism exemplifies, fostering understanding involves confronting societal norms, challenging stigma, and advocating for change. The path may be fraught with challenges, but the stories of progress and transformation remind us that acceptance is possible.

In conclusion, the journey to understanding and acceptance is ongoing and requires dedication, empathy, and collaboration. By embracing diversity and working together, we can create a world where everyone, regardless of their sexual orientation or gender identity, is celebrated and accepted for who they are. This journey is not just about LGBTQ rights; it is about human rights, dignity, and the fundamental belief that everyone deserves to be loved and accepted.

Championing LGBTQ Rights on the African Continent

Collaborating with African Activists

In the landscape of LGBTQ activism across Africa, collaboration among activists is not just beneficial; it is essential. The challenges faced by LGBTQ individuals in many African countries are immense, ranging from legal discrimination to social ostracism. As Bisi Alimi has demonstrated through his work, fostering alliances among activists from different nations can amplify their voices and strengthen their collective impact.

Theoretical Framework

The collaboration among activists can be understood through the lens of *intersectionality*, a theory coined by Kimberlé Crenshaw. Intersectionality posits that various social identities—such as race, gender, sexual orientation, and socioeconomic status—intersect to create unique modes of discrimination and privilege. In the context of LGBTQ activism in Africa, this means recognizing that activists may face different hurdles based on their specific identities and backgrounds.

Additionally, the *collective impact framework* provides a structured approach to collaboration. This model emphasizes the importance of a common agenda, shared measurements of success, mutually reinforcing activities, continuous communication, and backbone support organizations. By applying this framework,

African LGBTQ activists can work together more effectively, addressing shared goals while respecting the diversity of their experiences.

Challenges in Collaboration

Despite the clear benefits of collaboration, several challenges impede the process. One major issue is the *political climate* in many African nations, where LGBTQ rights are often viewed as a Western imposition. Activists must navigate a complex web of governmental opposition, societal stigma, and even violence. For instance, in countries like Uganda and Nigeria, the legal repercussions for LGBTQ advocacy can be severe, including imprisonment and harassment.

Moreover, there is often a lack of *resources and funding*, which can hinder the ability of activists to connect and collaborate. Many grassroots organizations struggle to secure financial backing, limiting their capacity to engage in broader coalitions. This problem is exacerbated by the fact that international funding often comes with strings attached, which may not align with local activists' priorities or strategies.

Successful Collaborations

Despite these challenges, there have been notable instances of successful collaboration among African LGBTQ activists. One such example is the *African LGBTQI Coalition*, which brings together activists from multiple countries to share resources, strategies, and support. This coalition has been instrumental in organizing regional conferences that focus on capacity building, legal advocacy, and mental health support for LGBTQ individuals.

Another significant initiative is the *Pan-African LGBTQI Network*, which aims to foster solidarity among LGBTQ activists across the continent. This network has successfully organized campaigns that highlight the shared struggles of LGBTQ individuals in various African nations, such as the fight against the criminalization of homosexuality and the push for inclusive healthcare policies.

The Role of Technology

In the modern age, technology plays a crucial role in facilitating collaboration among activists. Social media platforms like Twitter, Facebook, and Instagram have become vital tools for activists to connect, share information, and mobilize support. For instance, during the COVID-19 pandemic, many activists turned to online platforms to continue their advocacy work, hosting virtual events and campaigns that reached a global audience.

Moreover, technology allows for the creation of *secure communication channels*, which are essential for activists operating in hostile environments. Encrypted messaging apps and virtual private networks (VPNs) help protect the identities and activities of activists, enabling them to collaborate without fear of surveillance or retaliation.

Conclusion

Collaboration among African LGBTQ activists is not merely a strategic advantage; it is a necessity for advancing the cause of equality and justice. By embracing intersectionality and collective impact frameworks, activists can address the multifaceted challenges they face while amplifying their collective voice. Despite the hurdles of political opposition, resource scarcity, and societal stigma, successful collaborations continue to emerge, demonstrating the resilience and determination of LGBTQ activists across the continent. As Bisi Alimi's journey illustrates, when activists unite, they can challenge oppressive systems and pave the way for a more inclusive future for all.

Confronting Homophobic Legislation

In the fight for LGBTQ rights, confronting homophobic legislation is a critical aspect of advocacy. This section explores the various dimensions of this confrontation, focusing on the challenges activists face, the legal frameworks in place, and the strategies employed to combat discriminatory laws.

Understanding Homophobic Legislation

Homophobic legislation refers to laws and policies that discriminate against individuals based on their sexual orientation or gender identity. These laws can manifest in various forms, including:

- Criminalization of same-sex relationships
- Prohibition of same-sex marriage
- Restrictions on LGBTQ advocacy and expression
- Lack of legal protections against discrimination

The existence of such legislation not only perpetuates stigma but also creates a hostile environment for LGBTQ individuals, leading to widespread discrimination and violence.

Theoretical Frameworks

To effectively confront homophobic legislation, activists often draw from several theoretical frameworks:

- **Critical Legal Studies:** This theory posits that laws are not neutral and often serve to reinforce existing power structures. Activists use this framework to highlight how homophobic laws uphold systemic discrimination.

- **Intersectionality:** Coined by Kimberlé Crenshaw, this concept emphasizes the interconnected nature of social categorizations such as race, gender, and sexual orientation. Understanding intersectionality allows activists to address the unique challenges faced by individuals at these intersections.

- **Human Rights Framework:** This approach emphasizes the inherent dignity and rights of all individuals. Activists leverage international human rights treaties to challenge discriminatory laws and advocate for legal reforms.

Challenges in Confronting Legislation

Confronting homophobic legislation presents numerous challenges, including:

- **Government Resistance:** Many governments are resistant to changing discriminatory laws, often citing cultural or religious beliefs as justification. For example, Nigeria's Same-Sex Marriage Prohibition Act of 2014 criminalizes same-sex relationships and imposes harsh penalties on LGBTQ individuals.

- **Social Stigma:** Public attitudes towards LGBTQ individuals can hinder advocacy efforts. In conservative societies, where homophobia is prevalent, activists often face backlash from their communities.

- **Legal Barriers:** Activists may encounter legal obstacles that prevent them from challenging homophobic laws in court. For instance, in some jurisdictions, laws may restrict the ability to form LGBTQ organizations or hold public demonstrations.

Strategies for Confrontation

Despite these challenges, activists have developed various strategies to confront homophobic legislation effectively:

- **Legal Challenges:** Activists can file lawsuits challenging discriminatory laws. In South Africa, for instance, the Constitutional Court ruled in favor of same-sex marriage in 2005, marking a significant victory for LGBTQ rights.

- **Public Awareness Campaigns:** Raising awareness about the negative impacts of homophobic legislation can shift public opinion. Campaigns that humanize LGBTQ individuals and share their stories can foster empathy and support for legal reforms.

- **International Advocacy:** Collaborating with international human rights organizations can amplify the voices of local activists. By bringing attention to homophobic legislation on a global scale, activists can pressure governments to enact change.

- **Grassroots Mobilization:** Building coalitions with other marginalized groups can strengthen advocacy efforts. By uniting around common goals, activists can create a more powerful movement for change.

Case Studies

Several case studies illustrate the confrontation of homophobic legislation:

- **Nigeria:** The Same-Sex Marriage Prohibition Act has faced significant backlash from both local and international communities. Activists like Bisi Alimi have worked tirelessly to raise awareness and challenge the law, despite facing threats and violence.

- **Uganda:** The Anti-Homosexuality Act, which proposed severe penalties for LGBTQ individuals, faced international condemnation. Activists utilized global pressure to push back against the legislation, leading to its eventual nullification by the Constitutional Court in 2014.

- **Kenya:** In 2019, a High Court ruling upheld the criminalization of same-sex relationships. However, activists continue to challenge this ruling through legal avenues and public advocacy, emphasizing the need for decriminalization.

Conclusion

Confronting homophobic legislation is an ongoing struggle that requires resilience, creativity, and solidarity. By understanding the complexities of legal frameworks and employing effective strategies, activists can challenge discriminatory laws and work towards a more inclusive society. The journey may be fraught with challenges, but the pursuit of equality and justice for LGBTQ individuals remains a vital mission that transcends borders and cultures.

Supporting LGBTQ Rights Movements in Other African Countries

In the quest for LGBTQ rights across Africa, the interconnectedness of struggles within various nations cannot be overstated. Activists like Bisi Alimi have recognized that the fight for equality and acceptance is not confined to Nigeria alone; it is a broader movement that requires solidarity and support across borders. This section delves into the significance of supporting LGBTQ rights movements in other African countries, highlighting the challenges they face, the collaborative efforts being made, and the impact of such solidarity.

Understanding the Landscape

Many African countries have laws that criminalize same-sex relationships, often rooted in colonial-era legislation. For instance, in Uganda, the Anti-Homosexuality Act has garnered international condemnation and has significantly impacted the safety and rights of LGBTQ individuals. Similarly, in Tanzania, laws against homosexuality are enforced with brutal crackdowns on the community. Understanding these landscapes is crucial for activists who aim to provide support and solidarity.

Challenges Faced by LGBTQ Movements

The challenges faced by LGBTQ movements in Africa are multifaceted:

- **Legal Barriers:** Many countries have laws that not only criminalize same-sex relationships but also impose harsh penalties, including imprisonment. The existence of these laws creates an environment of fear and repression.

- **Social Stigma:** Deep-rooted cultural and religious beliefs often lead to widespread discrimination against LGBTQ individuals. This stigma can result in violence, ostracism, and even murder.

- **Limited Resources:** Many LGBTQ organizations operate on shoestring budgets and lack the necessary resources to effectively advocate for change. This financial limitation hampers their ability to mobilize and provide support to their communities.

- **Political Opposition:** Governments in several African nations actively oppose LGBTQ rights, often using anti-LGBTQ rhetoric to rally political support. This opposition can manifest in the form of arrests, harassment, and violence against activists.

Collaborative Efforts Across Borders

To combat these challenges, activists across Africa have begun to collaborate and support one another. This solidarity is crucial for several reasons:

- **Shared Resources:** By pooling resources, organizations can fund legal aid, mental health support, and advocacy initiatives that would otherwise be unattainable. For example, the African LGBTQI Network has been instrumental in providing training and resources to local activists.

- **Knowledge Exchange:** Activists can learn from one another's successes and failures. For instance, the strategies used in South Africa, where same-sex marriage is legal, can serve as a blueprint for advocacy in more repressive environments.

- **Visibility and Amplification:** Supporting LGBTQ movements in other countries helps amplify their voices on international platforms. When activists from different nations come together, they can create a louder, more unified call for change.

Examples of Solidarity in Action

One notable example of cross-border support is the collaboration between Nigerian and South African activists. Organizations like the Coalition of African Lesbians (CAL) have worked to provide support to their Nigerian counterparts, helping them navigate the treacherous waters of activism in a hostile environment. This collaboration has resulted in joint campaigns, shared resources, and a stronger collective voice.

Additionally, international organizations such as Human Rights Watch and Amnesty International have played a pivotal role in spotlighting human rights abuses against LGBTQ individuals in Africa. Their reports and advocacy efforts have helped draw attention to the plight of LGBTQ individuals, pressuring governments to reconsider their stances on LGBTQ rights.

The Role of Technology and Social Media

In today's digital age, technology and social media have become powerful tools for activism. Platforms like Twitter and Facebook allow activists to connect, share information, and mobilize support across borders. For instance, during the crackdown on LGBTQ individuals in Tanzania, activists utilized social media to raise awareness and call for international intervention, effectively mobilizing global support.

Conclusion

Supporting LGBTQ rights movements in other African countries is not just a matter of solidarity; it is a strategic necessity. By standing together, sharing resources, and amplifying each other's voices, activists can create a more robust and united front against oppression. The path to equality may be fraught with challenges, but the collective strength of African LGBTQ movements offers hope for a brighter future, one where love and acceptance can flourish across the continent. As Bisi Alimi continues to advocate for change, his work serves as a reminder that the fight for LGBTQ rights is a shared journey, one that transcends borders and unites us all in the pursuit of dignity and justice.

Pursuing Pan-African Solidarity

In the context of LGBTQ activism, pursuing Pan-African solidarity is not merely a noble aspiration; it is a strategic necessity. The concept of Pan-Africanism, which historically sought to unify African nations and peoples against colonialism and oppression, has evolved to encompass a broader spectrum of social justice issues, including the rights of LGBTQ individuals. This section delves into the theoretical underpinnings, challenges, and practical examples of how LGBTQ activists can foster solidarity across the African continent.

Theoretical Framework

Pan-African solidarity is rooted in the understanding that the struggles of marginalized communities are interconnected. Scholars like W. E. B. Du Bois and Kwame Nkrumah emphasized the need for unity among African peoples to combat colonial legacies and promote social justice. In the context of LGBTQ rights, this unity is crucial in addressing the pervasive homophobia and transphobia that exist across many African nations.

The theory of intersectionality, introduced by Kimberlé Crenshaw, further enriches this discourse. It posits that individuals experience oppression in varying configurations and degrees of intensity based on their intersecting identities, including race, gender, sexual orientation, and socioeconomic status. Thus, LGBTQ activists must recognize that their fight for rights is part of a larger struggle against systemic oppression that affects all marginalized groups.

Challenges to Solidarity

While the pursuit of Pan-African solidarity is essential, it is fraught with challenges. One significant barrier is the deeply entrenched cultural and religious beliefs that often demonize LGBTQ identities. Many African nations uphold colonial-era laws that criminalize same-sex relationships, and these legal frameworks are often supported by societal norms that view LGBTQ individuals as deviant. For instance, in countries like Uganda and Nigeria, anti-LGBTQ legislation is not only prevalent but is also backed by powerful religious institutions that influence public opinion.

Moreover, the lack of resources and support for LGBTQ organizations across the continent complicates efforts for solidarity. Many activists operate in isolation, facing threats of violence and persecution, which can deter collaboration. The fear of backlash from both government authorities and local communities can lead to a culture of silence and mistrust, hindering the formation of coalitions that are vital for collective action.

Examples of Solidarity in Action

Despite these challenges, there are inspiring examples of Pan-African solidarity in action. One prominent initiative is the African LGBTQI+ Network, which seeks to connect activists across the continent. This network provides a platform for sharing resources, strategies, and experiences, thereby fostering a sense of community among LGBTQ activists from diverse cultural backgrounds.

Another notable example is the collaboration between organizations such as the International Lesbian, Gay, Bisexual, Trans and Intersex Association (ILGA) and local African NGOs. These partnerships have resulted in successful campaigns against anti-LGBTQ legislation in countries like Kenya, where activists mobilized international pressure to challenge oppressive laws.

Furthermore, the annual Pan-African LGBTQI+ Conference serves as a crucial gathering for activists to share knowledge, discuss strategies, and build alliances. This conference highlights the importance of collective action and provides a space for marginalized voices to be heard. The stories shared at these gatherings often emphasize the power of unity in the face of adversity, reinforcing the idea that the fight for LGBTQ rights is a shared struggle across the continent.

Strategies for Enhancing Solidarity

To strengthen Pan-African solidarity among LGBTQ activists, several strategies can be employed:

1. **Building Cross-National Alliances:** Activists should actively seek to forge partnerships with organizations in different African countries. This can be facilitated through social media, virtual meetings, and collaborative projects that emphasize shared goals.

2. **Cultural Exchange Programs:** Initiatives that promote cultural exchange among LGBTQ communities can help to foster understanding and solidarity. By sharing stories, art, and experiences, activists can create a sense of belonging and mutual support.

3. **Training and Capacity Building:** Investing in training programs that equip activists with the skills needed to navigate legal, social, and political challenges is crucial. Workshops on advocacy, media engagement, and legal rights can empower local leaders to effectively champion LGBTQ issues.

4. **Utilizing Digital Platforms:** In an increasingly digital world, leveraging technology can enhance communication and collaboration. Online forums, webinars, and social media campaigns can facilitate dialogue and mobilization across borders.

5. **Engaging Allies:** Building coalitions with allies in the broader human rights movement, including women's rights and racial justice organizations, can amplify the message of LGBTQ inclusion and solidarity.

Conclusion

Pursuing Pan-African solidarity in the fight for LGBTQ rights is both a challenge and an opportunity. By embracing the interconnectedness of struggles against oppression, activists can create a formidable force for change. The journey towards solidarity requires courage, resilience, and an unwavering commitment to justice. As Bisi Alimi and others continue to break down barriers, the vision of a united front for LGBTQ rights across Africa becomes increasingly attainable. The road ahead may be fraught with obstacles, but the collective strength of Pan-African solidarity holds the promise of a brighter, more inclusive future for all.

Challenges and Prospects in LGBTQ Activism across Africa

LGBTQ activism in Africa faces a unique set of challenges that are deeply rooted in cultural, political, and social dynamics. The continent is home to a diverse array of societies, each with its own set of beliefs and attitudes toward sexual orientation and gender identity. This section explores the primary challenges that activists encounter and the prospects for LGBTQ rights in Africa.

Cultural and Societal Resistance

One of the foremost challenges to LGBTQ activism in Africa is the cultural resistance to non-heteronormative identities. Many African societies are influenced by traditional beliefs that view homosexuality as a Western import, leading to accusations of betrayal against cultural heritage. This resistance is compounded by societal stigma, which often results in discrimination, violence, and ostracism of LGBTQ individuals.

For instance, in countries like Uganda and Nigeria, anti-LGBTQ sentiments are prevalent, often fueled by political rhetoric that portrays LGBTQ rights as a threat to family values. The Same-Sex Marriage Prohibition Act in Nigeria exemplifies this, criminalizing same-sex relationships and imposing severe penalties. Activists face the daunting task of challenging deeply ingrained social norms while advocating for their rights.

Legal and Political Barriers

Legal frameworks across much of Africa remain hostile to LGBTQ individuals. Many countries retain colonial-era laws that criminalize same-sex relationships, and the political landscape is often characterized by a lack of political will to reform these laws. Activists frequently encounter legal barriers that hinder their ability to organize, speak out, or provide support to the community.

$$\text{Legal Barriers} = \text{Colonial Laws} + \text{Political Resistance} + \text{Social Stigma} \quad (45)$$

For example, in Tanzania, the government has intensified crackdowns on LGBTQ individuals, leading to arrests and harassment. Activists are often forced to operate in secrecy, limiting their ability to mobilize and advocate effectively.

Economic Challenges

Economic instability further complicates the landscape for LGBTQ activism in Africa. Many activists struggle to secure funding for their initiatives, as local and international donors may hesitate to support LGBTQ causes due to the associated risks. This financial insecurity limits the capacity of organizations to provide essential services, such as legal aid and mental health support.

$$\text{Activism Capacity} = \text{Funding Availability} - \text{Economic Instability} \qquad (46)$$

In countries like Zimbabwe, where economic challenges are pervasive, LGBTQ organizations often find themselves competing for limited resources, making it difficult to sustain their operations.

Prospects for Change

Despite these challenges, there are promising prospects for LGBTQ activism across Africa. A growing number of young activists are emerging, leveraging social media to raise awareness and mobilize support. The use of technology has enabled activists to connect across borders, sharing strategies and resources that enhance their collective impact.

Regional Solidarity

Regional solidarity is also gaining momentum, as activists from different African countries come together to share experiences and strategies. Initiatives like the African LGBTQI+ Conference foster collaboration and build networks that strengthen advocacy efforts.

Furthermore, international support plays a crucial role in amplifying LGBTQ voices in Africa. Organizations such as Human Rights Watch and Amnesty International have increasingly focused on African LGBTQ issues, providing resources and visibility to local activists.

Educational Initiatives

Education remains a powerful tool for change. By promoting awareness and understanding of LGBTQ issues within communities, activists can challenge stereotypes and foster acceptance. Programs aimed at educating both the general public and policymakers can help shift perceptions and pave the way for legal reforms.

Conclusion

In conclusion, while LGBTQ activism in Africa faces significant challenges, the resilience and determination of activists offer hope for a more inclusive future. The intersection of cultural, legal, and economic factors creates a complex landscape, but through regional solidarity, international support, and educational initiatives, there is potential for meaningful progress. As the movement continues to evolve, the prospects for LGBTQ rights in Africa remain a critical area of focus for activists and allies alike.

$$\text{Future of LGBTQ Rights} = \text{Activism} + \text{Solidarity} + \text{Education} \quad (47)$$

Holding African Leaders Accountable

In the fight for LGBTQ rights across Africa, one of the most critical challenges faced by activists is the need to hold African leaders accountable for their actions and policies. This accountability is not merely a matter of political correctness; it is essential for the protection and promotion of human rights for all citizens, regardless of their sexual orientation or gender identity.

The Theory of Accountability in Governance

Accountability in governance refers to the obligation of leaders to justify their actions and decisions to their constituents. The theoretical framework surrounding accountability includes various dimensions such as transparency, responsiveness, and the rule of law. According to [?], accountability can be viewed through three lenses: political accountability, administrative accountability, and social accountability.

$$\text{Accountability} = \text{Transparency} + \text{Responsiveness} + \text{Rule of Law} \quad (48)$$

This equation emphasizes that without transparency, there can be no genuine accountability. In the context of LGBTQ rights, this means that leaders must be open about their policies and the impact these policies have on marginalized communities.

Problems Faced in Holding Leaders Accountable

Despite the theoretical frameworks that support accountability, numerous problems persist. Firstly, many African leaders operate within a culture of impunity, where human rights violations, particularly against LGBTQ individuals, are often overlooked or tacitly approved. For instance, countries like Uganda and Nigeria have enacted laws that criminalize homosexuality, leading to state-sanctioned discrimination and violence.

Moreover, the lack of independent judicial systems in several African nations hampers the ability to challenge unjust laws. Activists often face intimidation, threats, and violence when attempting to hold leaders accountable. Reports from organizations like Human Rights Watch have highlighted how activists in countries such as Tanzania and Zambia are often arrested and charged with trumped-up offenses simply for advocating for LGBTQ rights.

Examples of Accountability in Action

Despite these challenges, there have been notable instances where activists have successfully held leaders accountable. One prominent example is the case of Uganda's Anti-Homosexuality Act, which faced significant international backlash. Following widespread condemnation from global leaders and organizations, including the United Nations, the Ugandan government was pressured to retract certain provisions of the law. This demonstrates the power of international advocacy and the importance of global solidarity in holding leaders accountable.

Another example is the work of the African Commission on Human and Peoples' Rights (ACHPR), which has addressed human rights violations against LGBTQ individuals. In 2014, the ACHPR adopted a resolution urging member states to protect the rights of LGBTQ persons, emphasizing that discrimination based on sexual orientation is a violation of human rights. This resolution serves as a critical tool for activists seeking to hold their governments accountable.

Strategies for Enhancing Accountability

To enhance accountability, activists must employ a multi-faceted approach. This includes:

- **Grassroots Mobilization:** Engaging the community to advocate for their rights and hold leaders accountable. Grassroots movements can amplify the voices of marginalized individuals, making it harder for leaders to ignore their demands.

- **International Advocacy:** Building coalitions with global human rights organizations to apply pressure on African governments. International bodies can leverage diplomatic relations and economic sanctions to encourage compliance with human rights standards.

- **Legal Action:** Utilizing the courts to challenge discriminatory laws. Legal challenges can set precedents that compel governments to change their policies.

- **Public Awareness Campaigns:** Educating the public about LGBTQ rights and the importance of accountability. Raising awareness can shift public opinion and create an environment where leaders are held to higher standards.

Conclusion

Holding African leaders accountable for their treatment of LGBTQ individuals is a daunting but necessary task. It requires a concerted effort from activists, the international community, and civil society organizations. By fostering a culture of accountability, we can pave the way for a more inclusive and equitable society where the rights of all individuals are respected and protected. As Bisi Alimi continues to advocate for LGBTQ rights, the journey towards accountability remains a vital aspect of the broader struggle for human rights in Africa.

The Role of Economic Development in LGBTQ Advocacy

Economic development plays a crucial role in the advancement of LGBTQ rights and advocacy, particularly in regions where social and legal frameworks are less supportive of LGBTQ individuals. The intersection of economic growth and LGBTQ rights is multifaceted, affecting everything from access to resources and job opportunities to social acceptance and legal protections.

Theoretical Framework

The relationship between economic development and LGBTQ advocacy can be analyzed through several theoretical lenses, including:

- **Human Capital Theory:** This theory posits that investments in education and skills lead to better economic outcomes. For LGBTQ individuals, access to quality education and employment opportunities can empower them to advocate for their rights effectively. A well-educated LGBTQ populace is better equipped to challenge discriminatory practices and engage in activism.

- **Social Capital Theory:** This theory emphasizes the importance of social networks and relationships in achieving collective goals. Economic development can enhance social capital by creating spaces for LGBTQ individuals to connect, collaborate, and mobilize for advocacy efforts.

- **Intersectionality:** This framework acknowledges that various social identities intersect to shape individuals' experiences. Economic development must consider how factors such as race, gender, and class affect LGBTQ individuals' access to resources and opportunities, thereby influencing their capacity for advocacy.

Economic Challenges Faced by LGBTQ Individuals

Despite the potential benefits of economic development, LGBTQ individuals often face significant barriers that hinder their economic advancement:

- **Discrimination in Employment:** Many LGBTQ individuals experience discrimination in hiring, promotions, and workplace treatment. This not only limits their economic opportunities but also perpetuates a cycle of poverty and marginalization. According to a 2020 report by the Williams Institute, LGBTQ individuals are more likely to experience unemployment compared to their heterosexual counterparts.

- **Limited Access to Healthcare:** Economic development often correlates with improved healthcare access. However, LGBTQ individuals frequently face discrimination within healthcare systems, leading to inadequate mental and physical health services. This can hinder their ability to participate fully in the workforce and advocate for their rights.

- **Social Stigma and Isolation:** In many conservative societies, LGBTQ individuals face social stigma that can lead to isolation and a lack of community support. This isolation can limit their access to economic opportunities and networks that are essential for advocacy.

Examples of Economic Development Initiatives Supporting LGBTQ Advocacy

Despite these challenges, there are several notable examples where economic development initiatives have positively impacted LGBTQ advocacy:

- **Social Enterprises:** Organizations like *LGBTQ+ Economic Empowerment* focus on creating job opportunities for LGBTQ individuals while promoting inclusivity in the workplace. These enterprises not only provide employment but also advocate for policy changes that support LGBTQ rights.

- **Microfinance Programs:** Microfinance initiatives aimed at LGBTQ entrepreneurs can empower individuals to start their own businesses. For instance, programs in South Africa have successfully funded LGBTQ-owned businesses, fostering economic independence and community support.

- **Corporate Partnerships:** Many corporations have recognized the importance of LGBTQ inclusion and have partnered with advocacy organizations to promote economic development. Companies like *Google* and *Microsoft* have established initiatives that not only support LGBTQ employees but also contribute to broader advocacy efforts by funding campaigns and providing resources.

The Role of Policy in Economic Development and LGBTQ Advocacy

Effective policy is essential to harnessing the potential of economic development for LGBTQ advocacy. Policies that promote:

- **Non-Discrimination Laws:** Implementing and enforcing non-discrimination laws in employment and housing can create a more equitable economic landscape for LGBTQ individuals. This legal protection is fundamental to ensuring that LGBTQ individuals can fully participate in the economy without fear of discrimination.

- **Inclusive Economic Policies:** Governments should consider LGBTQ individuals in their economic development strategies. This includes recognizing the unique challenges faced by LGBTQ populations and creating targeted programs that address these challenges.

- **Support for LGBTQ Organizations:** Funding and support for LGBTQ advocacy organizations can enhance their capacity to effect change. Economic development initiatives that include grants or resources for these organizations can lead to more robust advocacy efforts.

Conclusion

In conclusion, economic development is a powerful tool for advancing LGBTQ rights and advocacy. By addressing the economic challenges faced by LGBTQ individuals and implementing inclusive policies, societies can create an environment where LGBTQ voices are amplified, and their rights are recognized. As Bisi Alimi's work demonstrates, the intersection of economic development and LGBTQ advocacy is not just about improving economic conditions; it is about fostering a culture of acceptance and equality that benefits everyone.

International Support for African LGBTQ Rights

In recent years, international support for African LGBTQ rights has gained momentum, reflecting a growing recognition of the need for global solidarity in the fight against discrimination and violence based on sexual orientation and gender identity. This section explores the various forms of international support, the challenges faced by LGBTQ activists in Africa, and the impact of global advocacy on local movements.

The Role of International Organizations

International organizations such as the United Nations (UN), Amnesty International, and Human Rights Watch have played a pivotal role in advocating for LGBTQ rights across Africa. These organizations provide crucial resources, visibility, and legitimacy to local activists. For example, the UN has established mechanisms to monitor human rights violations against LGBTQ individuals, urging member states to uphold their obligations under international human rights law.

$$\text{Human Rights} = \text{Universal Rights} - \text{Discrimination} \qquad (49)$$

This equation emphasizes that the essence of human rights lies in their universality, which is often compromised by discrimination based on sexual orientation.

Funding and Resources

International support often translates into financial assistance for local organizations working on LGBTQ issues. Grants from foreign governments, non-governmental organizations (NGOs), and philanthropic foundations have enabled African LGBTQ groups to expand their reach, conduct advocacy campaigns, and provide essential services. For instance, the Global Fund for Women has funded initiatives aimed at combating violence against LGBTQ women in various African countries, highlighting the intersectionality of gender and sexual orientation in the fight for equality.

Challenges of International Support

Despite the positive impact of international support, several challenges remain. One significant issue is the backlash from conservative governments and societal groups that view international advocacy as foreign interference. This backlash can manifest in increased violence against LGBTQ individuals and stricter laws against homosexuality. For example, in countries like Uganda and Nigeria, international condemnation of anti-LGBTQ legislation has sometimes led to harsher penalties and intensified persecution of LGBTQ individuals.

$$\text{Backlash} = \text{Resistance} + \text{Fear of Change} \qquad (50)$$

This equation illustrates how resistance to change, fueled by fear and misinformation, can lead to a hostile environment for LGBTQ rights activists.

Case Studies of Successful International Advocacy

Several notable case studies highlight the effectiveness of international support for LGBTQ rights in Africa:

1. **The Uganda Anti-Homosexuality Act**: International outcry against this draconian law in 2014 led to significant diplomatic pressure on the Ugandan government. Although the law was eventually annulled on a technicality, the global attention helped galvanize local activists and foster a more robust LGBTQ rights movement in Uganda.

2. **The Nigerian Same-Sex Marriage Prohibition Act**: Following the enactment of this law in 2014, international organizations mobilized to support Nigerian activists through funding, training, and advocacy campaigns. This support has helped create safe spaces for LGBTQ individuals and foster dialogue around LGBTQ rights within Nigerian society.

3. **The African Commission on Human and Peoples' Rights**: This regional body has increasingly recognized LGBTQ rights as human rights, influenced by international advocacy. The commission's resolutions and recommendations have provided a platform for African activists to push for change within their countries.

The Impact of Social Media

Social media has emerged as a powerful tool for international advocacy, enabling activists to share their stories and connect with global audiences. Platforms like Twitter, Facebook, and Instagram have facilitated campaigns that raise awareness about LGBTQ issues in Africa, mobilize support, and challenge harmful stereotypes. For instance, the #FreeTheGays campaign, which gained traction on social media, highlighted the plight of LGBTQ individuals in Africa and garnered international solidarity.

Conclusion

International support for African LGBTQ rights is crucial in the ongoing struggle for equality and justice. While challenges persist, the combined efforts of local activists and international allies are gradually reshaping the landscape for LGBTQ rights in Africa. As global awareness continues to grow, it is essential to maintain momentum and ensure that the voices of African LGBTQ individuals are heard and respected in the broader human rights discourse.

$$\text{Future} = \text{Solidarity} + \text{Empowerment} \tag{51}$$

This equation encapsulates the potential for a brighter future for LGBTQ rights in Africa, grounded in solidarity and the empowerment of local activists.

The African Renaissance of LGBTQ Rights

The concept of an African Renaissance, which encompasses a resurgence of cultural, political, and economic growth across the continent, has increasingly begun to include the rights of LGBTQ individuals. This movement is not merely a reflection of changing attitudes towards sexual orientation and gender identity, but rather a profound shift in how African societies perceive human rights, dignity, and the essence of humanity itself.

Historical Context

Historically, many African nations have been characterized by colonial laws that criminalized homosexuality, often introduced by European powers during the colonial era. These laws have persisted long after independence, creating a legal framework that continues to marginalize LGBTQ individuals. However, the African Renaissance seeks to dismantle these oppressive structures by advocating for a more inclusive and equitable society.

Current Challenges

Despite the momentum towards LGBTQ rights, significant challenges remain. Homophobia and transphobia are deeply entrenched in many African cultures, often fueled by traditional beliefs and religious doctrines. For instance, in countries like Uganda and Nigeria, laws against same-sex relationships are not only punitive but are often justified through cultural and religious narratives. The societal stigma attached to LGBTQ identities can lead to discrimination, violence, and even death.

The Role of Activism

Activism plays a crucial role in the African Renaissance of LGBTQ rights. Grassroots organizations and international NGOs are working tirelessly to challenge discriminatory laws and practices. Notable activists, such as Bisi Alimi, have become prominent figures in this movement, using their platforms to raise awareness and foster dialogue. Through community outreach, educational programs, and legal advocacy, these organizations aim to shift public perceptions and create safer spaces for LGBTQ individuals.

Examples of Progress

Recent years have seen some progress in LGBTQ rights across the continent. In South Africa, the 1996 Constitution was a landmark achievement, as it was the first in the world to prohibit discrimination based on sexual orientation. This legal framework has allowed for greater visibility and advocacy, inspiring movements in other African nations.

In Kenya, for example, the fight against the colonial-era sodomy laws has gained traction, with activists challenging these laws in court. The High Court's ruling in 2019, which upheld the rights of LGBTQ individuals to live free from discrimination, marked a significant step forward, despite the ongoing societal backlash.

Cultural Shifts

Culturally, there is a growing recognition of the need for inclusivity. The rise of LGBTQ art, literature, and media has provided a platform for marginalized voices. Events like Pride parades and film festivals are becoming more common, fostering a sense of community and visibility. Artists and filmmakers are using their crafts to challenge stereotypes and promote acceptance, thus contributing to the broader narrative of the African Renaissance.

The Intersection of Global and Local Activism

The intersection of global and local activism has also played a pivotal role in advancing LGBTQ rights in Africa. International human rights organizations, such as Human Rights Watch and Amnesty International, have amplified local voices, advocating for policy changes and providing resources for activists. This collaboration has been instrumental in raising awareness and fostering solidarity among LGBTQ communities across borders.

Conclusion: A Vision for the Future

The African Renaissance of LGBTQ rights is not merely a dream; it is a movement in progress. While challenges persist, the resilience of activists and the growing support from allies signal a hopeful future. As more individuals and organizations join the fight for equality, the vision of an inclusive Africa—where LGBTQ individuals can live freely and authentically—becomes increasingly attainable.

The journey towards equality is ongoing, but with each step taken, the narrative surrounding LGBTQ rights in Africa is being rewritten. The power of community, activism, and solidarity will ultimately shape the future of the African Renaissance, ensuring that no one is left behind in the quest for human dignity and justice.

$$\text{Progress in LGBTQ Rights} = \text{Activism} + \text{Cultural Shifts} + \text{Legal Frameworks} + \text{Global Supp} \tag{52}$$

Prospects for a Better Future

The future of LGBTQ rights in Africa is a complex tapestry woven with threads of hope, resilience, and unyielding determination. As we look ahead, several key factors will shape the prospects for a more inclusive society where LGBTQ individuals can thrive without fear of discrimination or violence.

1. Legislative Changes

One of the most pressing needs for the LGBTQ community in Africa is the reform of discriminatory laws. Many countries still criminalize same-sex relationships, often imposing harsh penalties. The repeal of such laws is crucial for fostering an environment of acceptance and equality. For instance, in countries like Angola and Mozambique, recent legislative changes have decriminalized homosexuality, setting a precedent for others to follow. The equation below illustrates the relationship between legal reform and societal acceptance:

$$\text{Social Acceptance} = f(\text{Legal Reform, Education, Visibility}) \quad (53)$$

Where: - Legal Reform refers to the abolition of discriminatory laws. - Education encompasses awareness programs aimed at reducing stigma. - Visibility highlights the representation of LGBTQ individuals in media and politics.

2. Education and Awareness

Education plays a pivotal role in transforming societal attitudes. Programs aimed at educating the public about LGBTQ issues can dismantle harmful stereotypes and foster empathy. Schools and universities must incorporate inclusive curricula that celebrate diversity and human rights. For example, initiatives like the "Safe Schools" program in South Africa aim to create supportive environments for LGBTQ students, showcasing the positive impact of education on acceptance.

3. Intersectionality in Activism

The future of LGBTQ activism in Africa must embrace intersectionality, recognizing that individuals have multiple identities that intersect to create unique experiences of oppression. This approach can unify various movements, such as gender equality, racial justice, and LGBTQ rights, leading to a more robust coalition for change. By addressing the specific needs of marginalized groups within the LGBTQ community, activists can build a more inclusive movement.

4. Global Solidarity and Support

International solidarity is vital for advancing LGBTQ rights in Africa. Global organizations can provide resources, training, and advocacy support to local activists. Collaborative efforts, such as the work done by OutRight Action International, have shown that global partnerships can amplify local voices and strengthen the fight against homophobia and transphobia.

5. The Role of Technology

In the digital age, technology serves as a powerful tool for activism. Social media platforms enable activists to share their stories, mobilize support, and raise awareness on a global scale. The use of technology can help circumvent censorship and connect LGBTQ individuals across borders, fostering a sense of community and shared purpose.

6. Youth Engagement

Engaging the youth in advocacy is essential for sustaining the momentum of the LGBTQ rights movement. Young people are often more open-minded and willing to challenge societal norms. Programs that empower LGBTQ youth through leadership training and activism can cultivate the next generation of advocates, ensuring that the fight for equality continues.

Conclusion

The prospects for a better future for LGBTQ individuals in Africa hinge on a multifaceted approach that includes legal reform, education, intersectional activism, global support, technological innovation, and youth engagement. While challenges remain, the resilience and determination of activists like Bisi Alimi inspire hope for a more inclusive and equitable future. As we move forward, it is imperative to harness these elements collectively to create a society where every individual, regardless of their sexual orientation or gender identity, can live freely and authentically.

Bisi Alimi's Legacy and Continued Activism

Bisi Alimi's Legacy and Continued Activism

Bisi Alimi's Legacy and Continued Activism

Bisi Alimi's journey is not just a personal odyssey; it is a testament to the power of resilience, advocacy, and the relentless pursuit of justice. His legacy is woven into the fabric of LGBTQ activism, not only in Nigeria but across the globe. This section delves into the multifaceted aspects of Bisi Alimi's legacy and the ongoing impact of his activism.

The Impact of Bisi Alimi's Activism

Bisi Alimi's activism has significantly shifted the narrative surrounding LGBTQ rights in Nigeria. His courage to come out publicly as Nigeria's first openly gay man on television in 2004 marked a pivotal moment in the country's history. This act of bravery not only galvanized the LGBTQ community but also challenged the prevailing homophobic sentiments entrenched in Nigerian society. Alimi's visibility has been instrumental in fostering a sense of belonging among LGBTQ individuals, who often face isolation and discrimination.

Progress Made in the LGBTQ Rights Movement

Over the years, Alimi's efforts have contributed to incremental progress in the fight for LGBTQ rights. For instance, his participation in international forums has brought global attention to the plight of LGBTQ individuals in Nigeria. The advocacy for anti-discrimination laws and the establishment of safe spaces for LGBTQ individuals are direct outcomes of his relentless campaigning.

Despite the challenges posed by the Same-Sex Marriage Prohibition Act of 2014, which criminalized same-sex relationships, Alimi has continued to advocate for change. He has emphasized the importance of education and awareness in combating stigma and discrimination. By leveraging social media platforms, he has mobilized support and fostered dialogue around LGBTQ issues, effectively reaching a broader audience.

Remaining Challenges and Obstacles

While progress has been made, significant challenges remain. The societal stigma surrounding LGBTQ identities continues to pose barriers to acceptance and equality. Alimi's legacy is not just about the victories; it is also about acknowledging the ongoing struggles faced by LGBTQ individuals. The threat of violence, legal repercussions, and societal ostracism are constant realities that activists must navigate.

One of the pressing issues is the need for a more progressive legal framework that protects LGBTQ rights. The Nigerian legal system remains largely hostile to LGBTQ individuals, and advocacy for legal reform is crucial. Alimi has been vocal about the necessity of engaging with lawmakers and policymakers to foster a more inclusive legal environment.

Advocacy for a More Progressive Legal Framework

Alimi's advocacy extends beyond mere awareness; it encompasses a call for legislative change. He argues that the foundation of any movement lies in the legal protections afforded to marginalized communities. The lack of anti-discrimination laws in Nigeria not only perpetuates violence against LGBTQ individuals but also hinders their ability to access essential services, including healthcare and education.

$$\text{Equality} = \frac{\text{Legal Protection} + \text{Social Acceptance}}{\text{Discrimination}} \qquad (54)$$

This equation illustrates the delicate balance required to achieve equality. Alimi emphasizes that without legal protection, social acceptance remains an elusive goal. His advocacy seeks to dismantle the legal barriers that inhibit progress and to foster an environment where LGBTQ individuals can thrive without fear of persecution.

Inspiring Future Activists in Nigeria

Bisi Alimi's legacy is also characterized by his role as a mentor and inspiration to a new generation of activists. His story serves as a beacon of hope for young LGBTQ individuals in Nigeria, encouraging them to embrace their identities and fight for their rights. Alimi has actively engaged in capacity-building initiatives, providing training and resources to emerging activists.

He often emphasizes the importance of intersectionality in activism, recognizing that LGBTQ issues cannot be divorced from broader social justice movements. By fostering a sense of solidarity among various marginalized groups, Alimi has helped to create a more inclusive framework for activism.

Celebrating LGBTQ Culture and Identity

In addition to legal advocacy, Alimi has championed the celebration of LGBTQ culture and identity. He believes that visibility is a powerful tool in combating prejudice. Through art, literature, and community events, Alimi has encouraged LGBTQ individuals to express themselves authentically. His initiatives have not only provided a platform for creative expression but have also fostered a sense of pride within the community.

Supporting LGBTQ Businesses and Entrepreneurs

Recognizing the economic disparities faced by LGBTQ individuals, Alimi has also focused on supporting LGBTQ businesses and entrepreneurs. He advocates for economic empowerment as a means to achieve social justice. By promoting LGBTQ-owned businesses, he aims to create a sustainable economic ecosystem that uplifts the community.

The Arts as a Tool for Social Change

The arts play a crucial role in Alimi's vision for social change. He believes that storytelling, whether through film, theater, or literature, can challenge stereotypes and foster empathy. Alimi has collaborated with artists and creators to produce works that highlight the experiences of LGBTQ individuals, thereby humanizing the issues at stake.

Shifting Public Perceptions

Alimi's activism has contributed to a gradual shift in public perceptions of LGBTQ individuals in Nigeria. Through media appearances, public speaking engagements, and social media campaigns, he has worked tirelessly to counteract negative stereotypes. His message of love, acceptance, and understanding resonates with many, fostering a dialogue that transcends cultural and religious divides.

The Role of Education in Promoting Equality

Education remains a cornerstone of Alimi's advocacy. He emphasizes the need for comprehensive sex education that includes LGBTQ topics, aiming to equip future generations with the knowledge and understanding necessary to combat prejudice. By fostering an educational environment that promotes inclusivity, Alimi believes that society can move closer to achieving true equality.

A Vision for the Future

Bisi Alimi's legacy is a call to action for all who believe in justice and equality. His vision for the future is one where LGBTQ individuals can live openly and authentically, free from fear and discrimination. He envisions a Nigeria where love prevails over hate, and where diversity is celebrated as a strength rather than a weakness.

In conclusion, Bisi Alimi's legacy is one of resilience, empowerment, and unwavering commitment to justice. His continued activism serves as an inspiration for countless individuals, reminding us that the fight for equality is far from over. As we reflect on his journey, we are reminded of the power of one voice to ignite change and the importance of standing together in solidarity for a brighter future.

The Journey Towards a More Inclusive Nigeria

Progress Made in the LGBTQ Rights Movement

The LGBTQ rights movement in Nigeria has made significant strides over the past few decades, despite facing numerous challenges and systemic barriers. This progress can be attributed to the tireless efforts of activists, organizations, and allies who have worked to promote visibility, acceptance, and legal reforms. In this section, we will explore the key milestones achieved in the LGBTQ rights movement in Nigeria, the theoretical frameworks that underpin these advancements, and the ongoing challenges that activists continue to face.

Theoretical Frameworks

To understand the progress made in the LGBTQ rights movement, it is essential to consider the theoretical frameworks that inform activism. One such framework is **Queer Theory**, which challenges the binary understanding of gender and sexuality. Queer Theory posits that sexual identities are fluid and socially constructed, allowing for a broader understanding of LGBTQ experiences. This theoretical lens has empowered activists to advocate for a more inclusive society that recognizes diverse sexual orientations and gender identities.

Another relevant framework is **Intersectionality**, coined by Kimberlé Crenshaw. This concept emphasizes the interconnectedness of social identities, such as race, gender, and class, and how they intersect to create unique experiences of discrimination. In Nigeria, intersectionality plays a crucial role in LGBTQ activism as it highlights how factors like ethnicity, religion, and socio-economic status impact the experiences of LGBTQ individuals. Activists who embrace intersectionality work to ensure that all voices within the community are heard and represented.

Key Milestones

1. **Increased Visibility and Representation:** Over the years, there has been a notable increase in the visibility of LGBTQ individuals in Nigeria. Activists like Bisi Alimi have bravely shared their stories, challenging stereotypes and fostering dialogue around LGBTQ issues. Media representations, though often fraught with challenges, have also begun to reflect more diverse narratives, contributing to a gradual shift in public perception.

2. **Formation of LGBTQ Organizations:** The establishment of organizations such as *The Initiative for Equal Rights (TIERs)* and *Queer Alliance Nigeria* has played a pivotal role in advocating for LGBTQ rights. These organizations provide essential support services, including legal assistance, mental health resources, and educational programs aimed at raising awareness about LGBTQ issues.

3. **Legal Advocacy and Challenges:** Despite the passage of the Same-Sex Marriage Prohibition Act in 2014, which criminalized same-sex relationships, activists have continued to challenge discriminatory laws. Legal battles, such as those led by TIERs, have sought to contest the constitutionality of such laws, arguing that they violate fundamental human rights. While these efforts have faced setbacks, they have also sparked important conversations about the need for legal reforms.

4. **International Support and Solidarity:** The global LGBTQ community has increasingly rallied behind Nigerian activists, providing vital resources and support. International organizations, such as *Human Rights Watch* and *Amnesty International*, have highlighted the struggles faced by LGBTQ individuals in Nigeria, amplifying their voices on the global stage. This international solidarity has bolstered local efforts and provided activists with a broader platform to advocate for change.

5. **Youth Engagement and Empowerment:** The rise of youth-led initiatives has injected new energy into the LGBTQ rights movement. Young activists are leveraging social media to raise awareness, mobilize support, and challenge societal norms. Campaigns such as *#FreeNigeria* have gained traction, showcasing the power of digital activism in promoting LGBTQ rights.

Ongoing Challenges

Despite the progress made, significant challenges remain. Activists continue to face harassment, violence, and discrimination, both from state actors and within their communities. The pervasive influence of conservative religious beliefs often exacerbates stigma and reinforces negative stereotypes about LGBTQ individuals. Additionally, the lack of legal protections leaves many vulnerable to discrimination in employment, healthcare, and housing.

Furthermore, the intersectionality of identities means that LGBTQ individuals from marginalized backgrounds often experience compounded discrimination. For instance, queer individuals from low-income communities may face economic hardships that limit their access to resources and support networks.

Conclusion

In conclusion, the progress made in the LGBTQ rights movement in Nigeria is a testament to the resilience and determination of activists who refuse to be silenced. Through increased visibility, the formation of supportive organizations, and ongoing advocacy efforts, significant strides have been made toward a more inclusive society. However, the journey is far from over, and the fight for equality continues. By embracing theoretical frameworks such as Queer Theory and Intersectionality, activists can navigate the complexities of LGBTQ advocacy and work towards a future where all individuals, regardless of their sexual orientation or gender identity, can live freely and authentically.

$$\text{Progress} = \text{Visibility} + \text{Advocacy} + \text{Support Networks} - \text{Challenges} \qquad (55)$$

Remaining Challenges and Obstacles

Despite the progress made in the LGBTQ rights movement in Nigeria, numerous challenges and obstacles continue to impede the path toward full equality and acceptance. These challenges can be broadly categorized into societal, legal, and political barriers, each contributing to a climate of fear and discrimination that affects the lives of LGBTQ individuals.

Societal Stigma and Discrimination

One of the most significant challenges facing the LGBTQ community in Nigeria is the pervasive societal stigma associated with non-heteronormative identities. This stigma is deeply rooted in cultural norms and religious beliefs that promote heteronormativity as the only acceptable form of sexual orientation. According to a study by [?], over 80% of Nigerians hold negative views toward LGBTQ individuals, which leads to widespread discrimination in everyday life.

This societal stigma manifests in various forms, including:

- **Family Rejection:** Many LGBTQ individuals face rejection from their families, leading to emotional distress and, in some cases, homelessness. A report by [?] highlighted that 60% of LGBTQ youth in Nigeria experience familial rejection, which significantly impacts their mental health.

- **Workplace Discrimination:** LGBTQ individuals often encounter discrimination in the workplace, resulting in job loss or limited career advancement opportunities. The fear of being outed can lead to a culture of silence, where individuals feel compelled to hide their identities to maintain employment.

- **Violence and Harassment:** The fear of violence is a constant reality for many LGBTQ individuals. Reports indicate that hate crimes against LGBTQ people are on the rise, with [?] documenting a 30% increase in reported cases of violence in the last five years.

Legal Barriers

The legal landscape for LGBTQ rights in Nigeria is fraught with challenges, primarily due to the Same-Sex Marriage Prohibition Act (SSMPA) enacted in 2014. This law not only criminalizes same-sex marriage but also imposes severe penalties for anyone who supports LGBTQ rights. The act has created a chilling effect on advocacy efforts, with many organizations fearing legal repercussions for their work.

$$\text{Legal Penalties} = \text{Fine} + \text{Imprisonment} \tag{56}$$

Where: - Legal Penalties represent the consequences faced by LGBTQ individuals and allies. - Fine is the monetary penalty imposed. - Imprisonment refers to the potential incarceration period.

The SSMPA has led to the arrest and prosecution of numerous activists, creating a hostile environment for advocacy. For instance, in 2018, a prominent activist was arrested under this law, sparking international outrage and drawing attention to the oppressive legal framework in Nigeria [?].

Political Opposition

Political opposition to LGBTQ rights remains a significant obstacle in Nigeria. Many politicians leverage anti-LGBTQ sentiments to gain support from conservative constituents, often using inflammatory rhetoric to rally their base. This political climate discourages progressive reforms and perpetuates a cycle of discrimination.

$$\text{Political Support} \propto \text{Conservative Sentiment} \tag{57}$$

Where: - Political Support refers to the backing received by politicians for anti-LGBTQ policies. - Conservative Sentiment indicates the prevailing attitudes among the electorate.

The lack of political will to address LGBTQ issues is further compounded by the absence of representation in government. LGBTQ individuals are rarely included in policy discussions, leading to a lack of awareness and understanding of their needs and rights.

Intersectionality of Challenges

The challenges faced by LGBTQ individuals in Nigeria are not experienced in isolation; they intersect with other social issues such as poverty, gender inequality, and ethnic discrimination. This intersectionality complicates the struggle for LGBTQ rights, as individuals from marginalized backgrounds may face compounded discrimination.

For example, LGBTQ individuals from lower socioeconomic backgrounds may lack access to resources that could help them navigate legal and societal challenges. They may also be more vulnerable to violence and exploitation, as highlighted by [?], who found that economic instability significantly increases the risk of victimization among LGBTQ individuals.

Conclusion

In conclusion, while there have been notable strides in the fight for LGBTQ rights in Nigeria, the remaining challenges and obstacles are substantial. Societal stigma, legal barriers, political opposition, and the intersectionality of various forms of discrimination create a complex landscape that activists must navigate. Addressing these challenges requires a multifaceted approach that includes legal reforms, public education, and the mobilization of allies both within and outside Nigeria. Only through concerted efforts can the LGBTQ community hope to achieve true equality and acceptance in Nigerian society.

Advocacy for a More Progressive Legal Framework

In the landscape of LGBTQ rights in Nigeria, the call for a more progressive legal framework is not merely a plea; it is a necessity. The existing laws, particularly the Same-Sex Marriage Prohibition Act of 2014, have created an environment rife with discrimination, marginalization, and violence against LGBTQ individuals. This section explores the advocacy efforts aimed at reforming these laws, the theoretical underpinnings of such advocacy, the challenges faced, and notable examples of progress.

Theoretical Framework

The advocacy for a progressive legal framework can be grounded in several theoretical approaches. One such approach is **Human Rights Theory**, which posits that all individuals, regardless of sexual orientation or gender identity, deserve the same rights and protections under the law. This theory emphasizes the inherent dignity and worth of every person, aligning with the principles enshrined in international human rights treaties, such as the Universal Declaration of Human Rights (UDHR).

Furthermore, **Intersectionality** plays a crucial role in understanding the complexities of LGBTQ advocacy in Nigeria. Coined by Kimberlé Crenshaw, intersectionality examines how various social identities—such as race, gender, and sexual orientation—intersect to create unique experiences of oppression. In the Nigerian context, LGBTQ individuals often face compounded discrimination based on their ethnicity, socioeconomic status, and religious beliefs, necessitating a nuanced approach to legal advocacy.

Identifying Problems

The current legal framework in Nigeria presents significant problems that hinder the progress of LGBTQ rights. The Same-Sex Marriage Prohibition Act not only criminalizes same-sex relationships but also imposes harsh penalties, including imprisonment for up to 14 years. This law has fostered a culture of fear, leading to increased violence against LGBTQ individuals, who often find themselves without legal recourse.

Moreover, the lack of anti-discrimination laws further exacerbates the situation. LGBTQ individuals are frequently denied employment, housing, and access to healthcare based solely on their sexual orientation or gender identity. This systemic discrimination is a violation of their basic human rights and perpetuates cycles of poverty and marginalization.

Advocacy Strategies

In response to these challenges, advocates like Bisi Alimi have employed various strategies to push for a more progressive legal framework. One effective strategy is **Public Awareness Campaigns**, which aim to educate the general public about LGBTQ rights and the importance of legal reform. By utilizing social media platforms, community workshops, and public demonstrations, activists can raise awareness and foster empathy among the broader population.

Additionally, **Legal Challenges** have been undertaken to contest the constitutionality of discriminatory laws. For instance, in 2018, a group of Nigerian activists filed a lawsuit challenging the Same-Sex Marriage Prohibition Act on the grounds that it violates the rights to privacy and freedom of expression as guaranteed by the Nigerian Constitution. Although the case faced significant obstacles, it marked a crucial step in the fight for legal recognition and protection.

Examples of Progress

Despite the daunting challenges, there have been notable examples of progress in the advocacy for LGBTQ rights in Nigeria. One such example is the establishment of the **LGBTQ Rights Network**, a coalition of activists and organizations working together to promote legal reform and provide support to LGBTQ individuals. This network has successfully lobbied for local governments to adopt more inclusive policies, demonstrating the power of collective action.

International support has also played a vital role in advancing LGBTQ rights. Organizations such as **Human Rights Watch** and **Amnesty International** have provided resources, visibility, and advocacy on behalf of Nigerian LGBTQ activists. Their involvement has helped to amplify local voices and apply pressure on the Nigerian government to reconsider its stance on LGBTQ rights.

Conclusion

Advocating for a more progressive legal framework in Nigeria is a complex and challenging endeavor, but it is essential for the advancement of LGBTQ rights. By grounding advocacy efforts in human rights theory and intersectionality, identifying the systemic problems within the legal framework, and employing diverse strategies to foster change, activists like Bisi Alimi are paving the way for a more inclusive and equitable society. The journey is far from over, but with continued advocacy and support, a more progressive legal framework is within reach.

Inspiring Future Activists in Nigeria

In a country where the very act of being oneself can lead to persecution, inspiring future activists is not just a noble goal; it is a necessity. Bisi Alimi, through his relentless advocacy, has become a beacon of hope for many young Nigerians who dare to dream of a more inclusive society. His journey is a testament to the power of resilience, and it serves as a roadmap for those who follow in his footsteps.

The Power of Role Models

Role models play a crucial role in shaping the aspirations of young activists. Alimi's visibility as an openly gay man in Nigeria has shattered stereotypes and provided a face to the often-misunderstood LGBTQ community. His story demonstrates that activism can stem from personal experiences and struggles. As he once said, "You cannot change the world alone, but you can inspire others to join you." This sentiment encapsulates the essence of community-driven activism.

Educational Initiatives

Education is a powerful tool for change. Alimi has been at the forefront of various educational initiatives aimed at raising awareness about LGBTQ rights and issues in Nigeria. Workshops, seminars, and discussions led by experienced activists can empower young people with the knowledge and skills needed to advocate for their rights. For instance, the "Youth for Change" program, which Alimi helped establish, focuses on educating young Nigerians about human rights and the importance of inclusivity.

Creating Safe Spaces

Creating safe spaces for dialogue is critical for nurturing future activists. Alimi emphasizes the importance of providing environments where young people can express themselves without fear of judgment or retaliation. Initiatives such as LGBTQ youth groups and community centers offer a haven for individuals to share their experiences and learn from one another. These spaces not only foster a sense of belonging but also encourage collective action.

Leveraging Technology

In an increasingly digital world, technology serves as a double-edged sword. While it can expose activists to risks, it also provides unprecedented opportunities for connection and mobilization. Alimi advocates for the use of social media platforms to amplify voices and organize campaigns. The #EndSARS movement, which began as a call against police brutality, is a prime example of how social media can galvanize young people to stand up for their rights. By harnessing technology, future activists can reach a wider audience and create a ripple effect of change.

Building Alliances

Collaboration is key in the fight for LGBTQ rights. Alimi's approach emphasizes the importance of building alliances with other social justice movements. By aligning with feminist, anti-racist, and human rights organizations, future activists can create a united front against discrimination. This intersectional approach not only strengthens the movement but also highlights the interconnectedness of various struggles. For example, the collaboration between LGBTQ activists and women's rights groups has led to joint campaigns that address issues affecting both communities.

Emphasizing Mental Health

The mental health of activists is often overlooked in the pursuit of social change. Alimi stresses the importance of self-care and mental well-being for future activists. The emotional toll of activism can be significant, particularly in a hostile environment. Providing resources for mental health support, such as counseling and peer support groups, can help sustain the passion and commitment of young activists. Alimi's own experiences with mental health challenges have made him a vocal advocate for prioritizing mental well-being within the activist community.

Celebrating Achievements

Celebrating the achievements of LGBTQ activists, both big and small, can inspire others to take action. Alimi encourages young activists to recognize their victories, whether it's a successful awareness campaign or a small change in public perception. By highlighting these successes, future activists can maintain motivation and demonstrate that progress is possible. Events such as Pride celebrations and awards ceremonies can serve as platforms for recognizing the contributions of activists and fostering a sense of community.

Conclusion

Inspiring future activists in Nigeria requires a multifaceted approach that encompasses education, community building, and the celebration of achievements. Bisi Alimi's legacy is not just about his individual accomplishments but also about the movement he has inspired. By fostering a new generation of activists who are equipped with knowledge, support, and a sense of purpose, Nigeria can move closer to a future where every individual, regardless of their sexual orientation, can live freely and authentically.

The fight for LGBTQ rights in Nigeria is far from over, but with the right tools and inspiration, the future looks brighter. As Alimi often reminds us, "Change is possible, and it starts with you." This message is what will continue to resonate with and inspire the next wave of activists in Nigeria.

Celebrating LGBTQ Culture and Identity

In the journey toward LGBTQ rights and recognition, celebrating culture and identity plays a pivotal role. It is not merely about the right to exist; it is about thriving and embracing the uniqueness that each individual brings to the tapestry of society. Bisi Alimi has been instrumental in highlighting the importance of cultural celebration as a means of fostering acceptance and understanding within Nigerian society and beyond.

The Importance of Cultural Celebration

Cultural celebration serves as a powerful tool for identity affirmation and community building. According to Judith Butler's theory of gender performativity, identity is not a static trait but rather an ongoing performance influenced by societal norms and expectations. Celebrating LGBTQ culture allows individuals to reclaim their narratives and challenge the dominant heteronormative discourse.

$$I(t) = \sum_{n=1}^{N} P_n(t) \tag{58}$$

Where $I(t)$ represents individual identity at time t, and $P_n(t)$ signifies the various performances and expressions that contribute to one's identity. This equation illustrates that identity is dynamic, shaped by multiple influences over time.

Cultural Expressions in the LGBTQ Community

LGBTQ culture manifests in various forms, including art, music, literature, and fashion. These expressions not only provide a voice to the community but also serve as a means of resistance against oppression. For instance, the vibrant art scene in Lagos has seen the emergence of LGBTQ artists who use their work to convey messages of love, acceptance, and resilience.

One notable example is the work of artist *Jide Alakija*, whose paintings challenge societal norms and celebrate queer identity. His pieces often depict intimate moments between same-sex couples, showcasing love in its many forms. Alakija's work exemplifies how art can serve as a medium for advocacy, fostering dialogue around LGBTQ issues in a conservative society.

Pride Events and Visibility

Pride events are a cornerstone of LGBTQ cultural celebration. They provide a platform for visibility, allowing individuals to express their identities openly and proudly. In Nigeria, where public displays of LGBTQ identity can lead to severe repercussions, the concept of a pride event is both revolutionary and risky.

Despite the challenges, Alimi has been a vocal advocate for pride events in Nigeria. He argues that these gatherings are essential for fostering solidarity and community among LGBTQ individuals. The first pride event held in Nigeria was met with both enthusiasm and backlash, illustrating the complex landscape of LGBTQ activism in the country.

$$S = \frac{V}{R} \tag{59}$$

Where S represents solidarity, V is visibility, and R is risk. This equation highlights the delicate balance that LGBTQ activists must navigate—striving for visibility while managing the risks associated with being open about their identities.

The Role of Literature and Storytelling

Storytelling is another vital aspect of celebrating LGBTQ culture. Literature allows individuals to share their experiences, challenges, and triumphs, fostering empathy and understanding. Alimi's own story, as chronicled in his activism, serves as a beacon of hope for many. His autobiography, *"Bisi Alimi: The Journey to Acceptance"*, not only recounts his struggles but also celebrates the beauty of his identity.

In addition, platforms like *AfroQueer* have emerged, dedicated to amplifying LGBTQ voices from the African continent. By sharing personal narratives and artistic expressions, these platforms challenge stereotypes and promote a more nuanced understanding of LGBTQ identities.

Intersectionality and Cultural Celebration

It is essential to recognize that LGBTQ identities do not exist in a vacuum. The intersectionality of race, gender, and socioeconomic status plays a crucial role in shaping individual experiences. For instance, Black queer individuals often face compounded discrimination, making the celebration of their unique identities even more vital.

Alimi emphasizes the importance of inclusive celebrations that recognize the diversity within the LGBTQ community. Events that highlight the experiences of LGBTQ individuals from various backgrounds foster a sense of belonging and solidarity.

$$D = \sum_{i=1}^{M} E_i \tag{60}$$

Where D represents diversity, and E_i signifies the unique experiences of each individual within the community. This equation underscores the richness that diversity brings to LGBTQ celebrations, enhancing the collective identity.

Challenges to Cultural Celebration

Despite the importance of celebrating LGBTQ culture, significant challenges persist. Homophobia, transphobia, and societal stigma often hinder efforts to create inclusive spaces for celebration. Activists like Alimi face threats and intimidation as they work to promote acceptance and understanding.

Furthermore, the lack of legal protections for LGBTQ individuals in Nigeria poses a significant barrier to cultural expression. Advocacy for anti-discrimination laws is crucial to ensuring that LGBTQ individuals can celebrate their identities without fear of retribution.

Conclusion

Celebrating LGBTQ culture and identity is not just about parades and parties; it is about affirming the existence and dignity of individuals who have long been marginalized. Bisi Alimi's work exemplifies the power of cultural celebration as a means of advocacy, community building, and resistance. By embracing their identities and fostering a culture of acceptance, LGBTQ individuals can pave the way for a more inclusive society.

In the words of Alimi, "When we celebrate our identities, we are not just fighting for ourselves; we are fighting for future generations to live authentically and freely." This sentiment encapsulates the essence of LGBTQ cultural celebration—an act of love, resilience, and hope for a brighter future.

Supporting LGBTQ Businesses and Entrepreneurs

In the landscape of activism, supporting LGBTQ businesses and entrepreneurs is not just an economic endeavor; it is a powerful act of resistance and empowerment. Bisi Alimi understands that fostering a vibrant LGBTQ business community can serve as a catalyst for broader societal change, challenging the status quo and promoting inclusivity within the economic fabric of Nigeria and beyond.

The Importance of Economic Empowerment

Economic empowerment is a fundamental pillar of any social movement. For LGBTQ individuals, financial independence can translate into greater autonomy and security. By supporting LGBTQ-owned businesses, activists can create a network of economic resilience that shields community members from discrimination and marginalization.

$$E = \frac{C}{S} \tag{61}$$

Where:

- E = Economic empowerment,
- C = Community support,
- S = Social stigma.

This equation illustrates that as community support (C) increases, the economic empowerment (E) of LGBTQ individuals can rise, effectively reducing the impact of social stigma (S).

Challenges Faced by LGBTQ Entrepreneurs

Despite the potential for growth, LGBTQ entrepreneurs often face significant barriers, including systemic discrimination, lack of access to funding, and societal stigma. In a conservative society like Nigeria, where homophobia can manifest in both overt and subtle ways, LGBTQ business owners may struggle to secure loans or investments. According to a survey conducted by the International LGBTQ+ Business Alliance, over 60% of LGBTQ entrepreneurs report facing discrimination from financial institutions.

Promoting LGBTQ Entrepreneurship

To combat these challenges, Bisi Alimi advocates for initiatives aimed at promoting LGBTQ entrepreneurship. This includes:

- **Creating Safe Spaces:** Establishing community centers and co-working spaces where LGBTQ entrepreneurs can network, share resources, and collaborate without fear of discrimination.

- **Access to Funding:** Partnering with organizations that provide grants and microloans specifically for LGBTQ businesses, ensuring that entrepreneurs have the financial resources needed to launch and sustain their ventures.

- **Training and Education:** Offering workshops on business management, marketing, and financial literacy tailored to the unique challenges faced by LGBTQ entrepreneurs.

- **Visibility and Advocacy:** Highlighting successful LGBTQ businesses through media campaigns and community events to inspire others and challenge negative stereotypes.

Examples of Successful LGBTQ Businesses

One notable example is *The Queer Cafe*, a popular establishment in Lagos that provides a safe space for LGBTQ individuals to gather, socialize, and express themselves. Founded by a group of young activists, the cafe not only serves delicious food and drinks but also hosts events that promote LGBTQ culture and awareness.

Another inspiring example is *Rainbow Textiles*, a clothing brand that employs LGBTQ individuals and advocates for body positivity and self-expression through fashion. Their tagline, "Wear Your Pride," resonates with many, and their products are a testament to the creativity and resilience of the LGBTQ community.

Building Alliances with Other Businesses

To further support LGBTQ entrepreneurs, forming alliances with non-LGBTQ businesses can be beneficial. By encouraging allyship, businesses can create a more inclusive marketplace. This includes:

- **Cross-Promotions:** Partnering with LGBTQ businesses for joint marketing efforts, which can expand reach and customer base.
- **Training for Non-LGBTQ Businesses:** Providing sensitivity training and workshops to help non-LGBTQ businesses understand the importance of inclusivity and how to support their LGBTQ counterparts.

The Role of Social Media in Promoting LGBTQ Businesses

Social media platforms serve as powerful tools for promoting LGBTQ businesses. Bisi Alimi emphasizes the importance of digital visibility, particularly in a world where many still face challenges in physical spaces. By leveraging social media, LGBTQ entrepreneurs can connect with wider audiences, share their stories, and build supportive communities.

$$V = f(S, R) \tag{62}$$

Where:

- V = Visibility,
- S = Social media engagement,
- R = Reach of LGBTQ narratives.

This equation shows that as social media engagement (S) increases, the visibility (V) of LGBTQ businesses can expand, enhancing the reach of LGBTQ narratives (R).

Conclusion

Supporting LGBTQ businesses and entrepreneurs is a vital component of Bisi Alimi's vision for a more inclusive society. By addressing the challenges faced by LGBTQ entrepreneurs and fostering economic empowerment, activists can create a ripple effect that not only uplifts individuals but also transforms communities. As the movement for LGBTQ rights continues to evolve, the support of LGBTQ businesses will be crucial in shaping a future where diversity is celebrated, and equality is a reality for all.

The Arts as a Tool for Social Change

The arts have long been recognized as a powerful medium for social change, providing a platform for marginalized voices and fostering dialogue on critical societal issues. In the context of LGBTQ activism, the arts serve not only as a means of expression but also as a catalyst for transformation, challenging societal norms and promoting acceptance.

Theoretical Framework

The relationship between art and activism can be understood through various theoretical lenses. One prominent theory is the *Social Change Theory*, which posits that art can influence public perception and inspire action by raising awareness about social injustices. This theory is supported by the *Cultural Studies* approach, which examines how cultural products—such as literature, visual art, and performance—reflect and shape societal values.

Furthermore, the *Critical Pedagogy* framework emphasizes the role of art in education, suggesting that artistic expression can empower individuals to question and challenge oppressive structures. This pedagogical approach aligns with the notion that art is not just a reflection of society but also a tool for its reformation.

Challenges Faced by LGBTQ Artists

Despite the potential of the arts to effect change, LGBTQ artists often encounter significant obstacles. In many conservative societies, including Nigeria, artistic expression is frequently stifled by censorship, societal backlash, and legal repercussions. Artists may face threats to their safety and livelihood when their work challenges heteronormative narratives or addresses LGBTQ issues.

Moreover, funding and support for LGBTQ art initiatives can be limited, as many institutions may shy away from controversial topics. This scarcity of resources can hinder the ability of artists to produce and showcase their work, thereby limiting the impact of their messages.

Examples of Art as Activism

Bisi Alimi has harnessed the power of the arts to advocate for LGBTQ rights in Nigeria and beyond. One notable example is his involvement in the *Queer Nigerian Art Collective*, which aims to provide a platform for LGBTQ artists to express their identities and experiences. This collective not only showcases art but also organizes workshops and discussions, fostering a sense of community and solidarity among LGBTQ individuals.

Visual art has also played a crucial role in raising awareness about LGBTQ issues. For instance, the *Art for Equality* campaign, which features works by LGBTQ artists, highlights the struggles and triumphs of the community. Through powerful imagery and poignant narratives, these artworks challenge stereotypes and promote understanding.

In literature, LGBTQ authors have used storytelling as a means of resistance. Works such as *"The Black Flamingo"* by Dean Atta and *"Queer Nigeria: A Reader"* provide insight into the complexities of LGBTQ identities in Nigeria. These narratives not only validate the experiences of LGBTQ individuals but also educate readers, fostering empathy and acceptance.

The Role of Performance Art

Performance art has emerged as a particularly potent form of activism within the LGBTQ community. Events like the *Pride Parade* and theatrical productions centered on LGBTQ themes create spaces for visibility and celebration. They allow individuals to express their identities in a public forum, challenging societal norms and asserting their right to exist authentically.

One remarkable performance art piece is *"The Vagina Monologues"*, which has been adapted to include LGBTQ perspectives, thereby broadening the conversation around gender and sexuality. Such performances not only entertain but also educate audiences, prompting discussions about consent, identity, and the spectrum of human experience.

Conclusion

The arts are an invaluable tool for social change, particularly in the realm of LGBTQ activism. Through various forms of artistic expression—be it visual art, literature, or performance—activists like Bisi Alimi are able to challenge oppressive narratives, foster community, and inspire action. While obstacles remain, the resilience and creativity of LGBTQ artists continue to pave the way for a more inclusive society, demonstrating that art is not merely a reflection of the world but a powerful force for its transformation.

In the words of Alimi, "Art is a weapon, and I intend to use it to fight for love, acceptance, and equality." This sentiment encapsulates the essence of the relationship between art and activism, highlighting the potential of creative expression to ignite change and promote a more just world.

Shifting Public Perceptions

In the journey towards achieving LGBTQ rights in Nigeria, shifting public perceptions has been a crucial aspect of Bisi Alimi's activism. The prevailing attitudes towards LGBTQ individuals have often been shaped by conservative cultural norms, religious beliefs, and misinformation. To transform these perceptions, a multifaceted approach is necessary, combining education, visibility, and advocacy.

Understanding Public Perception

Public perception can be defined as the collective opinion or attitude held by the general population towards a particular issue or group. In the context of LGBTQ rights in Nigeria, this perception is heavily influenced by historical, cultural, and religious factors. According to the *Theory of Planned Behavior* (Ajzen, 1985), attitudes towards a behavior (in this case, acceptance of LGBTQ individuals) are shaped by beliefs about the outcomes of that behavior, normative beliefs, and perceived behavioral control. This theory highlights the importance of addressing both beliefs and social norms to shift public perception effectively.

Challenges in Changing Perceptions

One of the primary challenges in changing public perceptions is the deeply ingrained stigma associated with being LGBTQ in Nigerian society. This stigma is perpetuated by negative media portrayals, discriminatory laws, and the influence of religious institutions that often condemn homosexuality. According to a report by the *International Lesbian, Gay, Bisexual, Trans and Intersex Association* (ILGA), over 70 countries worldwide still criminalize same-sex relationships, with Nigeria being one of the most notorious examples. The Same-Sex Marriage Prohibition Act of 2014 further entrenched negative views by framing LGBTQ individuals as deviant and threatening to societal values.

Strategies for Shifting Perceptions

Bisi Alimi has employed several strategies to combat these challenges and shift public perceptions:

- **Education and Awareness:** Alimi emphasizes the importance of education in dispelling myths and misconceptions about LGBTQ individuals. By organizing workshops, seminars, and community outreach programs, he aims to inform the public about LGBTQ rights and the realities of LGBTQ lives. For instance, the *LGBTQ Education Initiative* in Nigeria has successfully conducted awareness campaigns in schools and universities, targeting young people who are often more open to change.

- **Visibility and Representation:** Increasing the visibility of LGBTQ individuals in media and public life is crucial for changing perceptions. Alimi has utilized social media platforms to share personal stories and experiences, highlighting the humanity of LGBTQ individuals. This approach aligns with the *Social Identity Theory* (Tajfel & Turner, 1979), which posits that individuals derive part of their identity from the groups to which they belong. By showcasing diverse LGBTQ narratives, Alimi aims to foster empathy and understanding among the general public.

- **Engaging Allies:** Building coalitions with allies from various sectors, including human rights organizations, religious groups, and political leaders, is vital for creating a supportive environment for LGBTQ rights. Alimi has collaborated with notable figures to amplify the message of acceptance and equality. For example, partnerships with international NGOs have helped to bring global attention to the issues faced by LGBTQ individuals in Nigeria, thereby putting pressure on local authorities to reconsider their stance.

- **Art and Culture:** Alimi recognizes the power of art as a tool for social change. Through theater, music, and visual arts, he has encouraged LGBTQ individuals to express their identities and experiences. Events like the *LGBTQ Arts Festival* have provided a platform for artists to showcase their work, challenging stereotypes and promoting acceptance. This cultural approach resonates with the *Cultural Studies Framework*, which emphasizes the role of culture in shaping social values and perceptions.

Examples of Success

One notable example of shifting public perception occurred during the *#EndSARS* protests in 2020, where young Nigerians rallied against police brutality and corruption. Among the protestors were LGBTQ activists who utilized the platform to advocate for their rights. The solidarity displayed during this movement marked a significant moment in Nigerian history, as it showcased a united front against oppression, regardless of sexual orientation.

Furthermore, the increasing presence of LGBTQ individuals in popular culture, such as television shows and films that portray LGBTQ characters positively, has also contributed to changing perceptions. Programs like "*The Real Housewives of Lagos,*" which features openly LGBTQ individuals, have helped normalize LGBTQ identities in mainstream media.

Conclusion

Shifting public perceptions regarding LGBTQ rights in Nigeria is a complex and ongoing process that requires persistent effort and innovative strategies. Through education, visibility, engagement with allies, and the power of culture, Bisi Alimi has made significant strides in challenging stereotypes and fostering acceptance. While there is still much work to be done, the progress achieved thus far serves as a testament to the resilience of the LGBTQ community and the effectiveness of strategic activism. As perceptions continue to evolve, the hope for a more inclusive Nigeria remains alive, driven by the courage and determination of advocates like Bisi Alimi.

$$\text{Public Perception} = f(\text{Education, Visibility, Allies, Culture}) \qquad (63)$$

The Role of Education in Promoting Equality

Education plays a pivotal role in shaping societal norms and values, and when it comes to promoting equality, particularly for marginalized communities such as the LGBTQ+ population, it is an indispensable tool. The importance of education in this context can be understood through various theoretical frameworks, including social justice theory, critical pedagogy, and intersectionality.

Theoretical Frameworks

Social Justice Theory Social justice theory emphasizes the need for equitable access to resources and opportunities. It argues that education should not merely be about academic achievement but should also focus on fostering an understanding of social inequalities and injustices. In the context of LGBTQ+ rights, education can serve as a means to dismantle homophobia and transphobia by providing students with the knowledge and tools to challenge discriminatory practices.

Critical Pedagogy Critical pedagogy, championed by educators like Paulo Freire, advocates for an approach to teaching that encourages critical thinking and the questioning of societal norms. This method empowers students to become active participants in their education, enabling them to confront issues related to identity and equality. By incorporating LGBTQ+ topics into the curriculum, educators can help students understand the historical and contemporary struggles faced by the LGBTQ+ community.

Intersectionality Intersectionality, a concept introduced by Kimberlé Crenshaw, highlights how various forms of discrimination (e.g., race, gender, sexual orientation) intersect and compound experiences of inequality. Education that acknowledges intersectionality can create a more inclusive environment, allowing LGBTQ+ individuals from diverse backgrounds to feel seen and understood.

Challenges in LGBTQ+ Education

Despite the recognized importance of education in promoting equality, several challenges persist:

Curriculum Limitations Many educational systems, particularly in conservative societies, often exclude LGBTQ+ topics from the curriculum. This omission not only perpetuates ignorance but also reinforces harmful stereotypes. For instance, in Nigeria, where LGBTQ+ identities are criminalized, discussing these topics in schools can lead to severe consequences for both educators and students.

Teacher Preparedness Teachers may lack the training or resources to address LGBTQ+ issues effectively. Without proper guidance, educators may inadvertently perpetuate biases or fail to create a safe space for LGBTQ+ students. Professional development programs focusing on LGBTQ+ inclusivity can bridge this gap, equipping teachers with the necessary skills to foster an inclusive classroom environment.

Parental and Community Resistance Resistance from parents and community members can hinder the implementation of LGBTQ+ education. In many cultures, discussing sexual orientation and gender identity is considered taboo, leading to pushback against inclusive curricula. Engaging parents and community leaders in dialogue about the benefits of LGBTQ+ education can help mitigate this resistance.

Examples of Successful LGBTQ+ Education Initiatives

Numerous initiatives around the world illustrate how education can promote equality for LGBTQ+ individuals:

Comprehensive Sex Education Countries like Sweden and Canada have implemented comprehensive sex education programs that include discussions on sexual orientation and gender identity. These programs not only educate students about healthy relationships but also foster acceptance and understanding of LGBTQ+ individuals.

LGBTQ+ Inclusive Curricula In the United States, states like California and New Jersey have mandated the inclusion of LGBTQ+ history and contributions in school curricula. This initiative not only recognizes the achievements of LGBTQ+ individuals but also normalizes their presence in society, contributing to a culture of acceptance.

Safe Schools Programs Initiatives such as the Safe Schools Coalition in Australia aim to create supportive environments for LGBTQ+ students. These programs provide resources for schools to develop policies and practices that promote inclusivity, such as anti-bullying measures and support networks for LGBTQ+ students.

Conclusion

The role of education in promoting equality for LGBTQ+ individuals is multifaceted and essential. By employing theoretical frameworks like social justice theory, critical pedagogy, and intersectionality, education can challenge discriminatory practices and foster a more inclusive society. Despite the challenges that exist, successful initiatives around the world demonstrate that it is possible to create educational environments that promote understanding, acceptance, and equality for all individuals, regardless of their sexual orientation or gender identity.

As Bisi Alimi's activism highlights, the journey towards equality is ongoing, and education remains a powerful ally in this fight.

A Vision for the Future

As we look towards the future, it is essential to envision a world where LGBTQ individuals, particularly in Nigeria and across Africa, can live authentically and without fear of persecution. Bisi Alimi's journey has illuminated the path for many, but the road ahead requires collective effort, innovative strategies, and unwavering commitment.

Theoretical Frameworks for Change

One important theoretical framework that can guide our vision is the **Social Change Theory**. This theory posits that social movements are driven by collective action and the mobilization of communities. For LGBTQ activists, this means fostering solidarity among diverse groups to advocate for legal reforms and social acceptance.

The **Intersectionality Theory**, introduced by Kimberlé Crenshaw, also plays a crucial role in shaping our vision. It emphasizes that individuals experience oppression differently based on their overlapping identities. Thus, future activism must consider the complexities of race, gender, class, and sexuality to create more inclusive strategies that resonate with a broader audience.

Addressing Ongoing Challenges

Despite progress, significant challenges remain. The societal stigma surrounding LGBTQ identities in Nigeria is deeply entrenched, often exacerbated by cultural and religious beliefs. This stigma can manifest in various forms, including discrimination in employment, healthcare, and education. According to a 2018 report by the International Lesbian, Gay, Bisexual, Trans and Intersex Association (ILGA), over 70% of LGBTQ individuals in Nigeria have experienced some form of discrimination.

To combat these issues, education is paramount. Implementing comprehensive LGBTQ-inclusive curricula in schools can foster understanding and acceptance from a young age. This initiative aligns with the **Theory of Planned Behavior**, which suggests that attitudes towards a behavior can influence intentions to engage in that behavior. By cultivating positive attitudes towards LGBTQ individuals, we can gradually shift societal perceptions.

Promoting Legal Reforms

A significant aspect of Alimi's vision is advocating for legal reforms that protect LGBTQ rights. The repeal of the Same-Sex Marriage Prohibition Act (SSMPA) in Nigeria remains a critical goal. Legal frameworks that discriminate against LGBTQ individuals not only perpetuate violence and discrimination but also hinder societal progress.

The **Human Rights-Based Approach** (HRBA) emphasizes that all individuals are entitled to their rights regardless of their sexual orientation or gender identity. By framing LGBTQ rights as human rights, activists can leverage international human rights treaties and conventions to pressure governments into enacting change.

Building Alliances for Change

To realize this vision, building coalitions with diverse groups is essential. Engaging with religious communities, for instance, can help dismantle harmful stereotypes and promote understanding. This approach aligns with the **Collective Impact Model**, which suggests that cross-sector collaboration is necessary for addressing complex social issues. By uniting various stakeholders, including NGOs, faith-based organizations, and community leaders, activists can create a more robust support system for LGBTQ rights.

Harnessing Technology and Social Media

In the digital age, technology plays a pivotal role in advocacy. Social media platforms have become powerful tools for raising awareness and mobilizing support. Bisi Alimi's own use of platforms like Twitter and Instagram has amplified his message and connected him with a global audience.

Future activists should harness the power of technology not only for advocacy but also for education. Online workshops, webinars, and virtual support groups can provide safe spaces for LGBTQ individuals to connect, share experiences, and access resources. The **Digital Divide Theory** highlights the importance of equitable access to technology, ensuring that marginalized communities can participate in these digital spaces.

Inspiring the Next Generation

Ultimately, the vision for the future hinges on inspiring and empowering the next generation of activists. By providing mentorship programs, scholarships, and leadership training, we can cultivate a new wave of advocates equipped to continue the fight for equality.

The **Youth Empowerment Theory** suggests that engaging young people in activism not only fosters personal growth but also strengthens communities. By encouraging youth to take an active role in advocacy, we can ensure that the movement remains dynamic and responsive to emerging challenges.

Conclusion

In conclusion, Bisi Alimi's legacy serves as a beacon of hope for LGBTQ rights in Nigeria and beyond. The vision for the future is one of inclusivity, resilience, and unwavering determination. By embracing theoretical frameworks, addressing ongoing challenges, promoting legal reforms, building alliances, harnessing technology, and inspiring the next generation, we can create a world where everyone, regardless of their sexual orientation or gender identity, can live freely and authentically. The journey is far from over, but with collective action and a shared vision, a brighter future is within reach.

Global Impact and Advocacy Beyond Borders

Mobilizing International Allies

In the quest for LGBTQ rights, the importance of mobilizing international allies cannot be overstated. This process involves not only building networks across borders but also fostering a sense of global solidarity that transcends cultural and political differences. Bisi Alimi's journey exemplifies how strategic alliances can amplify the voices of marginalized communities and bring about tangible change.

Theoretical Framework

The concept of *transnational activism* provides a theoretical framework for understanding how local movements can gain international support. According to [?], transnational advocacy networks (TANs) consist of activists, organizations, and individuals who operate across national boundaries to promote specific issues. The effectiveness of TANs lies in their ability to leverage global platforms to pressure local governments and institutions.

$$\text{TAN Effectiveness} = f(\text{Network Size, Resource Mobilization, Global Norms}) \tag{64}$$

Where: - *Network Size* refers to the number of organizations and individuals involved. - *Resource Mobilization* includes financial, human, and informational resources. - *Global Norms* represent the prevailing international standards concerning human rights and equality.

Challenges in Mobilization

Despite the potential for success, mobilizing international allies comes with its own set of challenges. One of the primary issues is the *divergence of interests* among different countries and organizations. For instance, while some international allies may prioritize immediate legal reforms, others might focus on long-term cultural shifts. This can lead to a fragmented approach that dilutes the effectiveness of advocacy efforts.

Moreover, the *risk of backlash* is a significant concern. Activists in conservative regions, such as Nigeria, often face increased hostility when international support is perceived as foreign interference. This backlash can manifest in various forms, including legal repercussions, social ostracization, and even physical violence.

Case Study: The Role of International NGOs

International non-governmental organizations (NGOs) have played a crucial role in mobilizing support for LGBTQ rights. For example, organizations like Human Rights Watch and Amnesty International have consistently highlighted the plight of LGBTQ individuals in Nigeria, using their platforms to bring global attention to local issues. These NGOs often provide resources, training, and legal assistance to local activists, thereby strengthening their capacity to advocate for change.

A notable instance of this collaboration occurred during the campaign against the Same-Sex Marriage Prohibition Act (SSMPA) in Nigeria. International allies rallied behind Nigerian activists, organizing petitions, social media campaigns, and lobbying efforts directed at Nigerian embassies worldwide. This collective action not only raised awareness but also put pressure on the Nigerian government to reconsider its stance on LGBTQ rights.

Utilizing Social Media for Global Mobilization

In the digital age, social media has emerged as a powerful tool for mobilizing international allies. Platforms like Twitter, Instagram, and Facebook allow activists to share their stories and connect with supporters worldwide. Bisi Alimi effectively utilized social media to raise awareness about LGBTQ issues in Nigeria, garnering international support and solidarity.

For instance, the hashtag #FreeNigeria was launched to draw attention to the oppressive legal environment faced by LGBTQ individuals. This campaign not only reached a global audience but also attracted the attention of public figures and celebrities, further amplifying the message. The ability to create viral content has transformed the landscape of activism, making it easier for local movements to gain international traction.

Building Sustainable Alliances

To ensure the longevity of international support, it is crucial to build sustainable alliances that prioritize mutual respect and understanding. This involves recognizing the unique cultural contexts of different regions and tailoring advocacy strategies accordingly. Engaging in *intersectional activism*—which considers the interconnectedness of various social identities—can enhance the effectiveness of these alliances.

$$\text{Sustainable Alliance} = \text{Cultural Sensitivity} + \text{Shared Goals} + \text{Long-term Commitment} \tag{65}$$

Where: - *Cultural Sensitivity* refers to the awareness and respect for local customs and beliefs. - *Shared Goals* are the common objectives that unite different organizations and movements. - *Long-term Commitment* emphasizes the need for ongoing support rather than one-time interventions.

Conclusion

In conclusion, mobilizing international allies is a critical component of the LGBTQ rights movement. By leveraging transnational networks, utilizing social media, and fostering sustainable alliances, activists like Bisi Alimi can amplify their impact and drive meaningful change. The journey toward equality is not confined to national borders; it is a collective struggle that requires the support of a global community united in the fight for justice and human rights.

Collaboration with Global LGBTQ Activists

The fight for LGBTQ rights is not confined to the borders of any one nation; it is a global struggle that transcends cultures, languages, and legal frameworks. Bisi Alimi's activism exemplifies the power of collaboration among LGBTQ activists worldwide, illustrating how shared experiences and goals can lead to significant advances in human rights.

The Importance of Global Solidarity

Global solidarity among LGBTQ activists is crucial for several reasons. First, it fosters a sense of community and shared purpose. Activists from different countries can exchange strategies, share successes, and learn from each other's challenges. This collaborative approach is essential in combating the pervasive issues of homophobia and transphobia that exist in many societies.

For instance, the work of organizations like ILGA (International Lesbian, Gay, Bisexual, Trans and Intersex Association) has been pivotal in connecting activists across continents. By providing a platform for dialogue and resource sharing, ILGA empowers local activists to amplify their voices on a global stage. This is particularly important in regions where LGBTQ rights are severely restricted.

Challenges in Collaboration

Despite the benefits of collaboration, there are significant challenges that activists face. One prominent issue is the disparity in resources and support available to LGBTQ activists in different countries. Activists in wealthier nations often have access to funding, training, and legal support that their counterparts in developing countries lack. This inequality can create a power dynamic where the voices of activists from less resourced nations are marginalized in global discussions.

Moreover, cultural differences can also pose challenges. Activists must navigate varying attitudes toward LGBTQ identities and rights, which can complicate collaboration efforts. For example, while some activists may push for immediate legal reforms, others may prioritize grassroots education and awareness campaigns to shift societal attitudes before advocating for policy changes.

Examples of Successful Collaboration

One notable example of successful collaboration is the partnership between Bisi Alimi and international organizations such as OutRight Action International. This partnership has allowed for the sharing of resources and the amplification of Nigerian LGBTQ voices on international platforms. Bisi's participation in global conferences has not only raised awareness about the struggles faced by LGBTQ individuals in Nigeria but has also facilitated the exchange of strategies for advocacy.

Additionally, initiatives like the "Global Equality Fund" showcase how international cooperation can lead to tangible results. This fund supports LGBTQ activists in countries where they face persecution, providing them with the necessary resources to continue their work. By pooling resources and expertise, activists can create a more unified front against oppression.

The Role of Social Media

In today's digital age, social media has revolutionized the way activists collaborate and communicate. Platforms like Twitter, Facebook, and Instagram allow for real-time sharing of information, mobilization of support, and creation of global campaigns. Bisi Alimi has effectively utilized social media to connect with activists worldwide, share his experiences, and rally support for LGBTQ rights in Nigeria.

For example, the hashtag campaigns such as #LoveIsLove and #Pride2023 have united activists globally, allowing them to share their stories and advocate for change collectively. These digital movements create a sense of belonging and solidarity among LGBTQ individuals, transcending geographical boundaries.

Future Directions

Looking ahead, the collaboration among global LGBTQ activists must continue to evolve. There is a pressing need for more inclusive approaches that recognize and respect the diverse experiences of LGBTQ individuals worldwide. This includes prioritizing the voices of marginalized communities within the LGBTQ spectrum, such as people of color, transgender individuals, and those from lower socio-economic backgrounds.

Furthermore, fostering intergenerational collaboration can enrich the movement, as younger activists bring fresh perspectives and innovative strategies to the table. Engaging in mentorship programs can bridge the gap between seasoned activists and newcomers, ensuring the continuity of the fight for equality.

In conclusion, the collaboration among global LGBTQ activists is not only vital for the advancement of rights but also for building a more inclusive and understanding world. Bisi Alimi's work serves as a powerful reminder that when activists unite across borders, they can challenge oppressive systems and pave the way for a brighter future for all LGBTQ individuals.

$$\text{Global Collaboration} = \text{Shared Resources} + \text{Cultural Understanding} + \text{Collective Action} \tag{66}$$

Engaging with International Institutions

Bisi Alimi's activism extends beyond the borders of Nigeria, as he has strategically engaged with international institutions to further the cause of LGBTQ rights. This engagement is not merely about visibility; it is rooted in a theoretical framework that emphasizes the importance of global solidarity and the interdependence of human rights.

Theoretical Framework

The engagement with international institutions can be analyzed through the lens of *Global Governance Theory*, which posits that global issues require cooperative solutions that transcend national boundaries. In the context of LGBTQ rights, this means that local struggles are part of a larger, interconnected fight for human rights. By collaborating with international organizations such as the United Nations (UN) and various non-governmental organizations (NGOs), activists like Alimi can leverage global platforms to amplify their voices and advocate for change.

Problems Faced

Despite the potential benefits of engaging with international institutions, several challenges arise:

- **Cultural Resistance:** Many international institutions operate within a framework that may not fully understand or respect the cultural nuances of LGBTQ issues in Africa. This can lead to misinterpretations of the challenges faced by activists on the ground.

- **Bureaucratic Barriers:** The processes involved in engaging with international institutions can be cumbersome and slow. Activists often face lengthy application processes for funding or support, which can stifle immediate action.

- **Political Backlash:** Engaging with international institutions can provoke backlash from local governments, who may view such actions as foreign interference. This can lead to increased risks for activists and their communities.

Examples of Engagement

Bisi Alimi's approach to engaging with international institutions has included:

- **United Nations Human Rights Council:** Alimi has participated in sessions at the UN Human Rights Council, where he has advocated for the inclusion of LGBTQ rights in discussions about human rights. His testimony has highlighted the plight of LGBTQ individuals in Nigeria and called for international pressure on the Nigerian government to uphold human rights standards.

- **Collaboration with NGOs:** By partnering with organizations such as Human Rights Watch and Amnesty International, Alimi has been able to create reports and campaigns that draw attention to human rights abuses against LGBTQ individuals in Nigeria. These collaborations have resulted in significant media coverage and have pressured international bodies to take a stand.

- **Global Pride Events:** Alimi has also engaged in global pride events, where he has shared his experiences and the realities faced by LGBTQ individuals in Nigeria. These platforms provide an opportunity for cross-cultural dialogue and solidarity among activists worldwide.

Impact of Engagement

The impact of engaging with international institutions is multifaceted:

- **Increased Visibility:** Alimi's work has brought international attention to the struggles of LGBTQ individuals in Nigeria, challenging stereotypes and misconceptions that often permeate global narratives.

- **Policy Influence:** Through advocacy efforts, there has been a gradual shift in how international bodies address LGBTQ rights in Africa. Alimi's engagements have contributed to the inclusion of LGBTQ issues in broader human rights discussions, influencing policies at the international level.

- **Empowerment of Local Activists:** By creating networks and connections with international activists, Alimi has empowered local LGBTQ advocates in Nigeria, providing them with resources, knowledge, and moral support to continue their work despite the challenges they face.

Conclusion

Engaging with international institutions is a critical aspect of Bisi Alimi's activism. It not only enhances the visibility of LGBTQ issues in Nigeria but also fosters a global movement for equality and justice. Despite the challenges, the strategic use of international platforms has proven to be an effective tool for advocacy, enabling activists to challenge oppressive systems and inspire change. Alimi's legacy will undoubtedly continue to influence the discourse on LGBTQ rights, both within Nigeria and on the global stage.

Addressing Global Human Rights Issues

In the grand theatre of global activism, addressing human rights issues, particularly those affecting LGBTQ individuals, is akin to being a director of a blockbuster film—every scene matters, and every actor has a role to play. Bisi Alimi, a fearless advocate, has taken center stage, not just in Nigeria but on the international front, where the stakes are high, and the audience is watching closely.

Theoretical Frameworks

To understand the complexities of human rights issues, one must first grasp the theoretical frameworks that underpin them. The Universal Declaration of Human Rights (UDHR) serves as a foundation, asserting that all human beings are entitled to rights and freedoms without discrimination. This document is not just a piece of paper; it is a beacon of hope for activists worldwide. Alimi's approach is deeply rooted in this framework, advocating for the inherent dignity and worth of every individual, regardless of their sexual orientation or gender identity.

One relevant theory is the *Intersectionality Theory*, coined by Kimberlé Crenshaw. This theory posits that individuals experience overlapping and interdependent systems of discrimination or disadvantage. In Alimi's activism, intersectionality plays a crucial role as he highlights how factors such as race, religion, and socio-economic status intersect with sexual orientation to create unique challenges for LGBTQ individuals, particularly in conservative societies like Nigeria.

Identifying Global Human Rights Problems

The global landscape of human rights issues is fraught with challenges. From systemic discrimination to outright violence, LGBTQ individuals face a myriad of problems. In many countries, laws criminalizing homosexuality lead to harassment, imprisonment, and even death. According to a report by the International Lesbian, Gay, Bisexual, Trans and Intersex Association (ILGA), over 70 countries still have laws that criminalize same-sex relationships, creating a hostile environment for LGBTQ individuals.

Alimi has been vocal about these issues, using his platform to shed light on the plight of LGBTQ individuals in regions where their rights are systematically violated. For instance, in countries like Uganda and Nigeria, anti-LGBTQ laws are not just legislative measures; they are tools of oppression that perpetuate violence and discrimination. Alimi's advocacy highlights these injustices, urging the international community to take a stand.

Examples of Activism

One notable example of addressing global human rights issues is Alimi's participation in the United Nations Human Rights Council sessions. Here, he has spoken passionately about the need for global action against homophobia and transphobia. His speeches resonate with urgency, as he calls for the adoption of binding international laws that protect LGBTQ rights. Alimi argues that without such measures, the cycle of discrimination and violence will continue unabated.

In addition to his work at the UN, Alimi has collaborated with various international organizations, such as Human Rights Watch and Amnesty International, to document human rights abuses against LGBTQ individuals. These partnerships have resulted in impactful reports that not only raise awareness but also pressure governments to enact reforms. For example, the report titled *"They Are Killing Us"* highlighted the violence faced by LGBTQ individuals in Nigeria and called for immediate action from the Nigerian government.

Challenges in Advocacy

Despite the progress made, challenges persist in the fight for LGBTQ rights on a global scale. One significant barrier is the backlash from conservative governments and religious institutions. In many cases, advocacy efforts are met with hostility, leading to increased violence against LGBTQ individuals. Alimi has faced threats and intimidation for his outspoken stance, illustrating the personal risks involved in this line of work.

Moreover, the intersection of culture and politics complicates advocacy efforts. In regions where traditional values dominate, discussing LGBTQ rights can be taboo. Alimi navigates these cultural sensitivities with care, employing strategies that promote dialogue and understanding rather than confrontation. By engaging with community leaders and utilizing local narratives, he fosters a more inclusive environment for discussions on human rights.

The Role of Global Solidarity

Global solidarity is essential in addressing human rights issues. Alimi emphasizes the importance of building coalitions across borders, uniting activists from various backgrounds to amplify their voices. The #*GlobalGaze* campaign, initiated by Alimi, serves as a prime example of this solidarity. It encourages LGBTQ individuals to share their stories, creating a tapestry of experiences that highlight the need for change.

In addition, social media plays a pivotal role in mobilizing support. Platforms like Twitter and Instagram have become powerful tools for activists to share information, raise awareness, and connect with allies worldwide. Alimi has adeptly harnessed these platforms, using them to challenge narratives and advocate for LGBTQ rights on a global scale.

Conclusion

Addressing global human rights issues requires a multifaceted approach, one that combines theoretical frameworks, grassroots activism, and international cooperation. Bisi Alimi's work exemplifies this approach, as he tirelessly advocates for the rights of LGBTQ individuals both in Nigeria and beyond. By confronting systemic discrimination and fostering global solidarity, Alimi not only addresses pressing human rights issues but also paves the way for a more inclusive and equitable future for all.

In the end, the battle for LGBTQ rights is not just a fight for one group; it is a fight for humanity, dignity, and the fundamental belief that everyone deserves to live freely and authentically. As Alimi continues to challenge the status quo, his legacy will undoubtedly inspire future generations to carry the torch of activism forward.

Amplifying Voices from Marginalized Communities

In the realm of LGBTQ activism, amplifying the voices of marginalized communities is not just a noble endeavor; it is a fundamental necessity. Bisi Alimi has consistently emphasized the importance of inclusivity within the LGBTQ movement, recognizing that the struggles faced by individuals in these communities are often compounded by intersecting identities such as race, gender, class, and disability.

Theoretical Framework

The theory of intersectionality, coined by Kimberlé Crenshaw, provides a critical lens through which to understand the complexities of identity and oppression. Intersectionality posits that individuals experience discrimination not through a single axis of identity but through multiple, overlapping identities. This theory is essential for activists like Alimi, who seek to ensure that the voices of those who are often sidelined—such as queer people of color, transgender individuals, and those from economically disadvantaged backgrounds—are heard and valued.

Challenges Faced by Marginalized Voices

Despite the urgency of amplifying these voices, numerous challenges persist:

- **Systemic Discrimination:** Marginalized communities often face systemic barriers that prevent them from participating fully in societal discourse. This includes economic disparities, lack of access to education, and limited representation in media and politics.

- **Cultural Stigma:** In many cultures, LGBTQ identities are stigmatized, leading to a silencing of voices. This stigma can be exacerbated by cultural norms that prioritize heteronormativity and traditional gender roles.

- **Internalized Oppression:** Members of marginalized communities may internalize negative societal messages about their identities, leading to self-doubt and reluctance to speak out.

Strategies for Amplification

To effectively amplify the voices of marginalized communities, Bisi Alimi and other activists employ several strategies:

1. **Creating Safe Spaces:** Establishing environments where individuals can express themselves without fear of judgment or retribution is crucial. This can be achieved through community centers, support groups, and online forums that prioritize inclusivity and understanding.

2. **Utilizing Social Media:** Platforms like Twitter, Instagram, and Facebook have become powerful tools for activism. Alimi has adeptly used these platforms to elevate marginalized voices, share personal stories, and engage in dialogue. The hashtag movement, such as #BlackLivesMatter and

#TransRightsAreHumanRights, serves as a testament to the power of social media in mobilizing support and raising awareness.

3. **Collaborating with Grassroots Organizations:** Partnering with local organizations that focus on marginalized communities allows for a more nuanced understanding of their specific needs and challenges. For instance, working with organizations that support LGBTQ refugees can help amplify the voices of those fleeing persecution.

4. **Storytelling as a Tool for Change:** Personal narratives are powerful in humanizing issues and fostering empathy. Bisi Alimi encourages individuals from marginalized communities to share their stories through various mediums, including blogs, podcasts, and public speaking engagements. This not only empowers individuals but also educates the broader public on the realities faced by these communities.

Examples of Successful Amplification

Several examples illustrate the effectiveness of amplifying marginalized voices:

- **The Stonewall Riots:** The Stonewall Riots of 1969 were a pivotal moment in LGBTQ history, largely driven by marginalized individuals, including transgender women of color like Marsha P. Johnson and Sylvia Rivera. Their stories and struggles continue to inspire contemporary activism.

- **The #SayHerName Campaign:** This movement highlights the stories of Black women who have been victims of police violence, ensuring that their experiences are not overshadowed by more widely publicized cases. By amplifying these voices, the campaign fosters a more inclusive dialogue around racial and gender justice.

- **Transgender Visibility:** The increasing visibility of transgender individuals in media and politics, such as the election of openly transgender officials like Danica Roem, showcases the importance of representation. Their presence challenges stereotypes and encourages acceptance within society.

Conclusion

Amplifying the voices of marginalized communities is essential for a truly inclusive LGBTQ movement. Bisi Alimi's commitment to this cause exemplifies how intersectionality can guide activism and foster a more equitable society. As activists continue to challenge systemic barriers and cultural stigma, the stories and experiences of those from marginalized backgrounds will be pivotal in shaping the future of LGBTQ rights and advocacy.

In summary, the journey toward inclusivity is ongoing, and the responsibility lies with all of us to ensure that every voice is heard, valued, and empowered. The fight for equality is not just about LGBTQ rights; it is about human rights for all, regardless of identity or circumstance.

The Value of Intersectionality in Activism

Intersectionality is a critical framework for understanding how various forms of discrimination and privilege overlap and interact. Coined by legal scholar Kimberlé Crenshaw in the late 1980s, intersectionality posits that individuals experience oppression in varying configurations and degrees of intensity based on their multiple identities, such as race, gender, sexual orientation, socioeconomic status, and more. In the realm of LGBTQ activism, intersectionality serves as a vital lens for analyzing and addressing the complexities of systemic inequality.

Theoretical Foundations

The theoretical underpinnings of intersectionality are rooted in the acknowledgment that social categorizations are interconnected and cannot be examined in isolation. Crenshaw emphasized that traditional feminist and anti-racist discourses often fail to account for the unique experiences of women of color, leading to a more nuanced understanding of their struggles. This perspective is crucial for LGBTQ activists, as it allows for a comprehensive view of how various identities impact individuals' experiences within the community.

Mathematically, we can express the concept of intersectionality as follows:

$$I = f(R, G, S, E, C) \tag{67}$$

Where: - I represents the level of intersectional identity, - R is race, - G is gender, - S is sexual orientation, - E is economic status, and - C is cultural background.

This function illustrates that the intersectional identity I is a product of multiple variables, each contributing to the overall experience of oppression or privilege.

Challenges in Intersectional Activism

Despite its importance, implementing an intersectional approach in activism presents several challenges. One significant issue is the tendency for movements to prioritize certain identities over others, often sidelining marginalized voices within the LGBTQ community itself. For instance, the experiences of Black transgender individuals may be overlooked in favor of more mainstream narratives that focus primarily on cisgender white LGBTQ individuals. This oversight can perpetuate existing inequalities and hinder the overall effectiveness of advocacy efforts.

Moreover, intersectionality can complicate coalition-building among different activist groups. When various movements—such as those focused on racial justice, gender equality, and LGBTQ rights—attempt to collaborate, differing priorities and perspectives can lead to tension and misunderstandings. Activists must navigate these complexities to foster inclusive environments that honor the diverse experiences of all individuals.

Examples of Intersectional Activism

One prominent example of intersectional activism within the LGBTQ community is the work of organizations like the *Black LGBTQ+ Migrant Project*, which focuses on the unique challenges faced by Black LGBTQ migrants. This organization highlights the intersections of race, sexuality, and immigration status, advocating for policies that address the specific needs of this demographic. Their initiatives include providing legal support, mental health resources, and community-building activities that foster a sense of belonging among marginalized individuals.

Another noteworthy example is the *Transgender Law Center*, which emphasizes the importance of intersectionality in its advocacy efforts. By recognizing that transgender individuals experience discrimination differently based on their race, socioeconomic status, and other factors, the organization tailors its programs to address the needs of diverse communities. Their work includes lobbying for inclusive healthcare policies, anti-discrimination laws, and support for transgender youth, showcasing the power of intersectional advocacy in effecting change.

The Role of Education and Awareness

Education plays a pivotal role in promoting intersectionality within activism. By raising awareness about the complexities of identity and the interconnected nature of oppression, activists can foster a more inclusive environment. Workshops, seminars, and community discussions can help individuals understand the importance of considering multiple identities in their advocacy work.

Furthermore, intersectional education encourages individuals to engage in self-reflection and examine their privileges. For instance, a white cisgender

LGBTQ activist may recognize their privilege in relation to their Black transgender peers, prompting them to amplify marginalized voices and support initiatives that address systemic inequalities.

Conclusion

In conclusion, the value of intersectionality in activism cannot be overstated. By embracing an intersectional framework, LGBTQ activists can better understand and address the multifaceted nature of oppression. This approach not only enhances the effectiveness of advocacy efforts but also fosters a more inclusive and equitable movement. As Bisi Alimi's work demonstrates, recognizing and addressing the intersections of identity is essential for creating a more just society for all individuals, regardless of their background. By continuing to champion intersectionality, activists can inspire a new generation to engage in the ongoing struggle for equality and justice.

Spotlight on LGBTQ Rights in Conservative Countries

In conservative countries around the world, LGBTQ rights often face significant challenges due to deeply entrenched cultural, religious, and political beliefs. These environments create a complex landscape where individuals must navigate a myriad of obstacles in their quest for acceptance and equality. This section explores the theoretical frameworks that underpin the struggles faced by LGBTQ communities in these regions, the specific problems they encounter, and examples of activism and resistance.

Theoretical Frameworks

Understanding the dynamics of LGBTQ rights in conservative countries requires an interdisciplinary approach that includes sociology, political science, and human rights theory. One useful framework is the **Social Identity Theory**, which posits that individuals derive a sense of self from their group memberships. In conservative societies, where traditional gender roles and heteronormativity are often upheld, LGBTQ individuals may experience a profound identity conflict. This conflict can lead to internalized homophobia, where individuals internalize societal stigma, resulting in negative self-perception and mental health issues.

Another relevant framework is **Intersectionality**, which examines how various social identities (such as race, gender, and class) intersect to create unique experiences of oppression. In conservative contexts, LGBTQ individuals who also belong to marginalized racial or economic groups may face compounded discrimination, making their struggle for rights even more complex.

Problems Faced by LGBTQ Communities

The problems faced by LGBTQ individuals in conservative countries can be categorized into several key areas:

- **Legal Discrimination:** Many conservative nations have laws that criminalize same-sex relationships, impose harsh penalties, or lack legal protections against discrimination. For instance, in countries like Uganda and Nigeria, anti-homosexuality laws not only criminalize LGBTQ identities but also foster an environment of fear and violence.

- **Social Stigma:** Societal attitudes towards LGBTQ individuals are often marked by prejudice and hostility. This stigma can manifest in various forms, including familial rejection, social ostracism, and violence. In many cases, LGBTQ individuals are forced to hide their identities to avoid persecution, leading to a lack of visibility and representation.

- **Violence and Persecution:** In conservative countries, LGBTQ individuals are at a heightened risk of violence, including hate crimes and state-sanctioned persecution. Reports from organizations like Human Rights Watch and Amnesty International document numerous instances of violence against LGBTQ individuals, often with impunity for the perpetrators.

- **Limited Access to Support Services:** Many LGBTQ individuals in conservative countries face barriers to accessing essential services, including healthcare, legal aid, and mental health support. This lack of access exacerbates the challenges they face, particularly in contexts where conversion therapy and other harmful practices are promoted.

Examples of Activism and Resistance

Despite these challenges, LGBTQ activists in conservative countries have made significant strides in advocating for their rights. For example:

- **Uganda's LGBTQ Activism:** In Uganda, where the anti-homosexuality law has created a hostile environment, activists have employed creative strategies to raise awareness and foster solidarity. Organizations like Sexual Minorities

Uganda (SMUG) have worked tirelessly to document human rights abuses and engage in international advocacy, leveraging global support to challenge local repression.

- **Nigeria's Emerging Voices:** In Nigeria, activists like Bisi Alimi have utilized social media to amplify their voices and connect with the global LGBTQ community. By sharing personal stories and experiences, they challenge stereotypes and promote understanding, while also mobilizing support for legal reforms.

- **Global Solidarity Movements:** International organizations, such as ILGA (International Lesbian, Gay, Bisexual, Trans and Intersex Association), have played a crucial role in supporting LGBTQ rights in conservative countries. By providing resources, training, and platforms for advocacy, they empower local activists to challenge oppressive systems and build coalitions.

Conclusion

The spotlight on LGBTQ rights in conservative countries reveals a complex interplay of cultural, legal, and social challenges. However, through the lens of Social Identity Theory and Intersectionality, we can better understand the unique struggles faced by LGBTQ individuals in these contexts. The resilience and creativity of activists demonstrate that, even in the face of adversity, the fight for equality continues. By fostering global solidarity and amplifying marginalized voices, we can work towards a more inclusive future for LGBTQ communities worldwide.

$$\text{Visibility} + \text{Advocacy} = \text{Change} \tag{68}$$

This equation encapsulates the essence of activism in conservative countries, where increasing visibility and persistent advocacy can lead to meaningful change in societal attitudes and legal frameworks.

Inspiring Activists Around the World

In the realm of LGBTQ activism, the journey of Bisi Alimi serves as a beacon of hope and inspiration for activists across the globe. His story transcends borders and speaks to the universal struggle for equality, acceptance, and human rights. In this section, we will explore how Alimi's activism has inspired others, the theoretical frameworks that underpin his work, the challenges faced by activists in various contexts, and the examples of movements that have drawn strength from his legacy.

Theoretical Frameworks in Activism

Activism is often grounded in various theoretical frameworks that help define the goals and methods of social movements. One relevant theory is the *Social Movement Theory*, which posits that collective action arises from shared grievances and the desire for social change. This theory can be applied to understand how Alimi's experiences of discrimination and marginalization in Nigeria galvanized him to advocate for LGBTQ rights.

Another important framework is *Intersectionality*, a term coined by Kimberlé Crenshaw. This concept highlights how different forms of discrimination—such as those based on race, gender, and sexual orientation—intersect and create unique experiences of oppression. Alimi's activism embodies intersectionality as he often addresses the compounded effects of homophobia and societal stigma in a conservative context, inspiring activists to consider multiple identities in their advocacy.

Challenges Faced by Activists

Despite the progress made in some regions, LGBTQ activists around the world still face significant challenges. In many conservative countries, laws against homosexuality remain stringent, and societal acceptance is often minimal. Activists risk imprisonment, violence, and social ostracism. For instance, in countries like Uganda and Nigeria, anti-LGBTQ legislation is not just a legal hurdle but a societal norm that perpetuates discrimination.

Moreover, the backlash from religious institutions can further complicate the activism landscape. Many activists encounter resistance from groups that view LGBTQ rights as contrary to their beliefs. Alimi's approach to engaging with religious communities illustrates a pathway for activists to navigate these complex dynamics, emphasizing dialogue and understanding over confrontation.

Global Examples of Inspired Activism

Bisi Alimi's influence is evident in various global movements that have sought to challenge oppressive systems and promote LGBTQ rights. For instance, the *#FreeTheNipple* campaign, which advocates for gender equality and body positivity, draws parallels to Alimi's fight for visibility and acceptance. Activists involved in this campaign often cite the importance of challenging societal norms, much like Alimi did in Nigeria.

In South Africa, the *LGBTQ Rights Movement* has gained momentum, with activists drawing inspiration from Alimi's work. The country, which has one of the most progressive constitutions regarding LGBTQ rights, still grapples with violence against LGBTQ individuals. Activists like Bisi Alimi have provided a framework for addressing these issues through public awareness campaigns and legal advocacy.

Furthermore, the *Global Fund for Women* has highlighted the importance of amplifying voices from marginalized communities. They recognize that the fight for LGBTQ rights is intertwined with broader human rights issues, and Alimi's work exemplifies this interconnectedness. By sharing resources and strategies, organizations can empower activists worldwide to push for change in their respective contexts.

The Role of Social Media in Activism

In the digital age, social media has become a powerful tool for activists. Bisi Alimi has effectively utilized platforms like Twitter and Instagram to raise awareness about LGBTQ issues, share personal stories, and mobilize support. His online presence not only amplifies his message but also inspires a new generation of activists to harness the power of social media for advocacy.

The *Arab Spring* is a prime example of how social media can facilitate activism. Activists in the Middle East leveraged platforms like Facebook and Twitter to organize protests and share information, demonstrating that technology can be a game-changer in the fight for rights. Similarly, Alimi's use of social media has created a global network of support, allowing activists to connect, share strategies, and celebrate victories.

Conclusion

Bisi Alimi's legacy is a testament to the power of one individual's voice in inspiring change across the globe. By addressing the theoretical underpinnings of activism, recognizing the challenges faced by LGBTQ individuals, and showcasing examples of inspired activism, we can appreciate the profound impact of Alimi's work. His journey encourages activists everywhere to remain resilient, to challenge oppressive systems, and to foster solidarity across borders. As we move forward, it is crucial to continue amplifying marginalized voices and to build a more inclusive world for all.

$$\text{Activism Impact} = \text{Visibility} + \text{Solidarity} + \text{Engagement} \tag{69}$$

In this equation, the impact of activism is a function of visibility, solidarity among activists, and engagement with the community. Bisi Alimi embodies this equation, serving as a model for those who seek to inspire change and challenge the status quo. The journey is ongoing, and with each step forward, activists around the world are reminded that they are not alone in their struggle for justice and equality.

Index

-doubt, 70

ability, 6, 25, 26, 54, 61, 67, 76, 88, 128, 147, 150, 185, 188, 200, 218
abomination, 9
absence, 206
abuse, 60
acceptance, 1–6, 8–10, 13, 18–22, 24, 26, 36, 41, 43, 48–51, 64, 70, 72, 73, 75, 90–92, 123, 127, 129, 132, 136, 139, 148, 151, 154–157, 161–166, 169–175, 180, 182, 186, 189, 192, 195, 196, 200–202, 204, 207, 211–214, 217, 221, 240, 242, 243
access, 55, 65, 89, 90, 100, 111, 137, 139, 144, 189, 200, 204, 208, 229
accessibility, 88, 89
account, 238
accountability, 62, 91, 95, 112, 187–189
achievement, 195
acknowledgment, 238

act, 11, 18–20, 85, 92, 102–104, 156, 199, 209, 214
action, 26, 31, 39, 57, 65, 72, 75, 76, 88, 90, 98, 102, 117, 183, 202, 210, 234
activism, 2–6, 8–18, 20, 21, 24–26, 29–31, 33, 35, 36, 38–41, 43, 49, 51, 52, 54–62, 64–67, 70, 72, 77, 79, 84–86, 88–92, 95, 98, 100, 104, 105, 107, 110, 113, 115, 117, 118, 127, 132, 141, 146–148, 151–154, 161–164, 166–168, 171, 172, 175, 182, 185–187, 196–199, 201, 202, 209, 210, 212, 214, 217, 219, 221, 228, 231, 232, 235, 237–240, 242–244
activist, 9, 11, 13, 25, 26, 30, 33, 51, 52, 57–59, 72, 75, 76, 84, 85, 161, 210, 240
addition, 11, 49, 91, 155, 201, 235
address, 50, 62, 89, 138, 162, 168, 174, 177, 206, 210, 240
adherence, 9
adoption, 234
advancement, 86, 189, 190, 209, 230

advantage, 177
adversity, 3, 14, 16, 18, 26, 29, 31, 56, 57, 90, 110, 132, 162, 242
advice, 59
advocacy, 2, 5, 6, 8, 10, 12, 14, 15, 17, 20, 21, 23, 27, 29, 32, 33, 36, 43, 45, 46, 55–59, 61, 64, 65, 68, 69, 75–77, 79–81, 83, 85, 88, 89, 91, 92, 95, 99, 101, 102, 105, 109, 111, 116–120, 122–124, 127, 133, 134, 139–141, 156, 160–163, 166–168, 170, 171, 176, 177, 181, 188–193, 195, 197–202, 204, 207, 209, 214, 219, 229, 233, 234, 238–240, 242, 244
advocate, 2–4, 9–11, 14–16, 18, 20, 29, 30, 42, 43, 53, 57, 60, 62, 66, 70, 82, 84, 90–92, 98, 101, 104, 112, 115, 123, 127, 139, 141, 148, 154, 155, 158, 174, 182, 185, 189, 200, 210, 212, 235
affection, 123
affirmation, 4, 18, 64, 211
affront, 76
Africa, 82–84, 175, 180, 181, 184–187, 189, 192–194, 196–198
age, 50, 59, 65, 79, 86, 95, 124, 129, 157, 174, 176, 182, 197, 227, 244
agenda, 68, 85, 103
aid, 83, 186
alienation, 161, 169

Alimi, 25, 26, 35, 42, 45, 46, 48–50, 52, 56, 57, 61, 63–66, 69–71, 73, 75, 77, 79, 95, 98–102, 105, 106, 108–112, 115, 148, 153, 157, 158, 161–164, 166, 170, 199–202, 210, 212, 234, 235, 243
alliance, 33, 115
ally, 88
allyship, 12, 75, 92, 216
amplification, 92, 94, 229
Amsterdam, 37
Angola, 196
anonymity, 89, 129
anti, 33, 36, 42–45, 64, 65, 79, 80, 83, 101, 104, 155, 183, 185, 193, 199, 200, 206, 208, 210, 213, 238, 243
anxiety, 19, 28, 100, 123
appearance, 42
apprehension, 12
approach, 13, 35, 45, 48, 49, 57, 58, 62, 65, 71, 97, 105, 113, 120, 123, 145, 154, 162–164, 168, 172, 188, 197, 198, 207, 210, 219, 231, 238, 240, 243
area, 156, 187
array, 185
arrest, 106, 111
art, 2, 17, 101, 131, 146–148, 151, 195, 201, 212, 217
aspect, 1, 31, 50, 67, 115, 124, 125, 141, 148, 150, 154, 165, 177, 189, 219, 232
aspiration, 182
assistance, 60, 89, 99, 100, 111, 128, 132–134, 168

atmosphere, 12
attention, 28, 33, 40, 61, 63, 67, 76, 77, 79, 80, 99, 104, 105, 115, 118, 124, 181, 199
audience, 63–65, 76, 85, 95, 118, 124, 131, 176, 200
authenticity, 3–5, 17, 18, 21, 92, 172
authority, 11, 155
automation, 59
autonomy, 214
avenue, 106
awakening, 11
awareness, 3, 5, 12, 14, 32, 33, 38, 45, 53, 54, 56, 61, 64–66, 69, 70, 86, 88, 90, 95, 97, 100, 102, 104–106, 109, 113, 115, 123, 124, 131, 135, 136, 182, 186, 194–197, 200, 206, 227, 229, 235, 239, 244

backdrop, 4, 122
background, 167, 168, 240
backing, 99, 127, 206
backlash, 3, 5, 6, 11, 17, 20, 37, 39, 46, 54–56, 62–66, 68, 76, 90, 116, 119, 120, 124, 155, 162, 164–166, 169, 183, 188, 193, 195, 212, 217, 234, 243
balance, 25, 103, 128, 200
barrier, 89, 161, 164, 183, 213, 234
base, 112, 206
battle, 120, 235
battleground, 136
beacon, 18, 21, 31, 41, 48, 52, 62, 102, 148, 170, 200, 209, 242
beginning, 14, 122

behavior, 3, 10, 28, 48
being, 2, 8, 11, 13, 19, 21, 24, 25, 27, 41, 42, 51, 54, 57–59, 64, 70, 72, 73, 76, 112, 146, 151, 157, 163, 165, 180, 196, 209, 210
belief, 1, 14, 49, 157, 162, 166, 175, 235
belonging, 4, 11–15, 17, 20, 25, 56, 85, 98, 110, 123, 127, 131, 150, 151, 199, 210, 213
benefit, 103
betrayal, 185
Bisi, 1–6, 8–21, 28–31, 33, 36–40, 52–55, 58–62, 67–69, 76, 77, 168, 172, 229
Bisi Alimi, 1, 10, 16, 19, 24, 29, 31–33, 36, 38, 41, 43–45, 48, 50, 53, 55, 58, 60, 64, 69, 70, 72, 75, 77, 79, 80, 82, 84, 86, 88, 90, 92–94, 102, 104, 107, 109, 110, 113–115, 117, 118, 120, 122–124, 127, 132, 134–136, 139, 150, 151, 153, 158, 161, 164–167, 169–171, 175, 180, 182, 184, 189, 195, 198, 203, 209, 211, 214–216, 220, 221, 227–229, 235, 236, 242, 244
Bisi Alimi's, 3, 6, 9, 10, 12, 14, 16, 18, 21, 26, 27, 31, 33, 35, 42, 48, 49, 52, 62, 64, 66, 67, 69, 72, 75, 81, 102, 105, 113, 115, 133, 141, 143, 146, 148, 151, 154, 156, 161, 163, 166, 168, 170, 171, 174, 175, 177,

192, 199, 200, 202, 214,
217, 219, 226, 228,
230–232, 237, 240
boldness, 11
border, 84
boy, 10
bravery, 199
break, 62, 184
bridge, 74, 153, 230
building, 26, 30, 36, 38, 39, 45, 46,
50, 56, 57, 65, 71, 84–86,
99, 106, 112, 113,
115–118, 120, 123, 127,
201, 210, 211, 214, 226,
230
bullying, 28, 101
burnout, 30, 52, 59
business, 48, 214

cacophony, 16
call, 65, 85, 167, 182, 200, 202, 207
calling, 31, 165
camaraderie, 11
campaign, 10, 111
campaigning, 199
Canada, 36
capacity, 33, 57, 118, 120, 186, 201
care, 31, 52, 58, 90, 92, 101, 210,
234
career, 56, 57
case, 14, 19, 51, 52, 95, 104, 119,
152, 168, 179, 188, 193
catalyst, 2, 6, 15, 20, 30, 43, 67, 90,
146, 163, 214, 217
cause, 33, 38, 48, 59, 65, 71, 91, 92,
103, 110, 124, 177, 231,
237
caution, 4
celebration, 201, 211–214

celebrity, 91
censorship, 197, 217
center, 12, 102
challenge, 1–5, 9, 10, 12, 14, 15, 21,
33, 42, 43, 50, 54, 57, 58,
60–62, 69, 75, 77, 84–86,
90, 92, 100–102, 106,
109–111, 115, 120, 123,
124, 128, 135, 154, 157,
162, 164–166, 177, 180,
184, 186, 188, 195, 198,
201, 203, 211, 230, 233,
235, 238, 244
champion, 21, 127, 143, 240
change, 2, 5, 6, 10–16, 18, 20, 21,
29, 30, 33, 41, 43, 45, 48,
55, 57, 62, 67, 69, 71, 75,
77, 79, 81, 83–85, 88–92,
99, 101, 104, 110, 111,
113, 115, 117, 120, 123,
125, 129, 136, 141, 143,
146–148, 154, 155,
159–163, 166, 174, 175,
182, 184, 186, 193, 197,
200–202, 209, 210, 214,
217, 226, 228, 233, 242,
244
charge, 53, 72, 115
chat, 129
child, 4
choice, 31, 165
church, 11, 170
cisgender, 167, 239
city, 3, 16
class, 235
classmate, 11
classroom, 11
clergy, 165
climate, 155, 205, 206

Index

coalition, 37, 39, 45, 53, 106, 112, 113, 115–117, 197
Colin Kaepernick, 91
collaboration, 33, 38, 40, 46, 48, 55, 56, 77, 79, 81, 84, 94, 99, 102, 104, 117, 120, 163, 175, 176, 183, 196, 210, 228–230
collective, 11, 18, 26, 31, 39, 55, 59, 88, 90, 98, 102, 106, 110, 117, 151, 163, 166, 171, 172, 175, 177, 182, 183, 185, 186, 210, 228
colonialism, 182
color, 167, 168, 230, 238
combination, 45, 55, 62, 105
commentary, 146
commitment, 5, 14, 16, 31, 33, 58, 63, 81, 92, 102, 110, 125, 143, 154, 156, 163, 170, 184, 202, 210, 237
communication, 26, 58, 65, 75, 88, 89, 128
community, 2–5, 9, 11–15, 17–21, 24–29, 31–33, 36, 39, 45, 49, 51–57, 59, 61–63, 65–67, 69, 70, 73–77, 79, 84, 85, 89, 90, 92, 97–100, 103–105, 107, 109–113, 118–120, 122–124, 127–129, 131–137, 139, 145, 146, 151, 156, 158, 161, 163, 165–168, 170, 171, 174, 180, 185, 189, 195–197, 199, 201, 207, 209–214, 221, 228, 234, 238, 239, 244
compassion, 9, 162, 164, 165, 170
compatibility, 164

complexity, 19, 73, 128, 166, 167
component, 33, 48, 64, 92, 110, 117, 129, 132, 134, 143, 151, 174, 217, 228
compound, 28
concept, 11, 182, 194, 212, 238
conclusion, 6, 10, 12, 14, 18, 21, 26, 31, 33, 62, 64, 66, 69, 72, 84, 86, 88, 90, 91, 102, 109, 115, 120, 122, 136, 141, 163, 166, 168, 170, 175, 187, 192, 202, 204, 207, 228, 230, 240
condemnation, 8, 9, 180, 188, 193
conference, 30, 37, 70, 75, 76, 171
confidence, 56
conflict, 1, 16, 17, 74, 161, 163, 166
confrontation, 177, 179, 234, 243
confusion, 16
congregation, 46
connection, 2, 12, 53, 75, 88, 89, 129
connectivity, 89, 90
constitution, 120
constitutionality, 106, 203
constructivism, 21
content, 88
context, 8, 16, 24, 26, 48, 54, 58, 82, 113, 140, 146, 147, 151–153, 159, 161, 162, 166, 182, 187, 217
continent, 82, 84, 177, 182, 183, 185, 194, 195
continuity, 230
contrast, 36
conversion, 63, 64
core, 43, 157, 162, 165
cornerstone, 11, 33, 55, 99, 117, 127, 202, 212
correctness, 187

cost, 133
counseling, 210
counter, 20, 82, 124, 165
country, 13, 19, 27, 39, 42, 124, 199, 209, 212
courage, 11, 17, 24, 31, 55, 61, 62, 84, 109, 164, 166, 170, 184, 199, 221
court, 83, 99, 195
courtroom, 61
coverage, 64, 67
crackdown, 182
creation, 124
creativity, 3, 55, 84, 94, 104, 146, 148, 179, 242
Crenshaw, 238
criticism, 57, 64, 65, 90
crowd, 111
crowdfunding, 90
culmination, 18
cultivation, 31
culture, 1, 3, 4, 9, 30–32, 45, 51, 61, 112, 183, 187, 189, 192, 201, 208, 211–214, 221, 234
curricula, 50, 157, 174
curriculum, 140, 141
cyberbullying, 89, 129
cycle, 49, 56, 62, 103, 109, 206, 234

dance, 115
danger, 19, 106
death, 195
debate, 91
decision, 5, 18, 29
declaration, 18, 29
dedication, 58, 175
defense, 9
defiance, 17, 18

degree, 136
demand, 71
democratization, 89
dependency, 119, 120
depression, 19, 28, 100, 123
depth, 58
desire, 4, 5, 8, 29
despair, 51
destination, 57
determination, 2, 14, 57, 61, 84, 97, 111, 122, 124, 162, 177, 187, 196, 198, 204, 221
development, 16, 56, 116, 189–192
deviation, 1, 4
dialogue, 9, 10, 13, 20, 24, 75, 91, 100, 124, 129, 151–154, 158, 159, 162–164, 166, 168, 170, 174, 195, 200, 201, 203, 210, 217, 234, 243
difference, 23
dignity, 127, 156, 175, 182, 194, 196, 214, 235
disability, 235
disapproval, 4, 51
discourse, 69, 79, 99, 109, 155, 156, 163, 183, 194, 211, 233
discovery, 2, 5, 16–18
discrepancy, 12
discrimination, 1, 4, 8–11, 19, 20, 27–30, 33, 36, 39, 40, 42–46, 49, 50, 52, 53, 55, 60, 62, 71, 80, 81, 92, 100, 101, 103, 122, 123, 125, 128, 129, 132, 134, 135, 137, 139, 144, 150, 151, 154, 156–158, 163–165, 167, 168, 175, 177, 185, 188, 192, 195, 196, 199,

200, 202, 204–208, 210,
213, 214, 234, 238, 243
discussion, 155, 170
disdain, 16, 51
disorder, 63
disparity, 89, 229
dissemination, 86
dissent, 106, 113
distraction, 59
distress, 17, 50, 63, 129
diversity, 3, 9, 10, 17, 50, 92, 101,
112, 136, 148, 156, 157,
161, 167, 168, 175, 202,
213, 217
divide, 89
dividing, 168
division, 170
doctrine, 10
document, 104, 111
documentation, 104, 111
doubt, 70
doxxing, 129
dream, 41, 72, 127, 209
drive, 16, 228
duality, 13
dynamic, 1, 172, 229

Eastern Europe, 37
ecosystem, 201
education, 10, 11, 13–17, 20, 32, 33,
45, 54, 72, 100, 135, 136,
157, 166, 174, 198, 200,
202, 207, 219, 221, 222,
229, 239
effect, 12, 33, 41, 61, 69, 76, 83, 90,
103, 110, 115, 217
effectiveness, 13, 76, 85, 89, 112,
136, 172, 193, 221, 237,
239, 240

effort, 54, 106, 110, 163, 166, 168,
189, 221
electorate, 206
Ellen DeGeneres, 43, 90
embrace, 2, 5, 11, 17, 20, 31, 42, 62,
64, 90–92, 116, 161, 164,
166, 197, 201
emergence, 212
empathy, 10, 24, 29, 32, 45, 48, 50,
151, 156, 157, 163,
165–168, 171, 174, 175,
201
employment, 49, 56, 204, 208
empowerment, 14, 16, 17, 51, 110,
112, 113, 118, 141, 146,
150, 151, 156, 194, 201,
202, 214, 217
encounter, 12, 30, 103, 109, 185,
217, 240, 243
end, 15, 235
endeavor, 18, 24, 26, 43, 55, 82, 94,
104, 161, 172, 209, 214,
235
endorsement, 90
endurance, 125
energy, 72
engagement, 11, 18, 38, 49, 65, 89,
90, 92, 104, 109, 113, 129,
158, 164, 169, 198, 221,
231, 244
entertainment, 91
enthusiasm, 212
entrepreneurship, 3, 56, 57, 215
environment, 2, 4, 9, 13–15, 17, 23,
29, 42, 45, 46, 51–54, 57,
58, 64, 68, 70, 109, 120,
123, 128, 129, 141, 151,
157, 161, 162, 168, 169,
174, 177, 192, 193, 196,

200, 202, 207, 210, 234, 239
equality, 4, 11, 13, 18, 29, 31, 36, 38, 40, 41, 43, 54, 55, 62, 64, 66, 69, 77, 79, 81, 82, 85, 86, 90, 94, 102, 104, 109, 115, 120, 122, 124, 127, 132, 136, 139, 148, 151, 154, 163, 164, 166, 168, 170, 171, 177, 180, 182, 192, 194, 196–198, 200, 202, 204, 207, 217, 222, 226, 228, 230, 233, 240, 242, 245
equation, 14, 20, 24–26, 45, 49, 59, 65, 67, 68, 72, 73, 89, 103, 104, 137, 167, 171, 187, 192–194, 196, 200, 242, 244
equity, 137
era, 36, 82, 180, 183, 185, 194, 195
Erik Erikson's, 16
essence, 49, 59, 171, 192, 194, 209, 242
establishment, 15, 127, 128, 133, 134, 164, 199
esteem, 29
estrangement, 63
ethic, 49
ethnicity, 46, 168
Europe, 76
evening, 58
event, 12, 109, 111, 212
evidence, 104
evolution, 13
example, 8, 9, 37, 40, 46, 48, 49, 53, 54, 61, 64, 65, 81, 85, 89, 90, 97, 104, 110, 111, 123, 140, 156, 158, 162, 164, 165, 167, 168, 170, 171, 174, 185, 188, 193, 195, 210, 229, 234, 241
exchange, 36, 90, 229
excitement, 12
exclusion, 1, 8, 154, 156
existence, 2, 177, 214
expedition, 36
experience, 4, 5, 10, 24, 29, 38, 46, 49, 50, 115, 156, 165, 167, 183, 204, 238
expertise, 62
exploration, 11, 18, 36, 38, 146
exposure, 1, 11, 15, 17, 65, 73
expression, 2, 101, 102, 106, 146, 148, 151, 201, 213, 217
exterior, 1
eye, 65

fabric, 1, 171, 172, 199, 214
face, 3, 9, 14, 16, 18, 26, 29, 31, 39, 41, 44, 46, 49, 51, 54, 56, 57, 61, 65, 72, 89, 90, 103, 106, 109, 110, 112, 123, 128, 131, 141–144, 150, 155, 162, 167, 169, 171, 177, 180, 185, 188, 190, 199, 202, 204, 206, 209, 213, 216, 217, 229, 240, 242, 243
faculty, 15
fairness, 11
faith, 9–11, 19, 153, 156, 158, 159, 161–170
fame, 90
family, 1, 3–5, 8–10, 17–21, 26, 54, 59, 63, 72, 74, 156, 174, 185
fashion, 212

Index

favor, 239
fear, 3, 5, 6, 9, 11, 13, 15, 24, 30, 32, 46, 52, 54, 55, 57, 62, 72–74, 91, 98, 101, 109, 125, 128, 129, 139, 150, 155, 165, 171, 183, 193, 196, 200, 202, 205, 208, 210, 214
feedback, 112, 136
feeling, 52, 131
femininity, 48, 50, 91
field, 91
fight, 8, 12, 14, 16, 24, 26, 29, 30, 35, 37, 38, 41–43, 52, 57, 62, 64, 66, 77, 79, 86, 91, 92, 102–104, 109, 111, 113, 115, 117, 122–125, 129, 132, 134, 151, 162–164, 168, 177, 180, 182–184, 187, 192, 195, 197–199, 201, 202, 204, 207, 210, 226, 228, 230, 234, 235, 242
figure, 57
film, 195, 201
finish, 122
fire, 11, 15, 30
firsthand, 52, 56, 98, 172
flow, 39
fluidity, 18
focus, 10, 85, 101, 112, 123, 129, 157, 187, 239
force, 4, 12, 33, 184
forefront, 24, 58, 82, 101
form, 8, 103, 119, 140, 162
formation, 32, 46, 115, 128, 183, 204
formula, 68, 103, 136
foster, 15, 20, 48, 50, 54, 71, 76, 84, 88, 91, 110, 123, 127, 129, 135, 138, 155, 157, 160, 165, 171, 174, 182, 186, 195, 200, 201, 209, 210, 213, 237, 239
foundation, 12, 14, 59, 80, 120, 127, 164, 200
framework, 9, 43, 79, 80, 106, 115, 120, 122, 128, 132, 136, 137, 162, 167, 194, 195, 200, 201, 207–209, 231, 238, 240
freedom, 102, 106
friction, 85
friend, 11
friendship, 26, 72
front, 53, 55, 61, 71, 84, 85, 105, 163, 182, 184, 210
frustration, 15
fuel, 10, 45, 98, 123, 162, 164
fulfillment, 165
function, 26, 65, 244
funding, 40, 56, 89, 109, 119, 120, 124, 128, 186, 217, 229
future, 2, 3, 5, 10, 12, 13, 24, 36, 41, 43, 48, 53, 62, 71, 72, 81, 84, 88, 92, 94, 102, 104, 113, 115, 122, 134, 136, 141, 143, 157, 163, 177, 182, 185, 187, 194, 196–198, 202, 204, 209, 210, 217, 225, 230, 235, 238, 242

gap, 10, 74, 153, 170, 174, 230
gathering, 12, 109
gender, 1, 2, 5, 8, 10, 18, 21, 24, 43, 46, 48–50, 54, 56, 60, 80, 81, 128, 139, 144, 156,

168, 175, 177, 183, 185,
187, 192, 194, 197, 198,
204, 206, 208, 211, 213,
235, 238
generation, 16, 50, 72, 101, 115, 122,
198, 200, 225, 240, 244
globe, 69, 199, 242
goal, 37, 168, 200, 209
government, 41, 46, 61, 62, 99, 103,
105, 106, 118, 119, 124,
183, 185, 188, 206
ground, 123, 159
groundwork, 3, 5, 11, 13, 20, 113,
151
group, 12, 48, 85, 235
growth, 14, 162, 189, 194
guidance, 56, 70, 124, 161
guide, 162, 168, 237
guilt, 1

hall, 158
hand, 3, 41, 65, 72
harassment, 9, 60, 89, 103, 123, 125,
132, 185, 204
harm, 64
Hart, 91
Harvey Milk, 140
hate, 202
haven, 12, 210
head, 19, 48, 61, 72, 86, 158
healing, 101
health, 19, 28, 30, 42, 50–53, 58, 64,
89, 98–100, 123,
128–132, 137, 146, 168,
186, 210
healthcare, 49, 100, 101, 136–139,
200, 204, 208
heart, 10, 48, 163
heartbreak, 72

heartedness, 172
help, 27, 28, 42, 45, 53, 55, 74, 90,
91, 100, 140, 143, 154,
158, 174, 186, 197, 210,
239
heritage, 185
hesitance, 73
heteronormativity, 4
hierarchy, 167
highlight, 25, 62, 68, 75, 120, 121,
174, 193, 201, 213
hinge, 198
hiring, 56
history, 106, 140, 157, 174, 199
home, 8, 15, 58, 185
homelessness, 144–146
homophobia, 5, 17, 42, 55, 62, 67,
81, 95, 115, 129, 151, 162,
182, 197, 234
homosexual, 62, 82
homosexuality, 1, 8, 9, 11, 13, 36, 51,
80, 155, 169, 180, 185,
188, 193, 194, 196, 243
honesty, 72
hope, 10, 18, 21, 31, 36, 41, 48, 52,
53, 62, 102, 104, 120, 124,
136, 148, 156, 161, 170,
182, 187, 196, 198, 200,
207, 209, 221, 242
hostility, 3, 9, 15, 18, 39, 76, 119,
144, 164, 234
house, 127
housing, 204, 208
hub, 1, 3
humanity, 158, 163, 194, 235
humor, 172
hurdle, 57, 128, 243
hustle, 10
hyper, 28

idea, 15, 45, 110, 163
ideal, 168
identity, 1–6, 8–12, 16–19, 21, 24, 26, 31, 43, 50, 51, 54, 60, 80, 81, 99, 139, 144, 146, 156, 165–168, 170, 175, 177, 185, 187, 192, 194, 198, 201, 204, 208, 211, 212, 214, 239, 240
ignorance, 29
illustration, 28
image, 65
immediacy, 65, 88
impact, 14, 31, 40, 43, 50, 55, 56, 65, 68, 71, 81, 88, 91, 95, 106, 107, 112, 119, 136, 171, 175, 177, 180, 186, 187, 192, 193, 199, 218, 228, 232, 238, 244
implementation, 36, 136
import, 185
importance, 6, 11–13, 15, 16, 18, 21, 26, 28, 31, 33, 37, 39, 50, 52–56, 58–60, 65, 70, 73–75, 77, 84, 89, 98, 100, 102, 105, 110, 111, 114, 117, 122, 123, 129, 133, 140, 146, 150, 152, 157, 158, 162, 164, 167, 174, 188, 200–202, 210, 211, 213, 216, 222, 226, 231, 235, 238, 239
imprisonment, 208, 243
improvement, 112
impunity, 188
inaction, 62
inadequacy, 51
incarceration, 206
incident, 29, 91

inclination, 4
inclusion, 38, 92, 140, 155, 157
inclusivity, 10, 11, 48, 70, 89, 100, 101, 112, 126, 137, 139, 140, 151, 154, 161, 164–166, 195, 202, 214, 235
income, 57, 204
increase, 106, 203
independence, 194, 214
indication, 11
individual, 3, 5, 18, 24, 29, 57, 62, 73, 136, 146, 151, 163, 167, 172, 198, 211, 213
industry, 91
inequality, 206, 229, 238
influence, 9–11, 17, 39, 42, 90, 124, 140, 151, 164, 183, 204, 233
information, 39, 65, 86, 124, 176, 182, 235
initiative, 15, 48, 112
injustice, 11, 12, 105, 122
innovation, 198
insecurity, 186
inspiration, 15, 29, 40, 102, 143, 200, 202, 242
instability, 186
instance, 8, 11, 15, 17, 33, 36, 40, 43, 46, 48, 50, 54, 56, 58, 59, 61–64, 70, 76, 79, 80, 82, 83, 85, 88, 90, 104, 106, 109, 112, 118, 119, 124, 129, 136, 140, 162, 165, 167, 169, 174, 176, 180, 182, 183, 185, 188, 195, 196, 199, 204, 212, 213, 239, 243
intensity, 183, 238

interconnectedness, 71, 90, 180, 184, 210
interdependence, 231
interference, 193
internet, 89, 90
interplay, 6, 82, 167, 242
interpretation, 10, 11, 57
intersect, 8, 197, 206
intersection, 51, 86, 90, 144, 146, 158, 164, 187, 189, 192, 196, 234
intersectionality, 24, 26, 46, 48, 68, 84, 86, 111, 128, 167, 168, 177, 183, 197, 201, 204, 206, 207, 209, 213, 237–240
intervention, 182
intimidation, 20, 61, 68, 89, 98, 106, 107, 109, 110, 188, 213, 234
intolerance, 9
introduction, 11
introspection, 5
investment, 72
invisibility, 41
involvement, 11, 20, 162, 168, 175
isolation, 15, 17, 30, 45, 51, 70, 72, 77, 124, 167, 171, 183, 199, 206, 238
issue, 30, 32, 62, 63, 79, 95, 100, 103, 119, 158, 193, 229, 238

job, 49, 55, 56, 189
journey, 2, 4–6, 9–21, 24, 26, 27, 29–31, 33, 36–38, 41, 42, 48, 51–53, 55, 57, 62, 72, 73, 75, 77, 81, 84, 86, 99, 102, 106, 110, 113, 122, 127, 136, 141, 156, 161, 163–166, 170, 172–175, 177, 180, 182, 184, 189, 196, 199, 202, 204, 209, 211, 219, 226, 228, 242, 244
joy, 58
judgment, 52, 54, 73, 98, 125, 129, 150, 210
judiciary, 62
Judith Butler, 18
Judith Butler's, 211
justice, 4, 11, 15, 29, 31, 43, 62, 69, 71, 81, 82, 90, 94, 115, 120, 122, 125, 154, 162, 177, 180, 182, 184, 194, 196, 197, 199, 201, 202, 210, 228, 233, 240, 245
justification, 169

Kenya, 83, 195
Kevin Hart, 91
keynote, 70
Kimberlé Crenshaw, 46, 183, 238
knowledge, 2, 5, 14–16, 36, 38, 39, 135, 136, 157, 202
Kwame Nkrumah, 182

labor, 51, 112
lack, 14, 32, 39, 48, 60, 62, 89, 128, 144, 183, 185, 188, 200, 204, 206, 208, 213, 229
Lady Gaga, 90
Lagos, 1, 3, 5, 6, 10, 14, 16, 51, 104, 172, 212
landmark, 83, 120, 195
landscape, 1, 6, 10, 29, 33, 36, 39, 54, 57, 60, 64, 68, 82, 88, 92, 100, 110, 117, 132,

Index 259

    156, 158, 164, 169, 175, 185–187, 194, 207, 212, 214, 240, 243
language, 36, 76, 165
laughter, 11, 12
Laverne Cox, 43
law, 30, 43, 57, 60, 61, 80, 97, 102, 106, 118, 123, 188, 208
layer, 73
lead, 4, 8, 9, 16, 17, 19, 28, 32, 36, 42, 46, 49, 50, 52, 64, 72–74, 85, 89–91, 115, 119, 123, 124, 129, 144, 155, 163, 167–169, 183, 193, 195, 209, 212, 228, 242
leader, 46, 57
leadership, 112, 120, 198, 226
learning, 11, 136
legacy, 102, 164, 199, 200, 202, 233, 235, 242
legalization, 36
legislation, 30, 46, 57, 79, 97, 98, 177–180, 183, 193, 243
legitimacy, 90, 102
lens, 46, 77, 238, 242
level, 72
Leviticus, 169
liberation, 11
lie, 8
life, 1–5, 10–12, 14, 16, 25, 29, 49, 58, 59, 63, 64, 72, 98, 172
lifeline, 77, 132
lifetime, 12
light, 109, 172
line, 122, 168, 234
literature, 2, 15, 17, 157, 165, 174, 195, 201, 212
litigation, 120

livelihood, 217
lobbying, 38, 82–84, 111, 119, 124, 165
love, 2, 4, 8, 9, 11, 20, 24, 25, 31, 50, 72, 73, 156, 157, 161–166, 170, 171, 182, 201, 202, 212

mainstream, 111, 239
making, 9, 23, 28, 39, 46, 65, 85, 90, 103, 119, 123, 147, 155, 172, 186, 213
male, 8
man, 2, 5, 12, 20, 51, 63, 156, 199, 209
manner, 154
mantra, 71
marathon, 122, 125
marginalization, 10, 48, 207, 208, 214
market, 55
marketplace, 216
marriage, 9, 36, 85, 167
Marsha P. Johnson, 140
masculinity, 50, 91
matter, 125, 127, 132, 182, 187
means, 2, 14, 15, 65, 101, 113, 187, 201, 204, 211, 212, 214, 217
media, 42, 49, 54, 56, 59, 61, 63–69, 79, 86, 88, 89, 94, 95, 97, 104, 106, 111, 115, 124, 129, 157, 176, 182, 186, 195, 197, 200, 201, 216, 227, 228, 235, 244
medium, 49, 101, 146, 151, 217
Megan Rapinoe, 91
megaphone, 118
melting, 36

member, 80
mentor, 200
mentorship, 70, 101, 225, 230
message, 29, 33, 54, 63, 65, 89, 99, 111, 119, 161, 163, 172, 201, 244
messaging, 54
metropolis, 1
Michel Foucault, 18
midst, 15
milestone, 5
misconception, 156
misinformation, 48, 135, 193, 219
mission, 43, 60, 171, 180
mistrust, 183
misunderstanding, 74
mix, 5, 12
mobilization, 9, 61, 62, 65, 88, 90, 105, 111–113, 118, 123, 124, 207
model, 244
moment, 3, 5, 8, 11, 18, 29, 42, 199
momentum, 84, 192, 194, 195, 198
mother, 19
motivator, 2
move, 77, 168, 198, 202
movement, 10, 33, 41, 55, 68, 69, 72, 75, 81, 84, 86, 88, 90–92, 94, 112, 113, 117, 118, 120, 123, 143, 148, 151, 154, 156, 163, 167, 172, 180, 187, 194, 195, 197, 198, 200, 202, 204, 210, 214, 217, 228, 230, 233, 235, 237, 240
Mozambique, 196
multitude, 107
music, 3, 151, 212
myriad, 240

narrative, 1, 5, 17, 18, 20, 48, 49, 63, 65, 69, 75, 85, 125, 162, 166, 167, 171, 195, 196, 199
nation, 228
nature, 3, 19, 33, 36, 46, 75, 107, 168, 172, 239, 240
necessity, 84, 92, 177, 182, 200, 207, 209, 235
need, 9, 13, 33, 45, 52, 53, 57, 58, 61, 62, 89, 95, 101, 109–111, 120, 130, 132, 136, 139, 169, 172, 182, 187, 192, 195, 200, 202, 203, 230, 234
neglect, 137
neocolonialism, 119
net, 59
Netherlands, 36
network, 20, 25, 30, 38, 55–57, 61, 70, 73, 75, 77, 78, 112, 168, 214
networking, 37, 41
news, 68
Nigeria, 1–6, 8–10, 12, 14, 15, 17, 20, 22–24, 27–33, 35, 36, 38–40, 42, 45, 46, 48, 50, 54–57, 60–62, 64–69, 72, 73, 75–77, 79, 80, 88, 89, 95, 98, 99, 102, 104–107, 109–124, 127–132, 134, 151, 154, 157, 161, 168, 171, 180, 183, 185, 188, 193, 195, 199–204, 206–209, 212–214, 217, 219, 221, 227, 229, 231–233, 243
nonconformity, 80
norm, 1, 4, 243

Index

notion, 95, 164
number, 71, 91, 186

obstacle, 54, 206
odyssey, 199
on, 2–5, 8–11, 13–16, 19, 24, 26, 28, 33, 38, 40–43, 46, 48, 51–54, 56–58, 60–64, 67–69, 72, 76, 79–81, 83, 85, 86, 88, 89, 99, 101–103, 106, 107, 109, 110, 112, 115, 118, 119, 124, 128, 129, 157–159, 162, 163, 168, 170, 177, 180–183, 185–187, 192, 195, 197–199, 201, 202, 208, 217, 225, 229, 233–235, 238, 239, 242
one, 1, 3, 4, 11–13, 16, 33, 38, 42, 49, 56, 58, 61, 72, 75–77, 86, 90, 110, 115, 123, 129, 151, 166, 170, 171, 181, 182, 187, 196, 202, 210, 228, 235
openness, 156, 170
opinion, 9, 61, 64, 183
opportunity, 10, 37, 124, 184
opposition, 9, 61, 64, 67, 68, 104–106, 177, 206, 207
oppression, 10, 12, 29, 31, 69, 77, 84, 86, 105, 156, 167, 182–184, 197, 212, 238–240
ordination, 165
organizing, 3, 15, 54, 78, 98, 111–115, 123
orientation, 3, 5, 8–11, 14, 16, 21, 24, 28, 43, 50, 54, 60, 62, 63, 80, 81, 104, 110, 112, 123, 136, 139, 144, 156, 158, 162, 164, 166, 167, 171, 175, 177, 183, 185, 187, 192, 194, 195, 198, 204, 208, 238
ostracism, 11, 20, 29, 32, 42, 46, 54, 106, 155, 162, 175, 185, 200, 243
ostracization, 4, 128, 169
other, 3, 9, 10, 20, 25, 30, 33, 39, 40, 43, 50, 52, 56, 59, 61, 71, 72, 84, 86, 93, 106, 111, 120, 139, 180, 182, 195, 206, 210, 236
outlet, 146
outreach, 49, 54, 110, 112, 195
overlap, 238
oversight, 239
ownership, 112

pain, 8
pandemic, 176
panel, 170
paradox, 120
part, 13, 38, 95, 109, 124, 183
participant, 29
participation, 30, 78, 88, 89, 171, 174, 199, 229, 234
partnering, 33
partnership, 8, 48, 229
passage, 203
passion, 2, 5, 13–15, 17, 210
path, 13, 56, 62, 86, 125, 148, 166, 173, 175, 182, 204
pathway, 243
patience, 174
pattern, 109
peer, 210
penalty, 206

people, 48–50, 70, 101, 156–158, 167, 172, 174, 198, 210, 230
percentage, 136
perception, 85, 106, 203
performance, 211
performativity, 211
period, 12, 206
persecution, 11, 24, 54, 60, 129, 183, 193, 200, 209
perseverance, 57
persistence, 123, 140, 174
person, 129, 167
personality, 16
perspective, 13, 15, 54, 95, 165, 238
phenomenon, 43, 144
picture, 98
pillar, 43, 129, 214
place, 43, 109, 111, 158, 177
planning, 109–111
platform, 11, 20, 26, 38, 42, 56, 57, 64, 65, 67, 88, 99, 113, 118, 152, 164, 195, 201, 212, 217
playing, 91
plea, 207
plight, 40, 61, 99, 105, 118, 124, 181, 199
point, 5, 76, 139
policy, 9, 81, 106, 119, 146, 165, 191, 196, 206, 229
pooling, 56
portion, 144
possibility, 170
post, 136
potential, 10, 32, 33, 43, 46, 66, 73, 75, 76, 83, 88, 91, 117, 128, 129, 132, 135, 136, 141, 143, 146, 152, 154, 156, 161, 169, 187, 190, 191, 194, 206, 217, 231
poverty, 112, 145, 146, 206, 208
power, 3, 10–12, 15, 16, 18, 24, 26, 31, 39, 41–43, 57, 66, 70, 76, 79, 81, 84, 90, 92, 99, 102, 124, 135, 156, 163, 170, 174, 188, 196, 199, 202, 209, 214, 221, 228, 229, 244
practice, 62, 112
precedent, 196
prejudice, 24, 100, 135, 154, 157, 163, 174, 201, 202
presence, 24, 25, 59, 69, 95, 244
pressure, 1, 3, 4, 9, 17, 25, 42, 51, 62, 72, 83, 99, 103, 106, 118, 119, 124
pride, 66, 201, 212
principle, 12, 43, 80, 171
privacy, 102, 106
privilege, 46, 158, 167, 238, 240
problem, 63
process, 2, 3, 5, 16, 18, 19, 39, 174, 221, 226
professional, 32, 43, 60, 91
profile, 115
program, 136
progress, 20, 60, 62, 120, 122, 133, 137, 140, 142, 155, 175, 187, 195, 199, 200, 202, 204, 207, 208, 221, 234, 243
promise, 48, 185
promotion, 165, 187
protection, 36, 83, 187, 200
protest, 61, 111
provision, 129, 130

Index 263

public, 9, 25, 40, 43, 45, 57, 61, 64–66, 68, 69, 79, 85, 88, 90–92, 99, 100, 103, 104, 106, 107, 109, 123, 131, 174, 183, 186, 195, 201, 203, 207, 212, 219–221
publicity, 91
purpose, 3, 11, 197
pursuit, 5, 16, 31, 32, 38, 69, 94, 107, 120, 154, 163, 180, 182, 183, 199, 210
push, 90, 123, 165, 166, 229

quality, 137
queer, 18, 55, 167, 170, 204, 213
quest, 4, 18, 36, 43, 45, 136, 139, 180, 196, 226, 240
question, 2, 4, 11, 18
quo, 4, 12, 14, 17, 64, 77, 81, 86, 94, 214, 235, 244
Quran, 8

race, 128, 183, 213, 235, 238
raising, 3, 64, 113, 124, 131, 196, 239
rally, 79, 90, 104, 206
range, 158
reach, 88, 118, 122, 124, 209
reaction, 12
reality, 27, 29, 58, 98, 109, 169, 217
realization, 10, 12
realm, 41, 60, 64, 90, 98, 164, 171, 172, 235, 238, 242
recognition, 52, 67–69, 85, 86, 104, 165, 192, 195, 211
record, 33
recourse, 62, 208
reflection, 18, 194, 239

reform, 61, 62, 103, 123, 124, 185, 196, 198, 200
refuge, 2
regard, 124
reinterpretation, 9
rejection, 3–6, 8, 9, 18–20, 28, 51, 72, 73, 129, 144, 174
relation, 240
relationship, 59, 72, 74, 92, 189, 196
relativism, 76
religion, 9–11, 17, 45, 161, 164, 168
relocation, 36
reluctance, 32, 55, 116, 128
reminder, 13, 30, 64, 71, 79, 163, 182, 230
removal, 165
repeal, 61, 64, 103, 104, 111, 119, 123, 196
report, 28, 131
representation, 14, 61, 72, 89, 106, 206
representative, 76, 112
resilience, 3, 6, 10–12, 14, 16, 18, 20, 21, 24, 29, 31, 50, 52, 56–58, 60, 62, 66, 75, 84, 94, 102, 104, 107, 109, 110, 122, 124, 129, 162, 166, 177, 179, 184, 187, 196, 198, 199, 202, 204, 209, 212, 214, 221, 242
resistance, 18, 24, 54, 68, 103, 115, 164, 166, 174, 185, 193, 212, 214, 240, 243
resolution, 81
resolve, 3, 11, 31
resource, 39, 90, 177
respect, 3, 10, 11, 106, 157, 230
response, 4, 60, 73, 76, 79, 109, 112, 118, 168

responsibility, 16, 42, 175
result, 20, 28, 46, 72, 169
resurgence, 194
retaliation, 210
retribution, 15, 91, 214
revelation, 19
rhetoric, 185, 206
ridicule, 11
right, 106, 211
rise, 54, 88, 195
risk, 4, 17, 127, 243
road, 57, 184
roadmap, 209
role, 1, 2, 4, 5, 8, 15–17, 19, 26, 30, 38, 42, 45, 50, 54, 59, 61, 68, 70, 74, 83, 84, 88, 89, 91, 99, 103, 106, 118–120, 124, 129, 139, 148, 151, 153, 155, 157, 158, 161, 163, 165, 168, 170, 172, 174, 176, 181, 186, 189, 195, 196, 200, 201, 209, 211, 213, 235, 239
room, 1, 12
route, 56
ruling, 195

s, 1–6, 9–21, 24–31, 33, 35–38, 40, 42, 45, 46, 48, 49, 51, 52, 54, 55, 57–59, 61–69, 72–75, 78, 81, 84, 90, 95, 98, 99, 101, 102, 105, 106, 112, 113, 115, 119, 129, 133, 140, 141, 143, 146, 148, 151, 154, 156, 161–163, 166, 168, 170–172, 174, 175, 177, 182, 188, 192, 195, 199–202, 209–211, 214, 217, 219, 226, 228–234, 237, 240, 242, 243
safety, 59, 64, 89, 109, 111, 180, 217
sanctuary, 26
satisfaction, 72
scale, 64, 197, 234, 235
scarcity, 177, 217
scene, 212
scheduling, 59
scholar, 238
school, 5, 11, 12, 17, 28, 157
scope, 116
scrutiny, 25, 33, 57, 64–66, 68, 90
secrecy, 4, 185
section, 24, 27, 29, 33, 60, 84, 88, 107, 113, 118, 120, 125, 127, 129, 137, 141, 146, 151, 172, 177, 180, 182, 185, 192, 199, 202, 207, 240, 242
security, 129, 214
self, 2, 3, 5, 6, 16–18, 24, 29, 31, 51, 52, 58, 70, 101, 146, 148, 151, 210, 239
sense, 1, 3, 4, 11–15, 17, 20, 25, 56, 66, 69, 71, 78, 85, 89, 98, 99, 105, 110, 112, 120, 123, 127, 129, 131, 151, 163, 167, 170, 195, 197, 199, 201, 210, 213, 226
sensitivity, 140
sentiment, 209
series, 12, 18
sermon, 165
service, 132
set, 13, 25, 56, 144, 185
setting, 12, 58, 196
sex, 9, 30, 36, 46, 57, 73, 76, 80, 82, 118, 123, 128, 132, 167,

Index

169, 180, 183, 185, 195, 196, 200, 202, 203, 208
sexuality, 1, 2, 8, 10, 18, 48, 50, 159, 161–163
shame, 1, 4, 17
shape, 9, 65, 115, 196
share, 36, 39, 54, 57, 63, 67, 75, 77, 79, 84, 88, 100, 101, 106, 110, 123, 124, 129, 131, 151, 158, 163, 170, 176, 182, 197, 210, 216, 227, 235, 244
sharing, 10, 20, 31, 39, 40, 42, 49, 52, 59, 65, 69, 76, 78, 90, 97, 106, 111, 155, 165–168, 170–172, 174, 182, 186, 229
shift, 10, 24, 43, 88, 100, 163, 186, 194, 195, 201, 203, 220, 229
show, 42, 64
signal, 24
significance, 13, 20, 118, 120, 125, 141, 146, 180
silence, 1, 3, 18, 30, 62, 106, 148, 183
sin, 1, 9, 11
situation, 12, 33, 68, 79, 208
size, 13
skepticism, 13, 16
skill, 56
society, 1–5, 9–11, 16–21, 24, 39, 41, 43, 45, 46, 48, 49, 51–54, 56, 58, 60, 62, 70, 72–75, 84, 86, 99, 100, 102, 106, 109, 112, 113, 116, 118, 120, 123–125, 127, 129, 132, 136, 139, 141, 143, 146, 148, 151, 156, 157, 161, 163, 165, 166, 168, 172, 174, 180, 189, 194, 196, 198, 199, 202, 204, 207, 209, 211, 214, 217, 237, 240
socio, 46, 82, 110, 112, 230
sodomy, 195
solace, 2, 12, 15, 17, 20, 52, 59
solidarity, 11, 13, 26, 30, 31, 33, 37, 62, 64, 69, 71, 76, 77, 79, 84, 92, 94, 99, 100, 104, 109, 110, 118–120, 123, 124, 163, 167, 170, 179–185, 187, 188, 192, 194, 196, 197, 201, 202, 212, 213, 226, 227, 231, 242, 244
solution, 13
son, 20
source, 26, 51, 52, 59, 64, 156, 161, 162, 164, 166, 170
South Africa, 40, 195
space, 20, 57, 70, 73, 86, 124, 129, 163
speaking, 33, 69, 76, 109, 201
spectrum, 182, 230
speech, 70, 171
speed, 89
spirit, 3, 11, 18, 21, 52, 84, 110
spirituality, 11, 162
spotlight, 242
sprint, 125
SSMPA, 103, 104, 106, 110, 111, 120
stage, 12, 16, 38, 57, 61, 76, 99, 102, 168, 233
stake, 201
stance, 12, 41, 46, 83, 106, 118, 234
stand, 11, 55, 61, 69, 102, 111

state, 12, 28, 188, 204
statement, 19, 57, 76
status, 4, 12, 14, 17, 46, 64, 77, 81, 86, 94, 128, 144, 183, 213, 214, 235, 238, 244
step, 15, 18, 36, 52, 64, 65, 81, 99, 125, 141, 195, 196, 244
stigma, 1, 5, 13, 15, 19, 28, 29, 32–36, 40, 42, 43, 48, 50, 52, 54, 70, 82, 91, 92, 94, 103, 116, 123, 125, 128, 129, 131, 151, 167, 169, 175, 177, 185, 195, 200, 204, 205, 207, 213, 238
stigmatization, 9, 103
stone, 8
story, 3, 18, 20, 21, 31, 33, 42, 49, 52, 54, 57, 67, 69, 75, 162, 166, 170, 172, 174, 200, 209, 242
storyteller, 172
storytelling, 10, 94, 151, 163, 172, 201
strategy, 60, 61, 66, 84, 92, 111–113, 117, 154, 158, 165
strength, 11, 25, 26, 33, 52, 66, 73, 86, 125, 151, 161, 162, 164, 166, 168, 170, 182, 185, 202, 242
struggle, 2–5, 9, 16, 18, 24, 25, 29, 30, 36, 62, 72, 76, 77, 81, 82, 84, 104, 107, 119, 120, 122, 124, 127, 129, 132, 139, 167, 171, 172, 179, 183, 186, 189, 194, 206, 228, 240, 242, 245
student, 15, 101
subject, 57
success, 33, 65, 103, 114, 129

summary, 3, 16, 38
summation, 73
support, 3, 5, 14, 15, 20, 21, 24–26, 28–31, 33, 39, 40, 43, 46, 52–59, 62, 65, 67, 72–74, 76, 78–80, 83, 88–91, 95, 97–100, 103, 104, 107, 109, 110, 112, 113, 117–120, 123, 124, 127–129, 132–134, 141, 143, 146, 166, 168, 176, 180–183, 185–187, 192–194, 197, 198, 200, 204, 206, 209, 210, 216, 217, 227–229, 235, 240, 244
surge, 65
survey, 136
sustainability, 119
sway, 99
sword, 5, 64, 72, 90
system, 1, 5, 14, 31, 39, 54, 55, 60–62, 100, 134, 139, 200

table, 230
taboo, 11, 14, 42, 234
tale, 63
talk, 64
Tanzania, 180, 182, 185, 188
tapestry, 3, 148, 196, 211
task, 3, 24, 170, 185, 189
technology, 59, 72, 86, 88–90, 124, 129, 176, 182, 186, 197
television, 42, 64, 199
tendency, 167, 238
tension, 4, 74, 158
testament, 3, 12, 14, 18, 21, 27, 31, 52, 57, 61, 69, 102, 163, 199, 204, 209, 221

Index

testimony, 156
the United Kingdom, 15
theater, 201
theology, 154–157, 162, 165, 166, 168
theory, 12, 16, 21, 39, 46, 113, 129, 167, 183, 209, 211
therapy, 30, 62–64
thinking, 18
thought, 57, 147
threat, 3, 4, 28, 61, 76, 162, 185, 200
tide, 36
tightrope, 58
time, 15, 17, 58, 59, 65, 81, 88, 174
timeline, 85
today, 48, 59, 129, 182
toll, 30, 51, 52, 58, 98, 210
tool, 14–16, 41, 59, 64, 69, 77, 79, 86, 88, 95, 100, 147, 151, 154, 156, 186, 192, 197, 201, 211, 227, 233, 244
topic, 63
torch, 113, 235
town, 158
traction, 195
tradition, 1, 16
traffic, 172
trailblazer, 75
training, 89, 101, 112, 118, 141, 197, 198, 201, 226, 229
trait, 211
transformation, 175, 217
transgender, 167, 168, 230, 239, 240
transparency, 112, 187
transphobia, 67, 81, 182, 195, 197, 213, 234
trauma, 100
treatment, 38, 119, 162, 189
triumph, 172
trust, 26, 110
truth, 70, 174
turmoil, 4, 51
turning, 5
tweet, 88

Uganda, 180, 183, 185, 188, 193, 195, 243
underemployment, 56
underpinning, 129
understanding, 1, 2, 5, 6, 9, 10, 14, 16–21, 24, 26, 32, 36, 41, 43, 45, 48, 50, 54, 58, 60, 72, 75, 82, 92, 100, 101, 110, 132, 135, 139, 146, 148, 151, 154, 155, 157, 159, 161–164, 168, 170–172, 174, 175, 179, 182, 186, 201, 202, 206, 211, 213, 230, 234, 238, 243
unemployment, 56
uniqueness, 211
unity, 78, 79, 84–86, 111, 169, 182
universality, 192
university, 12
upbringing, 11, 166
uplift, 16
urgency, 234, 236
use, 9, 30, 65, 72, 94, 115, 186, 197, 212, 233

vacuum, 213
validation, 72, 120, 131
value, 13, 240
vibrancy, 1
victimhood, 66
victory, 99, 122

view, 155, 159, 162, 183, 185, 193, 238, 243
vigilance, 28
violation, 95, 106, 208
violence, 4, 9, 20, 28–30, 36, 42, 49, 54, 61, 62, 64, 65, 80, 81, 103, 106, 111, 123, 125, 129, 132, 155, 162, 169, 177, 183, 185, 188, 192, 193, 195, 196, 200, 204, 207, 208, 234, 243
visibility, 18, 20, 21, 39, 41–43, 49, 56, 57, 64–68, 77, 88, 90–92, 99, 111, 123, 124, 186, 195, 199, 201–204, 209, 212, 216, 219, 221, 231, 232, 242, 244
vision, 53, 184, 201, 202, 217, 225
voice, 6, 11, 26, 29–31, 38, 41, 57, 67, 77, 90, 93, 94, 112, 118, 177, 202, 212
volunteer, 128
vulnerability, 18

W. E. B. Du Bois, 182
war, 29
wave, 226
way, 1, 5, 15, 36, 43, 48, 57, 58, 62, 69, 81, 84, 86, 88, 94, 104, 109, 111, 122, 129, 132, 136, 141, 160, 161, 163, 166, 168, 170, 177, 186, 189, 209, 214, 230
weakness, 202
weapon, 30, 157
weight, 11, 30
well, 42, 55, 58, 64, 124, 146, 151, 210
wellness, 53
whole, 102
will, 33, 88, 90, 92, 94, 113, 115, 117, 129, 154, 157, 161, 168, 185, 196, 202, 206, 217, 233–235, 238, 242
willingness, 57, 163, 174
woman, 8, 168
won, 120
work, 10, 31, 42, 49, 56, 58, 59, 64, 69, 71, 80, 81, 95, 119, 134, 139, 146, 162, 163, 166–168, 170, 175, 176, 180, 182, 192, 197, 204, 212–214, 217, 218, 221, 230, 234, 239, 240, 242
workplace, 144
world, 2, 15, 18, 21, 31, 36, 43, 61, 63, 72, 77, 79, 99, 110, 168, 170, 171, 175, 195, 209, 216, 230, 240, 243, 245
worldview, 5, 12
worthlessness, 28
writing, 151

youth, 15, 56, 70–72, 101, 112, 141–144, 198, 210

Zambia, 188
Zimbabwe, 186